9/18

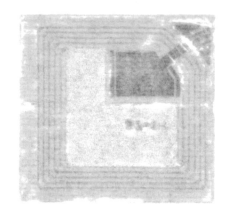

TILES

TILES

A GENERAL HISTORY

by

ANNE BERENDSEN

Marcel B. Keezer · Sigurd Schoubye

João Miguel dos Santos Simões

Jan Tichelaar

translated by Janet Seligman

A Studio Book

THE VIKING PRESS

New York

H. L.

FLIESEN: Eine Geschichte der Wand- und Bodenfliesen
von der Antike bis zur Gegenwart
Publisher's No. 139/1/363
Copyright 1964 Keysersche Verlagsbuchhandlung GmbH, München

TILES
English translation © Faber and Faber Limited, 1967

Published in 1967 by The Viking Press, Inc.
625 Madison Avenue, New York, N.Y. 10022
Printed in Western Germany by F. Bruckmann KG, München
Bound in Great Britain

Table of Contents

Foreword

Up to the present there has been no international survey of the history of ceramic tiles. Although there have been separate studies in abundance, there was clearly a need for a general work which would outline trends and relationships, direct attention to the rich artistic possibilities inherent in the raw materials, bring order into the scattered documentation of the subject and present the results in a new light.

In his *Guide to the Collection of Tiles*, published by the Victoria and Albert Museum in London, Arthur Lane laid the foundations of such a survey; but he was tied to the collections of his Museum. Forrer wrote a book on European tiles, which is now out of print and no longer complete and anyway, by definition, did not include Asia.

The present book sprang from the enthusiasm of a group of German and Danish connoisseurs. The Hamburg photographer, Walter Lüden, and Sigurd Schoubye, director of the Tönder Museum, discussed the matter and decided to bring out a fairly detailed book about the tiles they had known since their youth. These were for the most part of Dutch origin and the publishers wanted to see them presented in the context of the Dutch tile-manufacture as a whole. They therefore looked for a Dutch author to undertake this and I was all the readier to place myself at their disposal since Vis and de Geus's *Altholländische Fliesen*, which provides a survey of Dutch tiles, has long been among the rarities of the book-trade. The publishers then wanted a general introduction which would define the position of Dutch tiles within the international framework. The late Arthur Lane offered to write this.

But Lane was unable to contribute to this book and his death caused the plans to be changed. I took over what was to have been his part and it was soon agreed that the emphasis of the book should be on the international context presented in a suitably comprehensive manner. J. M. dos Santos Simões promised to collaborate and has written the chapters on Spain and Portugal and that on the influence of Dutch tiles in the Portuguese countries. Marcel B. Keezer was persuaded to undertake the chapter on Antwerp, while the discussion of the export of Dutch tiles to Germany and Denmark and of the indigenous manufacture of these countries is the work of Sigurd Schoubye. For the highly informative chapter on materials and methods of production we have to thank Jan Tichelaar, proprietor of the Makkum factory. There will probably be no objection to the fact that, in view of the comprehensive intention of the book, a number of illustrations of tiles have been included which may almost be regarded as folk-art, for the charm of the primitive and untutored is much prized today. Moreover, these are tiles which the collector may still from time to time obtain for reasonable prices. Reproductions of such specimens will be found side by side with illustrations of the more distinguished wares of the Dutch factories. This is one of the reasons why the chapters on Dutch tiles are more profusely illustrated than some of the others; another reason for this arose from our desire to provide an accurate impression of the many blues and mauves which are found on tiles, and for this purpose the Dutch tiles are the most suitable. A third reason is that Dutch wares were highly influential in the international development of tiles and, most compelling of all, that they show a particularly wide variety of decoration. The tiles of the Persian mosques, of the palaces and pools of Spain and Portugal, may have been more impressive than the wares of the Netherlands, but this is due to the fact that these were large-scale compositions. In a book about tiles as such, however, the individual piece is important and it was principally these which were produced in the Netherlands. Except for purposes of export to Spain or Portugal or, to a lesser extent, for certain tile-decorated rooms in other foreign countries, the tiles produced in the Netherlands were primarily individual pieces and for this reason these tiles have been discussed in the text mainly from the point of view of their iconographical significance.

Although this book is not intended to be a definitive presentation of the subject, I have tried to include as much unknown and unusual material as possible, so that it may be not only a guide but a source of information for connoisseurs. For the purposes of the book, tiles are defined as glazed, or at any rate fired, building-components. Thus glazed pillars have been included but not plaques which are glazed on one side and hang loose on the wall; nor do tiled stoves find a place in the book since these do not strictly belong to the architecture of the house, while tile-covered fire-places do and are included. Two further facts should also be mentioned: special tiles are sometimes displayed in frames in museums and in these cases the edge of the tile which is covered by the frame is missing on the plate; also, it is not always the best known and most celebrated tiles which have been reproduced in large size and in colour – for there is no reason not to cater also for the tastes of the more modest amateur.

In addition to the information available in the specialised literature of the subject, I have found much apposite material in the travel-books of which the English writers are the chief masters. Sacheverell Sitwell has descriptions of colours which have never been bettered. And in the books of Robert Liddell and Robin Fedden I have also found accounts which have entirely confirmed my own ideas. One cannot do better than to read their books in order to gain an impression of the splendour of the use of tiles in oriental architecture. It would clearly have been impossible to express my gratitude for their writings at every description of Asiatic work and I should therefore like to take this opportunity of doing so.

As regards tile scholarship, I express my thanks first and foremost to the late Arthur Lane. His *Guide*, in which he carried on the tradition of that pre-eminent authority, Bernard Rackham, has helped me at innumerable points. I have also had the active assistance of two distinguished authorities: Mr. Charleston, the present Keeper of the Department of Ceramics at the Victoria and Albert Museum, and Jonkheer H. van der Wijk, of the Dutch Bureau for the Conservation of Monuments, who is familiar with numerous outstanding treasures which he has brought together for me. I further express my gratitude to the many museums from which I have received the help of colleagues: the Vliesshuys in Antwerp (F. Smekens), the Musées Royaux d'Art et d'Histoire, Parc du Cinquantenaire, Brussels (Madame Marien-Dugardin), the Museum van Oudheden in Leiden (Juffrouw van de Velde), the Gemeentemuseum at The Hague (Dr. B. Jansen and Juffrouw J. Gallois), the Boymans-van Beuningen Museum, Rotterdam (Juffrouw B. R. M. de Neeve and A. Westers) and the Musée de la Céramique at Sèvres (H. Fourest). In addition to these, there are the many museums and collections, mentioned by name in the captions to the plates, whose willingness to help has contributed greatly to the successful completion of the book.

In conclusion, I should like to recall Voltaire's words about his epic poem, *La Henriade*: "Ce que j'ai à leur dire, c'est que lorsque je ferai imprimer, quelque tard que je le donne, je leur demanderai toujours pardon, de l'avoir donné trop tôt."

Anne Berendsen

EGYPT

It was the practice in the ancient Orient from very early times to decorate the houses – which were built of clay bricks dried in the air or baked – with glazed bricks or tiles. As far as is known, the first coloured glazes were produced in Egypt in the fourth millennium B.C.; these were blue copper glazes. The Egyptians did not, however, achieve the high quality in the production of faience on which so much store was set in later centuries. Their technique was limited in the main to inlaying, by which clay of different colours was incrusted on to the surface. By the reign of Amenhotep III (c. 1411–1375 B.C.) this technique was fully developed. There is in existence a celebrated arm-band with brilliant blue inlaid emblems which once belonged to this pharaoh.

Sir W. M. Flinders Petrie excavated fragments of faience of various sizes at Tell el Amarna. They date from the period of the eighteenth dynasty (1580–1335 B.C.) and are fascinating for the delicacy of the observation of nature which they reveal, particularly the pieces of the time of Akhenaton (1375–1358 B.C.). Some of the colours are strong, but the Flinders Petrie Collection also contains a large tile (17 cm. in length) with inlaid daisies in natural colours on a light yellow ground. The flowers were finished first and then inlaid into the tile. The brown stems, the outlines of the flowers and the delicate cornflowers between them represent the processes of growth very vividly – which shows that that feeling for nature which was so essential a part of Egyptian culture found its expression in ceramic art as in other spheres.

As far as is known, the Egyptians preferred a deep blue glaze to all other colours. The choice of colours was presumably limited at the time and since this blue also occurs on gravestones, we may perhaps conclude that it was related to current conceptions of divine power and eternal life. In the National Museum at Athens there is a fragment of a monument of this kind on which the figures appear greenish against this deep blue background. The Egyptian glaze was more transparent than that of Asia Minor and this effect was achieved by the application of layers of colour of varying thickness, a method seldom used in ceramic art but one which is familiar from the *champlevé* technique of medieval enamel-work; and it must not be forgotten that Egypt was the cradle of glass-making. In contrast to China, where ceramics were of far greater importance than glass, in Egypt knowledge which had been gained in the manufacture of glass was also adapted to pottery.

By a logical development from the foregoing, lines came to be scratched in the clay before glazing, so that the pattern or design stood out mysteriously in a deeper blue against the turquoise colour of the background. This technique made its first appearance during the reign of Seti I (1308–1298 B.C.) and was later adopted by the Byzantines and Romans. It was so effective that it was still being widely used in mediaeval times and persists to this day. In Egypt it was used mainly in the rendering of royal cartouches.

The most important wall-tiles were found in the Nile Delta at the temple of Medinet Habu near Tell el Yehudia (14). At the site of a palace begun by Rameses II and probably completed by Rameses III (c. 1180 B.C.), tiles were found which must have served to decorate a small chamber or passage-way. They represent human figures, probably those of prisoners of various races or peoples. They measure 30 cm. in height and have an extraordinarily life-like appearance. Of some, unfortunately, only fragments were found, a head or the upper part of a body. Since they are not very large, we may assume that the space they decorated was relatively small. These tiles do not, however, portray only human figures but also those of fabulous

*Cartouche on a tile of the time of Rameses III.
British Museum, London.*

beasts and real animals as well as symbolic signs and ornaments. The whole picture must have shown the pharaoh, either in his war-chariot or bringing a sacrifice to the altar, with the procession of prisoners to complete the scene. It must have been a splendid and extremely impressive work of art, for even the single figures with their picturesque garments show that the ancient Egyptians must have had a great sense of the dramatic. A royal cartouche of Rameses III in faience (22 cm. in height) has also been found (10). It reveals the existence of a highly developed technique: the deep and carefully incised inscription is filled with glaze in counter-relief. But pharaoh himself is not portrayed. This cartouche is now in London in the British Museum. Similar representations of prisoners have been found in Upper Egypt also, including Luxor and Coptos. They presumably came from the same workshop, but it is not yet known where this workshop was. Most of these outstanding finds are now in collections in Cairo or in the British Museum.

MESOPOTAMIA

As was only to be expected, the tiles found in Mesopotamia, the Iraq and Syria of today, differ considerably from the Egyptian tiles. There are no outstanding individual pieces here, but everything that has been found is of imposing effect and of a splendour which derives from the fact that the impulse to artistic expression was provided by religious feeling and experience. Between the years 1899 and 1917 R. Koldewey directed excavations at Babylon, in the course of which two huge series of glazed tile-reliefs were found: the Ishtar or Astarte gate and the throne-room of the south citadel.

In order to gain an idea of the cultural background and environment of these powerful works of art, it is necessary to recall that the precursors of the Babylonians and

Assyrians were the Sumerians, who, by about the year 2700 B.C., had reached a high level of civilisation. They built their houses of blocks of mud which they dried in the sun and by about 3000 B.C. were modelling figures from clay. As early as about 4000 B.C. ceramics with white and blue striped decoration and later with more varied patterns were produced in El Ubaid or Samarra. After 1950 B.C. Babylon crumbled into a number of small states, but under King Hammurabi (1728–1686 B.C.) it was reunited. In about the year 1415 B.C., when Babylon was conquered by the Kassites – it was at about this time that the celebrated Luristan bronzes were made in Elam – an impressive monument arose in the old Sumerian capital of Uruk, the present-day Warka. It is the base of a wall 2.10 m. in height made of baked bricks. Niches contain figures which represent, alternately, a bearded mountain deity and a river god. Between these niches a river is drawn in zigzag lines. This frieze has been reconstructed in the Berlin Museum. At this period nature deities and the spirits of fertility, who were connected with water, were revered above all others.

Sennacherib, a conqueror from Elam, laid Babylon waste and in the year 705 made Nineveh the capital. Further devastation followed, this time at the hands of the Chaldeans from the south. After the fall of Ninevah in 612 B.C., Babylon experienced a flourishing renaissance under the Chaldean kings, notably Nebuchadnezzar II (604–562 B.C.), familiar to us from the Book of Daniel in the Bible. The great complexes of the Ishtar gate, discovered by Koldewey, were produced at this time. They are comparatively late witnesses to a civilisation which, through two millennia, survived alternating periods of ascendancy and decline but which remained constant in essentials through many centuries, and the gates include numerous features which differ not at all from those of earlier Mesopotamian buildings.

The ziggurat erected in the reign of Nebuchadnez-zar (604–562 B.C.), the celebrated Tower of Babel of the Bible. Putative reconstruction after Koldewey.

Under the rule of Nebuchadnezzar, Babylon was the greatest metropolis of the Near East. Its name means "gate of god," indicating that it was the point at which heaven and earth met. The name probably derives from the great double gates – not the Ishtar gates – which led to the two great sanctuaries of the god Marduk. Those who passed through this gateway reached the Tower of Babel (11), a ziggurat with numerous terraces one above the other linked by a rising spiral ramp. The curves of this ramp corresponded to the courses of the stars, the details of which were familiar to astrologers. This parallel emphasises once again the cosmological character of the Babylonian civilisation. The most important parts of the ziggurat were the terraces which served as open-air altars for burnt offerings from which the smoke rose straight to heaven. For this reason these terraces were larger and more hallowed than a temple. At the centre of the tower there was probably a sanctified tomb symbolising death and resurrection. The Tower of Babel was a late example of such sanctuaries and the conception of the terrace serving as an altar had so far degenerated that a temple had been erected on the topmost terrace.

The second sanctuary reached through the gateway was the temple of Marduk. These edifices were built of blocks of mud faced at first with baked, and later with colour-glazed, clay bricks.

A system of primary colours was used to indicate the divine laws. The city walls were yellow, the gates sky-blue, the palaces brilliant red and the temples white. We have therefore to visualise the Ishtar gate surrounded by this complex of religious buildings. It was a double gate about 10.5 m. high in the double inner wall of the city of Babylon and thus the main means of access to the holy city. It was built in about 580 B.C. A passage-way led to the gate from a subterranean room. The approaching visitor was greeted by a relief of lions three metres high in brilliant colours on either side of the passage-way. The lions' manes must originally have been fiery red, though the red has now faded to a greenish yellow. Red pigments have always been difficult to fire and for this reason paint was probably used on this occasion. The lions were doubtless intended to instil fear into the visitor's heart and to warn him not to enter the holy places heedlessly but in a state of spiritual preparedness. The façades of the main building were decorated with series of bulls and dragons. These holy creatures are represented without foreshortening, taking no account of the position of the observer; thus only one horn is visible. The bulls, who have always symbolised new life and generative force, were intended as embodiments of the storm god Adad. The dragon Musrussu or Mush-Hush-Hushu (12) – the name echoes the hisses of the monster – serves the chief of the gods, Marduk. He has the body of a serpent, the fore-legs of a lion, an eagle's talons on the hind feet, the neck and mane of a bull and a serpent's head with forked tongue. This is no Homeric dragon but recalls rather the apocryphal chapters to the Book of Daniel, *The History of the Destruction of Bel and the Dragon.* The dragon was worshipped in the temple and the priest espoused the doctrine that it could eat and drink. "Then Daniel took pitch, and fat, and hair, and did seethe them together, and made lumps thereof: this he put in the dragon's mouth, and so the dragon burst in sunder: and Daniel said, Lo, these are the gods ye worship." There were altogether 575 figures of animals on the Ishtar gate, of which 152 have so far been found. The technique used in their execution differs fundamentally from the Egyptian. Each single tile was individually produced as a unit of the composition and subsequently fitted in to the whole relief.

The inner gate, built of unglazed blocks, still stands in Babylon. From the outer gate over 10,000 pieces, on which the glaze has survived through tens of centuries, have been taken to Berlin, where, in the museum on

11

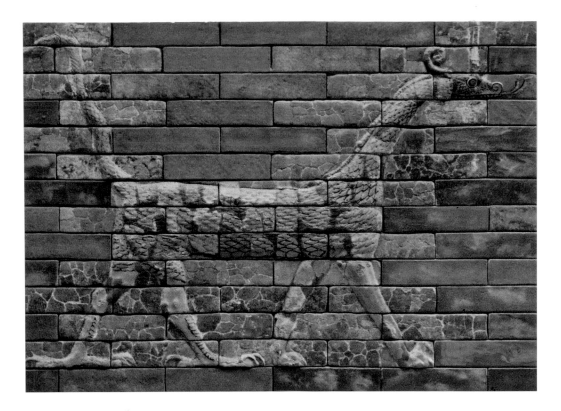

Top: *The dragon Musrussu from the Ishtar gate in Babylon. The creature is repeated many times on the walls of the gateway; it has the body of a serpent, the forefeet of a lion, the hind feet of an eagle, the neck and mane of a bull and the head of a serpent. It was the sacred beast of the chief of the gods, Marduk or Baal. c. 580 B.C. Height 1 m. Berlin (Sammlung der Vorderasiatischen Altertümer).*

Right: *Bodyguard of the Achaemenid princes at the palace of Artaxerxes II at Susa. c. 350 B.C. The degeneration of the ancient Mesopotamian culture into eclecticism may be clearly seen. Babylonian and Egyptian motifs characterise this grandiose representational art. The lotus flower, held sacred in Egypt, occurs in the inlaid and glazed work of that country and was already known in Babylon in the rigidly stylised form exemplified here. Susa was the winter residence, Persepolis the spring palace and Ecbatana, now Hamadan, the summer residence of the princes. Musée du Louvre, Paris.*

Below: *Lion in colour-glazed relief tiles from the processional street in Babylon, about 580 B.C. Sammlung der Vorderasiatischen Altertümer, Berlin.*

the island in the Spree (Sammlung der Vorderasiatischen Altertümer) the gate has been re-erected.

The throne-room of the South Citadel (52×17 m. in area, 20 m. in height) was the scene of Belshazzar's feast. It was here that the hand appeared to Belshazzar and wrote upon the wall "Mene, Mene, Tekel, Upharsin." Here also lions held watch. Stems and plants, probably the lotus, the sacred plant of Egypt, are reminiscent of Greek pillars. The idea of erecting pillars and capitals must have come from the Mediterranean. There was much magnificent colour, including a great deal of red, which has faded to green. The only groups of buildings known to us in Mesopotamia are isolated ones. A. Parrot has excavated the palace of Mari, the precursor of Babylon, on the banks of the Euphrates. Perhaps one day further glazed tiles will be found, yet the two great series already known to us suffice to give an impression of the vast vanished civilisation of Mesopotamia.

In the Greco-Roman world the use of tiles was restricted to semicircular roof-ornaments decorated with reliefs. The gorgon, a double-headed sphinx, and other fabulous creatures are depicted on these tiles which are multicoloured but unglazed.

PERSIA

When, in the year 539, Cyrus conquered Babylon, he took back a rich booty to Susa, capital of Elam. There, in the 5th century B.C., a palace of the Achaemenids was decorated with glazed reliefs or dried, multicoloured mud bricks. Lions and winged bulls remind us of Babylon, whereas the ceramics of the ancient Persians, which came into being two millennia earlier, probably with the vessels painted with water-birds from Nihàvand of the period 3000–2700 B.C. can have had virtually no successors.

The Achaemenids (559–331 B.C.), that is, Cyrus and his heirs, including Darius and Xerxes, immediately they came to power, built themselves great palaces in Pasargadae, Persepolis and Susa. They did not, however, provide any stimulus for an independent, indigenous art. It was customary at their courts to fabricate decorations from combined elements borrowed from Babylon, Assyria and Urardhu. Urardhu, part of present-day Armenia, had already been conquered by the Medes (675–559 B.C.), the forerunners of the Achaemenids. The principal purpose of their art was the glorification of their kings. The mud walls of the palaces display fired and glazed bricks, such, for example, as have been found at Susa (13). Gryphons, bulls, archers of the bodyguard – now in the Louvre – served as decoration; also rosettes, which, with their incrustations or filled-in counter-relief, remind one of Egyptian ceramics. Under the Seleucids (323–248 B.C.), successors of the Achaemenids, Hellenism penetrated into Persia, and this meant the end of the production of tiles and bricks. The Parthians, however, seceded and the production of ceramics became extremely widespread in their independent kingdom (247 B.C.–226 A.D.). The sarcophagi with the greenish-blue shimmering glaze are well-known. In these works the Scythian influence is noticeable in, for example, the figures of animals on the bronze fittings, and a characteristic east Persian style in art came into being. Under the rule of the Sassanians (224–642 A.D.) the resuscitation of Achaemenid culture resulted in an even more thoroughgoing eclecticism. The palace of Ktesiphon had a *liwan*, an antechamber enclosed on three sides and roofed by a barrel-vault, with a cupola in the middle. Vaults, cupolas, plaster walls, mosaic floors – these are the essential elements of an architecture the purpose of which was the display of power (cf. p. 33).

The main elements found on the tiles of later periods are those which also predominated in the textiles of

15

Leopard. Inserted relief-decoration of a tile from a grave-stone from the Chinese province of Honan. c. 1000 B. C.

that period: geometrical designs, flower garlands, medallions with religious symbols such as, for example, the tree of life. The walls were no longer faced with tiles as in the period of the Achaemenids, but were decorated with stucco incrustations of figures and stylised plants; this practice persisted into the Islamic period (after 641). Later on, a stucco facing was frequently combined with tiles and, when this happened, the form of the tiles was determined by the stucco decoration in question.

During the Islamic period, following the rule of the Sassanians, all methods of tile-decoration were brought to perfection in Persia. Glazed tile pavements also derive from Babylonian brick architecture, and were in use in many parts of Asia from the 6th to the 2nd century B.C. Mention may here be made of Mohenjo Daro and Harappa on the Indus. Stucco was also in general use in this region and the temple buildings are mainly constructed of natural stone and very seldom of brick.

CHINA

Still farther east, in China, the great centre of ceramic art, a fine white stone ware with the earliest Chinese glaze (16) was produced during the Shang-Yin dynasty (1523–1028 B.C.). Ceramic tomb-figures and pottery fired at a high temperature, a kind of forerunner of porcelain, are known from the Han dynasty (206 B.C.–221 A.D.). The tiles from the tombs (14) belong to the same category as the circular plaques which form the terminals of the sickle-shaped projecting eaves with their covering of tiles.

The Unsurpassed Tile-architecture
of Persia

GENERAL

The artists of the Islamic period were prepared to uphold the great traditions of the past. The Ummayads had lived in Damascus in extravagant Hellenistic fashion; they took no interest in buildings which derived their effect from the use of colour but cultivated an architecture consonant with their Greco-Roman civilisation based on the balanced interplay of thrust and support by which roofs and beams were supported by pillars. They were succeeded by the Abbasids (750–1258), whose capital was Baghdad, which lay much further to the east than Damascus; and their court was thus open to influences from Persia.

The walls of the palace of Samarra, built during the years 836–883 on the banks of the Tigris, were decorated with stucco in the manner familiar to us from Sassanian work at Ktesiphon and Kish.

The earliest tiles include squares with a plain brown or green lead-glaze and a composition in coloured glazes showing a cock in a wreath painted on squares and framed by oblong hexagons mottled to simulate marble. Both forms, the square and the oblong hexagon, promised much for the future. We shall encounter them repeatedly right up to the numerous Antwerp pavements of the sixteenth century, in which the large squares carry figures in wreaths or circles. The cockerel surrounded by the wreath is reminiscent of Sassanian textiles.

Trade from China to Baghdad was also of special importance during this period; it opened up many new possibilities and stimulated the making of pottery.

During the first centuries of Abbasid rule the craftsmen were notably independent. There was nothing to prevent their moving to those centres where they could expect important commissions. Wherever a workshop was established, it became a focal point for artists who had come from far and wide in search of an opportunity to put their abilities to use. Thus traditions from all over Asia met in a single workshop – a situation which persisted for centuries. When, in the tenth century, the glory of the caliphate of Baghdad began to pale, the pottery workshops were transferred to Egypt under the Fatimids (969–1171). Following Saladin's victory over the Fatimids, the workshops migrated further to northern Mesopotamia or to the cities of Persia, where the Seljuks then ruled. During the period, from 1219 onwards, of the invasions of the Mongols from the north-east Asian steppes, and under the rule of the khans (1259–1336), the ceramic artists and their traditions survived all oppression and exploitation. Nevertheless, craftsmen and their workshops were often abducted as part of the booty of war. All these migrations often make it impossible to distinguish between local and national traditions and styles in Asiatic ceramic production. And when another line of the Mongol dynasty came to power in China (1280–1368), contacts with Asia became still closer; it can be established that oriental ornamental designs made their way west, traversing all the Asiatic countries. The same is true not only of ceramics, but of all branches of decorative art.

EARLY MIGRATIONS

Tiles of the ninth century with opaque yellow, brown and, occasionally, red glazes have been found in Samarra and in Kairouan, near Tunis. Some of those found in Kairouan, decorations from the Mosque of Sidi Oqba, appear to be the local work of a potter who had emigrated from Baghdad. The objects in question are lustre tiles. This lustre technique, which originated in Mesopotamia and later appears to have been the monopoly of a group of ceramic artists in Fatimid Egypt, was here probably used not only for the decoration of vessels but also for that of tiles. The cruciform tiles which were

17

found in Constantine in Algeria may have been imported from Egypt.

In the year 1175, however, the irascible Saladin, the same warrior who was the terror of the crusaders, destroyed the works of art of the Fatimids and lustreware found a new home at Raqqa, on the northern frontier between Syria and Mesopotamia and in Rayy near Teheran, the Rages of the Book of Tobit. Here tiles in the shape of stars, crosses and hexagons were produced and they also had brown lustre on a blue or white ground (21).

The most important centre of tile production was, however, Kashan, south of Teheran.

LUSTRE TILES FROM KASHAN

In the book of Yaqut's travels (d. 1229), tiles are already called *kashi* or *kashani*, after the town of Kashan, and these words for tiles are still used in Persian. Indeed, the names of ceramic wares often derive from the places where they were produced or marketed, faience being, for example, named after Faenza, majolica after Majorca and Delft tiles after the town of Delft. In Kashan lived a man whose name is found on many tiles and who, in the year 1301 wrote a treatise on ceramic wares, Abulqasim. The substance of his treatise is reflected in those Kashan wares which have survived. The tiles of Kashan, of which some bear dates from 1208 to 1339, have brown lustre over decoration in relief with frequent additions of blue and turquoise (27). They were used with cruciform or star-shaped tiles, to face walls; each was painted with a complete design, while the upper part of the wall was separated by a frieze of oblong tiles with relief inscriptions in blue.

These tiles were also used for more esoteric purposes, including, for example, the *mihrab*, or the prayer-niche in a mosque. Complete *mihrabs* may be seen in the mosque of the Imam Reza in Mashhad in Iran (1216), in the Berlin Museum – removed from the Maidan mosque at Kashan (1226) – and in the Museum of the University of Pennsylvania – removed from the tomb of the Imam Gadeh Yahgya at Veramin naer Teheran (1265). Complete *mihrabs* faced with Kashan tiles are not rare (28). Many of them, as also many tiles with relief inscriptions, come from Natanz.

The tile industry of Kashan became a most brilliant phenomenon. The expressive power of these reliefs and the subtlety of delineation has never been surpassed. On the *mihrab* in the Berlin Museum (Staatliche Museen) we find the signature of the artist, al-Hasan ibn Arabshāh, on a flat background with delicate birds among scroll-work. Little hares also occur in the decoration of this period. Under the rule of Ghazan Khan (1295–1304), when the fateful ravages of the Mongols came to an end and the Khan himself went over to Islam, the revival of Persia's former artistic activity favoured the tile-industry as well; Chinese models regained importance and we find dragons, cloud-scrolls and lotus-flowers among the decoration (27).

Figure motifs were not so rare in the thirteenth century as is commonly believed. It was the fanatical adherents of the prophet, not Mohammed himself, who demanded that they should be abolished, but this was never accepted by the Mongol peoples. A pair of lovers in a garden, animals, trees and birds were among the permitted secular motifs. In the *mihrab*, however, it was the world of the unseen and unseeable god to which the devout submitted himself.

The thirteenth century dados of Kashan illustrate every feature of that world of legend which could be used for secular purposes. The artists had not yet turned their minds to the everyday, naturalistic motifs which we find in the fourteenth century. This period might be described as that of an intimate, late revival of the motifs of Sassanian textiles. The borders do not carry

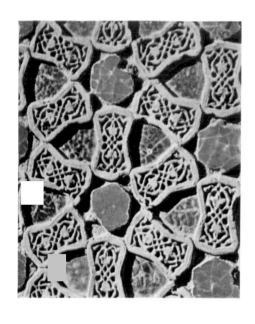

religious texts as they do in the mosques, but quatrains in the style of Omar Khayyam.[1] In the fourteenth century, however, a liking developed for border-tiles with scenes from Firdausi's version of the *Shah-nama* or *Book of Kings* (27) – depicting, for example, King Bahram Gur out hunting with Azada, his beloved, or a lion tearing an ox to pieces.[2] In general, however, this naturalism led to a loosening of style and to a simplification of detail. At the end of the thirteenth century blue and turquoise tones acquired more and more importance and this taste in colour also appears to be a mark of decadence. In about 1300, texts from the Koran were replaced by narrow blue lines and small curves which were no more than meaningless scribbles. Another sign that nearly always indicates decline is a coarsening of detail such as is to be seen in the borders, where the earlier powerful style of the inscriptions has degenerated and become crude. At the same time, the reliefs lost some of their expressiveness; they were now fairly flat and carried Chinese motifs such as lotus-flowers, dragons and birds in flight. Star-shaped tiles alternate with cruciform tiles carrying ornamentation in low relief on monochrome turquoise glaze (21).

Monochrome turquoise glaze and monochrome blue reliefs are, together with lustre-ware, typical of Kashan (21). There are whole *mihrabs* carried out in this technique. In the Victoria and Albert Museum in London there is a part of a niche showing riders on elephant-back, which was undoubtedly originally designed for religious purposes. It will not be difficult to understand how such strange pieces could have a place in sacred liturgy if we recall the great prestige of the Sassanian textiles. The Victoria and Albert Museum possesses a green-glazed tile with pierced decoration which probably served as a window-lattice. This piece was clearly influenced by stucco-work, which also derives from Sassanian tradition. It is worth pointing out, in this connection, that window-frames and lintels continued until

much later times to be made of glazed faience, as, for example, in Ebersbach and Hindelopen.

MINAI TILES

The so-called *minai* tiles with polychrome decoration which Abulqasim described as *haft paikar*, or "seven-colour" are probably typical products of Kashan and Rayy. They are sometimes dated to about the year 1200, and, in their extreme refinement, recall book-illustrations. Some of the colours were enamels fixed by a second short firing. It is possible that after the Mongolian invasions a group of ceramic artists from Rayy carried on their work among the Seljuks of Asia Minor, for pottery of the same kind though less accomplished, was found in the kiosk tower[3] of the citadel at Konya. Abulqasim also speaks of a simplified form of *minai* pottery, which he calls *lajvardina*: this technique involved the application of red, white, black and gold, fixed in a second short firing, to tiles with a dark blue ground *(lajvard)* or a turquoise glaze. The gold consisted of gold-leaf, which, as the outlines show, was cut into patterns with scissors (21; 27). These *lajvardina* tiles also carry the Chinese relief decorations which have already been mentioned in connection with the lustre tiles of Kashan. Thirteenth century tiles painted from a stencil in gold only were also found in Konya. The same form of decoration reappeared in Bursa and Istanbul in Turkey in the fifteenth century.

In about 1350 production at Kashan began to decline; large tiles were no longer produced; and by the fifteenth century there were only paltry remnants of this once so important industry.

STUCCO-EFFECTS IN SAMARKAND

When after 1369 Tamerlane, or Timur, and his successors rebuilt the city of Samarkand, glazed relief tiles were made which imitated the play of light and shade (20) so effective in stucco-work. Since stucco will not withstand weather, the demand for these new tiles was undoubtedly great. The same decorative technique is frequently found in and around Bukhara. The designs are in high and sharp relief and slightly undercut; so that the shadows appear extremely dark in contrast to the highlights. The surface is normally covered with a plain green or turquoise glaze, against which inscriptions and designs are rendered in contrasting whites, purples or blues. The best examples of this technique to have been found were designed for burial rites, among the most celebrated being the tombs in the graveyard of Shah Zindeh and, particularly, the grave of Timur's sister in Samarkand. This technique appears to have remained in use until the beginning of the fifteenth century.

TILE-MOSAICS IN PERSIA AND IN THE SELJUK CITY OF KONYA

Persia is the cradle of almost all the techniques employed in the production of tiles which were later used in Europe. The forerunners of the Spanish *alicatados*, or panels of tile-mosaic, were the Persian decorations in which the brickwork of the outer walls of the buildings was so bonded as to form patterns or Kufic inscriptions which were usually picked out in coloured glazes (20; 25). This technique entailed embedding the glazed components in a layer of mortar spread on the outer wall of a building. Combinations exist of bricks, glazed tiles and carved stucco ornaments. This method led to the practice of facing whole walls and cupolas with mosaics composed of sections of glazed slabs. At the beginning, simple geometric designs were carried out in this technique but later flowing lines and stylised plants were included. These mosaics derived their effect largely from colour contrasts. The mosaics of the Seljuks in and around Konya reached their greatest perfection (23) in the thirteenth century, at the time when the Mongolian invasions were making it impossible in Persia to undertake great projects in the sphere of the ceramic arts.

With Konya as capital, the Seljuks ruled from 1072 until 1327 a former Byzantine province, known as the Kingdom of Rum.[4] For a century before this they had lived within the Persian civilisation. They were highly skilled architects and built collegiate mosques, or madrassas, with an *iwan* or entrance hall, cupolas and elaborate vaults with stalactite ornament *(muqarnas)*. Exteriors were decorated with bricks and tiles bearing bold Kufic inscriptions.

These early Turkish mosaics have many connections with Persia. The material used was the same, while the mosaic of the Sirçali Madrassa[5] in Konya (1243) is signed by an artist from Tus in east Persia.

In and around Konya, inside walls, *mihrabs* and vaults were faced with tile-mosaics. There are documentary records of building-dates from 1220 onwards, and the earliest mosaics in the mosque of Ala'ed din surpass all those made in Persia up to that time. The elements of these splendid decorations are bands arranged in star-shaped figures, borders with inscriptions and stylised plant-designs. Once seen, the *mihrab*, so strongly suggestive of the heavens and the stars in their mysterious grandeur, will not easily be forgotten. One feels oneself undoubtedly closer to the Turkish than to the Persian spirit.

Important works of art were also produced in the Turk-

The iwan *or entrance-hall, with its tile-facing, of the tomb of Daniel in Susa, built in about the year 1300. According to the Bible, the prophet Daniel lived in Susa and was also buried there. His relics, venerated by the Mohammedans, are preserved in this mausoleum.*

25

ish city of Karaman. The range of colour here comprised a blackish-purple, a light turquoise, white, yellowish-brown and blue. It is tempting to see in this preference for ardent colours and in the powerful contours of the buildings an expression of Turkish mysticism. The principal technique used in Karaman involved scraping off the glaze from the background of the inscriptions, a technique which has persisted in Morocco for centuries. It achieved the strong contrasts pleasing to eyes accustomed to dazzling light. Mosaics with geometric designs composed of glazed slabs were especially highly prized in Egypt, North Africa and Spain from the end of the thirteenth century onwards.

In the fourteenth century tile-mosaics became fashionable in Persia. They are to be found in the great Yezd Mosque at Isfahan and others, dating from the fifteenth century, at the grave of Timur at Samarkand, a building which has also, according to Robert Byron, a ribbed dome "scattered with black and white diamonds". Another outstanding building is the Blue Mosque of Tabriz, completed in 1465 and once greatly celebrated though now badly damaged. Buildings continued to be decorated in the same style in all parts of Persia up to the beginning of the seventeenth century. The ornamental motifs included intertwining stems with arabesques, flowers and leaves, lotus-flowers and Chinese cloud-scrolls, flower-vases and sometimes birds as well. The colours, however, differ considerably from those we noted in Turkey in the thirteenth century, comprising as they do soft shades of blue, turquoise, yellowish, brown, green, white and purple; there is also a matt, unfired red which is painted on to the surface of the fired clay or on to a yellow glaze. These Persian mosaics are entirely different from the Turkish. Their splendid effect rests primarily on the fact that the glaze is unusually thick, so that the luminosity of the colours acquires full value. The special nature of the clay and the low firing temperature of the Persian biscuit tiles resulted in the glaze setting fairly thick. A colourless transparent glaze often enhanced the luminosity of the colours still further.

CUERDA SECA

Tile-mosaics were superseded at an early period by a technique to which in Spain the name *cuerda seca* was given (see p. 66). It was employed in North Africa as early as the eleventh century, although it did not become popular in Persia until the fourteenth. It has the disadvantage that the colours cannot be set so closely together. Very good examples of tiles in this style come from the madrassa of Bibi Hanum (1399–1404) in Samarkand. They are blue, turquoise, white, and some also show matt red and unfired gold-leaf.

Under the rule of Shah Abbas I (1587–1629) of the Safavid dynasty, the almost legendary prince who led Persia to renewed power and greatness, Isfahan became the brilliant centre of the kingdom. The early buildings of this reign were decorated with tile-mosaics but the *cuerda seca* technique was used as early as 1616 for the Imperial Mosque (33). Those celebrated blue skies seen through budding twigs, which are among the wonders of Persia, are carried out in this technique.

The *cuerda seca* process remained in general use. It was even employed for palace walls and garden-pavilions. Large panels of rectangular tiles which combined to represent a scene with human figures were completely new to Islamic architecture. For the first time painted tiles appear as parts of a larger decorative scheme. As is typical of Persian art of this period, the drawing and subject-matter are a little fulsome, but they are redeemed by the clear, brilliant colours in which bright yellow and apple-green predominate. Picnics in gardens were popular subjects and there are also large tiles showing a lynx or a hare and others painted

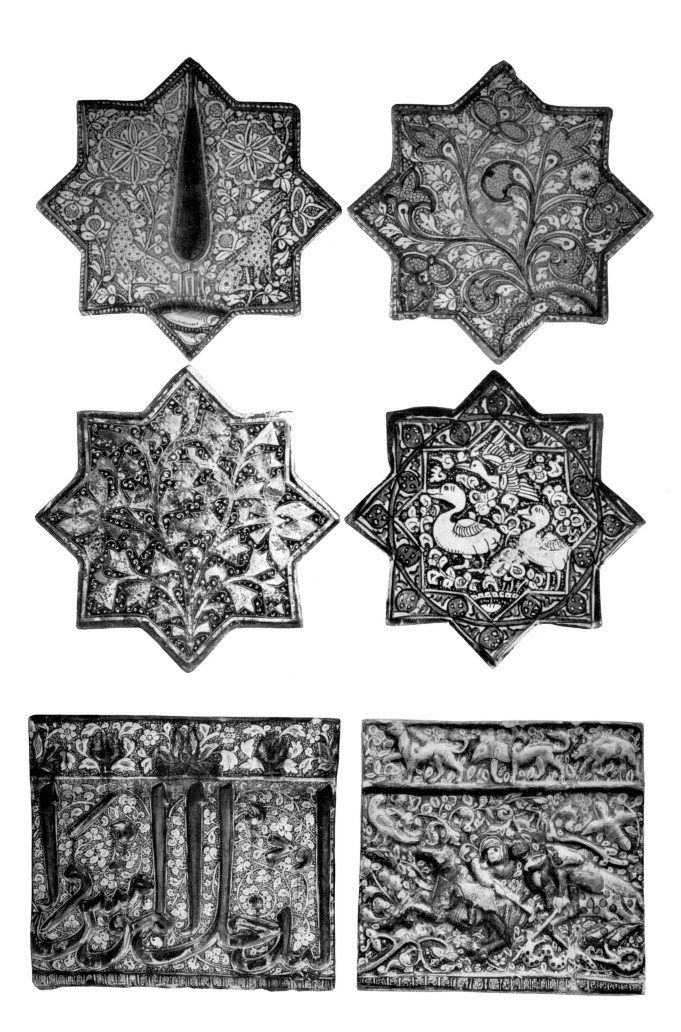

with parts of plant-compositions. Examples of these last occur in the Porcelain Hall built for Shah Abbas in Ardebil in the year 1611. Then in the seventeenth century the decline set in and the process has so far not been reversed: in the eighteenth and nineteenth centuries designs were coarse and the colours used – probably under the influence of the Chinese *famille rose* porcelain – were often an ugly yellow or pink.

Persian ceramic artists introduced the *cuerda seca* technique into Turkey too and worked on the Green Mosque in Bursa (1419–1424), the finest building in the city. The exterior was originally adorned by two minarets faced with emerald-green tiles. The interior, however, is of even greater beauty. The main nave is faced with sapphire-blue tiles. The transepts on either side are hung with hexagons showing delightful arabesques and flowers, in which emerald-green predominates. The *mihrab* is also faced with tiles as are the small galleries, one for the sultan and a smaller one below it. Here again sapphire-blue is the dominant colour There is an inscription in the Green Mosque which reads "Have made [it] the masters from Tabriz." The same inscription is to be seen on the octagonal Green Tomb or Yeşil Türbe (c. 1421) in Bursa. Here also the outer walls are faced with hexagonal green tiles. Inside the building, the walls gleam with hexagonal green, turquoise and blue tiles, stencilled over with patterns in unfired gold, though the gold has worn off and all that remains are the traces of the perforated pattern which was used. Other architectural features, such as *mihrabs*, borders and door-posts are decorated in the *cuerda seca* technique. We also find tile-mosaics and finally also relief-tiles with raised ridges which separate the colours from one another like the Spanish *cuenca* tiles; also tiles with "stalactite" ornaments in the style of stucco. In addition to the principal colours, apple-green, yellow and purple occur. The brilliance of the glazes is not enhanced by the grey earthenware on which they are laid and

this combines with the dull black outlines to produce a somewhat sombre effect.

In Edirne,[6] Ankara, Karaman and Istanbul tiles of the *cuerda seca* type were probably produced by Persians. It appears that this technique died out in Turkey in about 1470 and did not reappear until the year 1514 when, after his conquest of Tabriz, Selim I (the "Grim"), brought Persian ceramic artists to Istanbul. We find their small, neat patterns in the Mosque of the Sultan Selim. There is a marked difference between these and the *cuerda seca* tiles of the fifteenth century in Bursa, not only in the designs but also because in these the predominant yellow and apple-green produce a greater effect of brightness since they are applied to white clay; against this, however, the colours here are less strong because the glazes are fired in thinner layers. Here and there the glaze has been scratched in order to make room for an unfired red.

UNDERGLAZE PAINTING: THE "KUBACHI" TILES

As has already been said, the technique of overglazing with a transparent lead-glaze was known in Persia. Tiles of the thirteenth century decorated in this way have been found in Syria, Egypt and Turkey; at a later date they were painted blue and white, since imitation of Chinese porcelain had become fashionable. It is not certain whether these tiles were produced in Persia; it may, however, be assumed that the tiles still known as Kubachi-ware come not from the village of that name in the Caucasus but from Tabriz. The earliest pieces of the fifteenth century are painted blue and white or black under a transparent turquoise glaze. This treatment, however, was gradually superseded by a polychrome palette: black, brownish-red, ochre, green and blue were used, lightly applied, the black borders often being decorated in *sgraffito*, a technique which was widely used in Persia. The subjects represented – lions, angels, goats, plants – were taken from literary sources. In the time of Shah Abbas (1581–1629), the whole appearance of the tiles was much more fulsome – the same decline having taken place here as with the *cuerda seca* tiles. Occasionally the tiles, some of which were now square, bore painted portraits. The clothing of the subjects is often European, particularly Italian, from which it is evident that the European style was in vogue in Persia at this time – there was, in fact, a Dutch painter, Jan de Boer, working at the court of the Safavids. The large tiles from Khorasan with dancing girls on them derive from Persian miniatures. All these so-called Kubachi tiles are distinguished by a free, relaxed style. It is a striking fact that these tiles, dissimilar though they may otherwise be from contemporary Turkish tiles, have all assumed Turkish colouring, particularly the thick brownish-red. This adoption of Turkish elements is explained by the fact that more than once during the sixteenth century Tabriz came under Ottoman rule. From about 1630 onwards a further decline set in, as may be seen from specimens in which the material is coarse and the glaze has crazed.

Turkish colours were also used in Mashhad and Kermān, where a deep blue and an orange-red are found. Probably, however, tiles were not produced here in great numbers. There is in the Victoria and Albert Museum an overmantel for a fireplace which is typical of this special type of tile.

In the nineteenth century Teheran saw a renewal of the Safavid ceramic art. The polychrome tiles with black contours and thick glaze, sometimes with relief, are well-known. The popular subjects of the rider and scenes from the life of Shah Nahmeh are represented in an insipid, tasteless manner. It is difficult to describe them even as relics of the great golden age of Persian ceramics.

UNDERGLAZE PAINTING

Many instances were noted in the foregoing chapter of Persian ceramic artists working in the Turkish countries. They often settled down in their new surroundings and it must have been quite usual for Turks to have worked with them. In order to survey the history of Turkish tiles it is essential to consider the cities of Konya, Bursa, Edirne and Istanbul, the splendours of which were frequently mentioned in the course of the chapter on the tiles of Persia.

The town of Raqqa in northern Syria is, however, the true home of underglaze painting. Until Raqqa was destroyed by the Mongols in 1259, production was extremely active. Underglaze decorations in black and blue on a white ground played the leading role. In the fourteenth century imports from China increased, with the result that white pottery with blue underglaze painting also became fashionable. The Muslims followed the trend of the times and began to specialise in this technique. Imitation Chinese porcelain was produced in large quantities in Egypt and Syria and particularly in Damascus. Tiles made in Syria in this blue-and-white technique may still be seen in the Türbe or tomb of al-Tawrizi in Damascus (1423). These tiles are hexagonal and are set point to point. The interstices are filled with small, plain turquoise-coloured triangles. Other tiles which originate from Damascus are hexagonal and are painted with vases, birds and fruit-bearing plants all rising in flowing lines from the lowest point of the hexagon; these were perhaps produced for the Great Mosque of Damascus (31).

Tiles of another type – which are extremely beautiful – have Chinese designs with wavy stems, rosettes and tapering palmettes. A narrow turquoise-coloured border edged in blackish-brown lines is also often found. Yet another variety has designs in black under a pale turquoise-coloured glaze.

Syrian hexagonal tiles with underglaze painting. Plant-designs, the one on the left of Chinese origin. The bird is black under a turquoise-coloured transparent glaze. c. 1425. Victoria and Albert Museum, London.

Another group of tiles which also comes from Damascus is artistically less accomplished. These are blue, painted with arabesques, looped palmettes and radiating star-forms within blackish-brown outlines. These tiles are more or less geometric in design, in complete contrast to the graceful plant fantasies of the first category. Differently arranged, the turquoise-coloured triangular tiles become lozenges. These wares were undoubtedly exported to Cairo, although they were later probably made in Egypt also.

SYRIANS IN EDIRNE

Tiles of the same kind as those of the "Masters of Tabriz" in the Green Mosque of Bursa are found in the mosque of Murad I in Edirne, or Adrianople, which was completed in the year 1433, and were presumably products of the same workshop. There is in this mosque, however, also a wall faced with hexagonal tiles, which have blue and white underglaze decorations in the Chinese style.

In the *mihrab*, there are, among the *cuerda seca* tiles, smaller, specially shaped tiles which have either blue and white underglaze painting or black designs under a green glaze. Their shapes prove that they can only have been made locally, and they are so much like the tiles from Damascus that it must be assumed that they were produced in a workshop employing foreign craftsmen. No doubt it was Persian tile-makers from Tabriz who collaborated in their manufacture. This Syrian work can also be recognised in the underglaze painting in blue, turquoise, purple and black to be found in the Uch Sherefeli Mosque at Edirne (1437–1447).

ISNIK

It cannot be assumed that there was a connection between these Syrian tiles and those of Isnik, the ancient Nicaea, which were produced there from the end of the fifteenth century. The earliest tiles of Isnik are only a by-product of a ceramic industry which flourished in other spheres. The porous clay, which became white when fired, covered with a fine wash, provided the perfect base for a particularly brilliant glaze which developed no crackle when it was fired. The first period is characterised by blue and white decoration. In the Türbe of Prince Mustafa (d. 1474) in Bursa, presumed to have been decorated in 1512, the monochrome hexagonal tiles produced by the Persians are surrounded by long, narrow tiles which were probably made at the beginning of the sixteenth century. In the Türbe of Prince Mahmud unfired gold decorations in white medallions, similar to those made by the Persians, are found. In the second quarter of the sixteenth century, the tight arabesques gave way to more naturalistic plant-ornaments and polychrome painting, in which turquoise-blue predominated. This style of decoration was formerly wrongly attributed to Damascus. Once again the tiles are hexagonal and again they have designs under a green transparent glaze, this time with the same motifs which we find on vases: arabesques, cloud-scrolls and a kind of feathery leaf. The units of design are so carefully and neatly disposed that they suggest the use of stencils. The tiles were combined with triangular pieces to form panels, as, for example, in the Topkapi Saray in Istanbul. In about 1550 the designs began to be divided between a group of tiles, and the old hexagonals began to give way to rectangular shapes (35). Olive-green came into use as well as turquoise, and these were sometimes also supplemented by purple. Since, however, it was difficult to fire these colour-combinations, comprising dark blue, indigo blue,

olive-green and purple, which were not very full of contrasts, this colour-scheme was abandoned after a time. Feathery leaves and palmettes in their different variations remained the basic elements of the composition. Slight deviations are flowering twigs or Chinese motifs, such as ducks.

THE SEALING-WAX RED TILES OF ISTANBUL

In about the year 1550 a third style was evolved in Isnik and tiles were produced in great numbers. In the year 1453 the Turks had conquered Istanbul with the purpose of making it their capital in place of Edirne. This event naturally brought in its train many opportunities for tile-decoration, the great architectural projects being the mosques built by the Greek architect Sinan (1489–1588). The helmet-like shape of the domes gave a martial appearance to the exteriors of the mosques but the interiors were places of repose and relaxation. No trivial features break the surfaces of the domes, and the walls beneath them are faced with gardens of faience flowers, suggested perhaps by the experiences of the Turkish architects who, in the year 1545, had replaced the old mosaics of the Dome of the Rock at Jerusalem with tiles. In Istanbul, in the mosque of Süleyman I, the Magnificent, which was built between 1550 and 1557, the striking, thick red of Isnik appears for the first time. It was at first a little blotchy and brownish and was used beside manganese; since, however, this contrast was not particularly attractive, the manganese was abandoned. In the mosque of Rüstem Pasha, after 1561, tiles were used throughout the building not only on the walls, but also on pillars, in the *mihrab* and the *mimbar* or pulpit. The *mihrab* is full of budding trees "wreathed with lilies, tulips and carnations". Only the tiles of the Green Mosque and in the Green Tomb in Bursa can stand comparison with this display of richness and splendour. Turquoise is here used as the principal contrast to the red, which is beginning to shade into scarlet. In the Mosque of Sokollu Mahmud (1571), the celebrated masterpiece of the time of Shah Abbas, this scarlet is used in contrast with a bright bluish-green. And in the Blue Mosque of Sultan Ahmed I we find the same brilliance of colour.

These tiles correspond with the pottery vessels which used to be attributed to Rhodes. Tiles and vases show a similar degree of accomplishment; the colours within their black outlines contrasting with the cold white glittering background are extraordinarily brilliant. Up to this time in the Near East, as in Italy, the red pig-

Melody of a dervishes' dance of Konya symbolising the movements of the heavenly bodies. This unusual piece bears witness to the cosmic nature of the Seljuk religion and is characteristic of a whole civilisation, which is also expressed in their tile-faced buildings. (Reproduced from In the Steps of St. Paul *by H. W. Morton.)*

ment had become dull when it was fired because, due to the presence of iron-oxide, firing dissolved the lead particles of the glaze and it always took on a brownish tone. In Istanbul, however, they achieved a red of wonderful brilliance. It was applied in a thick layer, so that it stood out like a relief, and the Turkish lead-glaze stuck to it. This colour has been called sealing-wax red and it is illuminating to learn from Robert Liddell's book, *Byzantium and Istanbul*, that it was held to have been obtained from coral. The colour was such that this erroneous belief was possible. In addition to the old ornaments, tulips and carnations were used and sometimes birds as well. Panels with inscriptions show the characters against coloured backgrounds, some of which are red.

The designs must have originated in Istanbul and have been carried out in Isnik. Once again, the fact that the designs are repeated with such accuracy shows that they were executed with the aid of a stencil and the brush strokes also reveal that they were not carried out free-hand. In this respect, the Persian and Syrian tiles have a much more individual character than the Turkish. Lane writes that these tiles with their "improbable forms and barbarically splendid colour have a cruel fascination like that of hothouse plants."[1]

In the first half of the seventeenth century, the industry began to decline. The sultans had been the foremost patrons of the Isnik tile-makers and fewer buildings were being erected in Istanbul. In the year 1648 only nine workshops in Isnik were still in production whereas at the beginning of the century there had been as many as three hundred. The same decline may be observed in Istanbul, where, in the year 1639, the Baghdad Kiosk[2] and, in the year 1641, the Circumcision Room of the Topkapi Saray Palace were decorated with re-used tiles. And in the Yenim Valide Mosque (1663–1672) it is clear that work of the old quality was no longer available. Blue and turquoise are the only colours used and they lack brilliance just as the draughts-manship lacks rhythm. The large tile painted with the plan of the Kaaba in Mecca, which must date from the year 1665, already belongs to the period of decline (39). In the year 1724, the Vizir Daud Ibrahim attempted to launch a new tile-industry in Istanbul. He assembled in his capital the last remaining skilled craftsmen; their wares were good as regards colour, although they certainly had few first-class designs, and they carried on the industry through the eighteenth century in an adequate manner. Their designs show a great many European elements and reflect the European fashion which at that time dominated Turkey – just as the vogue for halls and baths decorated with tiles of Turkish inspiration was soon to dominate western Europe.

KÜTAHYA: ARMENIAN CHRISTIANS

In addition to these workshops, there existed in Turkey the tile-industry of Kütahya conducted by the Armenian Christians. In the year 1719 they painted over 160 tiles which had been commissioned for the Church of the Resurrection in Jerusalem but which, due to disputes, were never delivered. Thirty-seven of these tiles were later used for the Armenian Cathedral of St. James in Jerusalem, incorporated among blue-and-white tiles. They represent biblical scenes and figures, in colours which to some extent recall those of the Isnik ceramics, with the addition of a bright opaque yellow. The style is crude and primitive. Tiles of this type, even more naively executed, are found in many Armenian churches. The European influence is obvious: specimens with cherubs' heads and a cartouche reminiscent of German baroque art of about 1730 are preserved in the Victoria and Albert Museum, London (34). Imitations of Isnik ceramics are still being produced in Kütahya.

Plan of the sacred enclosure of Mecca.
Large tile of the period of the decline
of Isnik ceramic art, when sealing-
wax red was no longer used. Victoria
and Albert Museum, London.

SYRIA, EGYPT, THE MAGHRIB

In Syria, which came under Turkish rule in 1516, the tile-industry of Damascus continued to operate. When Süleyman the Magnificent directed that the mosaics of the Dome of the Rock at Jerusalem should be replaced by tiles, Persians, who probably came from Tabriz, started work in 1545 with the inscribed frieze immediately below the dome. They worked from the top downwards and at first adopted the *cuerda seca* technique; they then obviously began to experiment and transferred to underglaze painting. One tile, executed in this technique, is signed by Abdullah of Tabriz. It is probable that these Persian artists afterwards settled in Damascus and founded there an industry making tiles with underglaze painting. Such first-rate work, however, was not maintained. The influence of the Isnik tiles was strong, although the quality of the imitations does not equal that of the models; the drawing is slipshod and careless, in complete contrast to the rigorous discipline of Isnik. Favourite designs for important commissions in Syria were rows of cypresses or flower-vases with vertical branches against a blue background. These large panels are extremely beautiful, although the details have little charm. Imitations of Istanbul mosques are to be found everywhere: that built by the architect Sinan in 1585 diffuses an atmosphere of great calm. All these mosques were faced with tiles locally produced. The colours are confined to black outlines, turquoise, green and a manganese which replaces the red of Isnik. The glaze is thick and glassy and strongly crackled.

An offshoot of the tile-industry of Damascus operated during the seventeenth century in Egypt, which had become a part of the Ottoman Empire in 1517.

The Moorish countries of North Africa, the so-called Maghrib, did not distinguish themselves in the production of tiles. The Moors of Spain certainly derived no inspiration from this source. The Moors are closely related to the Arabs, who never had an art of their own. In their numerous relationships with the peoples of the Middle and Near East these desert-dwellers contributed their power of swift thought and their talent for Aristotelian logic and dialectic; but in the sphere of art they were the receivers, taking much from the Persians and the Seljuks in particular. Thus it is in no way surprising that, from the late thirteenth century onwards, the North African countries, influenced as they were by Arab culture, took over tile-mosaics from Asia.

What is more surprising is the existence of close, direct links between the Moors and the Christians of Spain and the Near East. There are to be found on Spanish façades glazed ornamental slabs such as were already in use in the Babylon of Nebuchadnezzar. In the extremely beautiful dome of the Convento de la Concepción Francisca in Toledo, stucco bands reflect the richness of arabesques, the Kufic script and other Islamic features, and we are reminded of many of the decorative slabs of the Seljuks with their complicated patterns, of similar work in Georgia and Armenia – much the same as the admirable work in the *mimbar* of Ulu Çami in Divriği. Zigzag lines, angular, geometric borders and interlace designs, such as were used in Rum and in the Caucasus and are probably of central Asiatic origin, reappear here. Stars occur frequently and should sometimes, perhaps, as in Rum, be regarded as connected with Venus, the great goddess of fertility. As in Asia, pillars are often of small architectural importance, their sole function being to lead the eye upwards into the higher parts of the building. Similar features may be observed in North Africa, whither they were taken by the Moors of Spain.

The abstract designs of the tiles of Granada are reflected in the Moorish tiles or *azulejos*. The best works of the Moorish potters in Africa are the public fountains of

Miniature from the Book of Festivities. *Turkish manuscript of the 16th century. In 1583, on the occasion of the circumcision of his son Mahmud, Sultan Murad III to display his power gave a feast in the hippodrome of Istanbul which lasted for 52 days and nights. The miniature shows the entry of the sultan into the hippodrome with his court, janissaries playing musical instruments, eunuchs dancing and jugglers. At the top left an acrobat may be seen. In the background stands the pavilion of the sultan with its facing of star-shaped and cruciform tiles. Near the sultan and holding a blue garment is a dervish.*

Marrakesh, especially El Mouasine, on which there is a cornice carved to a stalactite design of Persian origin and tiled facings showing suns with rays and parhelia, similar to those at Konya. There are numerous examples of this style to be found in Morocco. In the madrassas of Fez, such as, for example, the Attarine (1325), there are numerous tiled walls, which, in conjunction with wood-panelling and the many arches with stalactite edges exert a magical effect. Nevertheless, the tiles of the Maghrib remain entirely unoriginal. In the seventeenth century and later tiles were produced in great numbers in the coastal regions, but the craftsmen took their models from the European industry across the Mediterranean. Maiolica was imported from Italy and Spain; here, as in Spain, there was a demand for tiles with reliefs under green or light brown glazes. Under the fierce sun of the Maghrib delightful, even beautiful, works were made, but all were derivative.

Early English Tiles

From time immemorial, as far back, even, as the tents of the nomadic tribes, the peoples of Asia and Europe have covered their floors with rugs. Tiled floors are of infrequent occurrence in the East. Although tiles were made and decorated in practically every known way, including relief, lustre, stucco, mosaic, *cuerda seca*, *cuenca*, transparent glaze, underglaze and on-glaze painting and muffling, there was one technique which did not flourish in Asia: that of inlay. Tiles thus decorated are durable, provided that the designs are sufficiently deeply inlaid, and are therefore particularly well suited to floors.

In western Europe faience tiles did not become popular until a later date. The desire for bright colour to equal or outshine precious stones was satisfied by the work of the goldsmiths and by the stained glass windows of the cathedrals. The glazed tiles which, from the second half of the twelfth century onwards, were occasionally found in dwelling places, had usually been imported from Spain. The many links with the East forged by trade and the crusades had perhaps taught people to appreciate their beauty.

European taste, however, inclined rather towards the Latin tradition. Although but few Roman floor-mosaics had survived, some were nevertheless known, as were lead-glazes – which, however, were of course not used on the natural stones of the mosaics since these could not be fired. Theophilus in his *Schedula diversarum artium* (c. 1100) left instructions regarding the use of lead-glazes. When important commissions had to be executed, it was doubtless usual to think of copying Roman mosaics, using, however, less costly and locally available materials.

One may wonder whether there were, perhaps, no tiles at all for floors or for other purposes before the twelfth century. But terracotta tiles decorated in relief were certainly known. The monuments from Tours and Ulm discussed in the next chapter may provide an idea of the oriental splendour which, in this sphere as in others, had entered the experience of the new peoples of Europe. In central and western Europe during the later Middle Ages, tiles – and they were principally floor-tiles – seem to have been produced according to the following techniques: mosaic, inlay, *sgraffito* and *sgraffiato* and relief. The golden age of these floors was during the twelfth and thirteenth centuries, at the time, that is, when the finest Kashan tiles and the mosaics of Konya were being created; by the fourteenth century the vogue had lost its force. The dates, however, cannot be established with complete accuracy. The centres of origin of the medieval floors are also in the main difficult to ascertain, since, in the case of inlaid and relief tiles, the same blocks remained long in use. All that can in fact be stated with certainty is that the mythical content of the designs gradually disappeared and that in the fifteenth century a new style, characterised by the inclusion of domestic motifs and a more summary execution, made its appearance.

The English floors, especially when they are composed of inlaid tiles, are of a quality so much superior to those of the Continent that they should be discussed first. Their finer execution, sparkling fantasy and richness of decorative detail, their splendid display of heraldry and, above all, the evocative power of their figures, place them on a very much higher artistic level.

English mosaic floors are perhaps of not much later date than the first French ones, although a connection with the Continent should not necessarily be assumed. England had been an important province of the Roman Empire and many mosaics of natural stones had been made here. A single example, that of the villa at Fishbourne, near Chichester, excavated since 1961,[1] will suffice. An effect has here been attempted which is characteristic of declining cultures: the observer is deceived into believing that he sees before him a composition of rising blocks and towers whereas in reality the floor is quite flat. This floor, with its illusory effect, is only one noteworthy example of the surviving Roman models.

The tile-mosaics of the Middle Ages were not made, as those of Persia were, of assembled fragments of a fired slab but out of small pieces of clay which were shaped while they were soft and, after firing, were embedded in a layer of lime-mortar. They were usually of a simple geometrical shape; more complicated forms, such as that of the fleur-de-lis were composed of several pieces. Next, according to whatever pattern was desired, a slip of pipe-clay and the yellowish transparent lead-glaze, which always covered the upper surface and was coloured as required, were applied. The colour effect of the whole consisted of dark brown or red (the clay), yellowish-white (the slip, visible through the lead-glaze) and green or black (the coloured glaze).

These floors are often markedly Eastern in appearance. Viewed as a whole, they often resemble a series of oriental rugs laid side by side. There is, indeed, no reason why an Englishman of the thirteenth century should not have seen rugs so arranged in an Eastern mosque or why he should not have felt the inclination to lay out and decorate the floor in contrast, for once, to the Western, Roman manner, in such a way as to make good use of the available space. Since the time of the barbarian invasions a part of the population of Europe has always come from the East; it is, therefore, not surprising that Asiatic ideas and Asiatic ornament, divorced from its stylistic context, should reappear in Europe.

The question whether the tile-mosaics of the thirteenth century were confined to the Cistercian order has long been a subject of controversy. The monks undoubtedly laid many tiled floors, as, for example, those in the abbeys of Newbottle, Byland, Meaux, Fountains and Melrose. These mosaics, which, for all their simplicity, required a high level of skill in the craftsmen who laid them, harmonise excellently with the austere magnificence of the Cistercian churches.

Mosaic was the most ancient of the decorative techniques mentioned. A mosaic floor was still being laid in the chapel of Prior Crauden at Ely as late as the period 1321–1341. Yet about the year 1200 the need had begun to be felt for an alternative technique, in which figures could be represented with greater ease, and the inlaid floors which answered this need have become one of the glories of English art.

This style of decoration also was derived from stone floors. The design was drawn out on a stone slab. The background was then cut away in shallow counter-relief and into the sunken areas was pressed a resinous composition darker than the stone so that the figure stood out light against the dark ground. Details were engraved and likewise filled with dark resin. Tomb-slabs often bear the portrait of the deceased in outline only. A series of stone roundels, decorated in this manner, was at the beginning of the thirteenth century let into a mosaic floor, a pavement of the Cosmati school, in the retrochoir of Canterbury Cathedral. The work of the Cosmati of Rome had been well-known in England since Pietro Odorisio had executed a magnificent stone mosaic for the choir of Westminster Abbey, which had been brought from Rome to London in about 1267. Oderisio himself, or members of his family, worked thereafter in England. The roundels at Canterbury represent the occupations of the months and the signs of the zodiac. The cycle resembles that of the early thirteenth-century pavement at St. Omer in France. The stylistic and technical similarities between the two are so great that the known existence of close links between the clergy of the two churches can only confirm the supposition that the same artists must have worked in both places.

The technique was now developed further. The idea occurred of impressing a pattern in the clay by means

 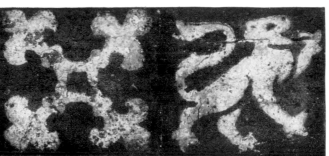 

of a wooden block, the resulting impression being filled with pipe-clay. This simplified system replaced the more laborious technique of engraving and cutting away the natural stone. The tiles were finally covered by a transparent glaze and fired.

In the Chapter House of Westminster Abbey a very fine example of this technique has been preserved almost untouched. It dates from the years 1253–1259 and bears a "rose-window", hunting scenes and the por-traits of Henry III, his queen Eleanor and Archbishop Richard of Crokesley, while minstrels enhance the courtly atmosphere. The inlaid tiles are arranged in long bands, two of them showing the arms of England. The whole is enriched by roundels, lions and quadri-lobes; here again, the composition is suggestive of ori-ental carpets. In the Chapter House of Salisbury cathe-dral the tiles were laid in cross-formation. The Old Choir School at Worcester Cathedral has a pavement[2] arranged in three parallel fields, which, although it dates from the fourteenth century, possesses much of the austerity of thirteenth-century compositions. Black tiles alternate with inlaid tiles showing heraldic motifs and ornaments; in the central field, lozenges appear between black tiles.

The shape of the individual pieces, although important in mosaic, is only of subsidiary significance in the new technique. The tiles become square and substantially larger in size. The pavement of the Chapter House at Westminster was probably executed in the same work-shop as the tiles found on the site of Chertsey Abbey in Surrey (48). The tiles from Chertsey have not the rec-tangular uniformity of shape of those at Westminster. Tiles of the Chertsey type were also found at Hayles Abbey in Gloucestershire, built by Richard of Cornwall, brother of Henry III – a further indication of the con-nection between this pottery and the court.

In Chertsey, where the tiles were perhaps intended for a royal chapel, the decoration included roundels sur-rounded by rectangular frames. In one series, in addi-tion to hunting and battle scenes, there are episodes from the legendary history of Richard Lion-Heart; in another series, perhaps of slightly later date, scenes from the romance of Tristan and Isolde are shown. The drawing is bold, foliage and fabulous creatures are im-aginatively and carefully executed. The Richard series provides an example of the survival of the tile-mosaic technique in the fact that the inscriptions are composed of small tiles, bearing only one letter apiece. This link with the earlier mosaic tradition appears to be nothing unusual for the workshop. The British Museum possesses small, round tiles from Chertsey, some with heads, others with the labours of the months, which are surrounded by tiles of the most varied shapes with inlaid foliage designs.

The Chertsey tile-kiln was found on the site of the Abbey. At the Premonstratensian Abbey of Halesowen, near Birmingham, the same stamps were used as at Chertsey and the same scenes from the Tristan legend were portrayed. The tile-makers probably travelled about with their tools and set up kilns where necessary. There were also, however, small workshops which pro-vided for local needs. Members of the monastic orders certainly did not engage in tile-making after it became an industry; from that moment onwards, if not before, it was in the hands of laymen.[3] Another important fact emerged from the excavations at Halesowen. One tile carries the inscription, "Istud opus Nicholas Matri Christi dedit Abbas Vigeat absque Chao, mater, dona Nicholao" (This work the Abbot Nicholas gave to the mother of Christ. That he may flourish without confusion, mother, grant to Nicholas). This Nicholas died in 1298 and the Halesowen pavement must have been laid before then. The inscription makes it possible, therefore, to date the two Chertsey series to about 1270. Most of the cathedrals and parish churches of England must have been decorated with inlaid tiles although

Left and right: Tiles from Chertsey Abbey, Surrey. 13th century. Middle: Portrait of Henry III on a tile from Westminster Abbey.

only a few have survived the wear of centuries. But in the abbeys which were dissolved at the Reformation many splendid tiles have been preserved. The foliate designs of Keynsham Abbey in Somerset (46) are les elaborate than the decoration at Chertsey or Halesowen but are still vigorous and pleasing. Roundels enclosing fabulous creatures from the same abbey and a tree between two birds from Tintern are examples of the more unpretentious tiles which were produced all over England. Models were often furnished by textile designs as, for example, in the case of a tile carrying a double-headed eagle which probably came from Lyme Regis; or by heraldic devices such as the swan-badge which Henry IV adopted from his first wife's family of De Bohun and which was found on a fragment of tile at Kenilworth. A curious use of letters sometimes suggests that the tile-maker was illiterate. As time went on, design and execution became increasingly simplified. The St. Paul under a canopy from Whitmore Park near Coventry (46) is only an uninspired reminiscence of the splendid figures of Chertsey and Westminster; representations of architecture were also simplified. The tile-makers became so indifferent to general changes in style and revolutions in architecture that the floors of the fifteenth century are often indistinguishable from those of the fourteenth. A very handsome tile-pavement, dated 1455, was laid in front of the high altar of Gloucester Cathedral (46). Smooth black tiles divide the field into squares of four, nine or sixteen inlaid tiles.

The change in style which took place in the course of the fifteenth century was accompanied by a falling-off in technique. For a long time the pipe-clay had ceased to be pressed into the counter-relief but was instead poured in. As the decline continued, the white clay was sometimes smeared over the surface of the block before the impression was made. There is here an obvious analogy with the woodcut and the practice of inking the block. As this development proceeded, the applied layer became increasingly thinner and therefore increasingly prone to wear.

A large number of tiles of the fifteenth century were found at Great Malvern Priory in Worcestershire. Many of these had been placed in an unusual position, upright and covering the lower part of the church wall. A unit composed of five rectangular tiles formed a Gothic canopy under the successive arches of which heraldic shields, the sacred monogram and the Pelican in her Piety, the symbol of Christ, appear.[4] An inscription which mentions the thirty-sixth year of the reign of Henry VI enables us to date the composition to the year 1457 or 1458. Inscriptions on this type of tile were frequent.

Delightful as the inlaid tiles of the fifteenth century are, they have lost, for all their attractive homely realism, the greatness inherent in the mythical creations of the thirteenth century. The monkeys and squirrels which now appear are the creatures of a new world. In the fourteenth century the attempt was already being made to achieve a richer colour-effect on a flat ground by the use of partial glazing. Parts of the geometrical design were filled with clay and covered with a green glaze. By this means, a green design on a red, unglazed ground was obtained.

Evidence of the work of Flemish craftsmen is occasionally found. This statement touches upon a subject which has not yet been systematically investigated, namely, the export of wares from the Netherlands to the British Isles and the emigration of Flemish craftsmen to England. Documents record that such links existed. There are, for instance, tiles from the church at Edmonton with the Dutch inscription: "Die tijt is cort/Die doot is snel/Wacht U vā sonden/Soe doedi wel" (Time is short, Death is swift, Waken from sin, So do thou good). As was only to be expected, links between England and the Netherlands have persisted through the centuries.

Not many inlaid tiles were made in England after the Reformation. Churches were no longer being built, the monasteries were dissolved; and what was needed for repairs could be obtained from the ruins. One of the last commissions for a tile-pavement was given in 1511 by the last Duke of Buckingham of the Stafford line for Thornbury Castle in Gloucestershire (56); but it was never completed, for in 1521 Henry VIII arrested the Duke. Nevertheless, tiles were still being made late enough for Renaissance decoration to appear on them. It is possible that Holbein drew designs for them; at all events they were influenced by him. After the sixteenth century the technique continued to be revived from time to time. The potters who produced slip-ware used the same materials as had been used for the medieval tiles and when they made tiles themselves they fell back on the old methods. Thus inlaid tomb-slabs may bear dates in the seventeenth or eighteenth centuries.

The tiles engraved in the *sgraffito* and *sgraffiato* techniques are particularly beautifully and carefully made. In the *sgraffito* technique an engobe of contrasting colours was applied; the design was engraved in the engobe so that the contrasting colour of the body showed through. The *sgraffiato* technique consisted in scraping away whole areas of the top coat so that the body was laid bare and formed, not the design, but the background. Well-known examples of these rare medieval *sgraffiato* tiles, which came from Tring Church in Hertfordshire, are today preserved in the British Museum and the Victoria and Albert Museum. The late Dr. Montague James showed that their themes were taken from a vernacular version of the Apocryphal Infancy Gospels describing the childhood of Christ. They were identified by comparing them with a manuscript in the Bodleian Library, Oxford.[5] The following miracles from the childhood of Christ are reproduced on the tiles: 1) Jesus raising the boys who played with him on a hill and fell; 2) Jesus and some boys drawing water;

3) the parents of a boy who imitated Jesus sliding on a sunbeam remonstrating with Joseph; 4) the boy being brought to life. Another tile in the Victoria and Albert Museum shows the surprise of the dyer when he discovered that when his apprentice, Jesus, put all the clothes into one vat they still came out with the right colours. The tiles are numbered on the back and since the numbers XXX and XXXVI occur, it is possible that all fifty-nine scenes of the Oxford manuscript were reproduced.

With *sgraffito* and *sgraffiato*, each tile is an original which cannot be reproduced by mechanical means. This technique was therefore used only for special commissions. One of these was the chapel built by Prior Crauden at Ely (1321–1341), in the lavish ornamentation of which the most various techniques of tile-decoration were used. A large part of the floor is paved with mosaic-tiles – according to Lane perhaps the latest example of the use of this technique in England. There are also large slabs in *sgraffiato* decorated with the Temptation of Adam and Eve and with heraldic beasts. It is possible that the *sgraffiato* technique was also used for tombs to take the place of monumental brasses. Two monumental tomb-slabs of this kind of the period of Henry VIII were found at Lingfield in Surrey.

Tiles with relief decoration came into use in England at the beginning of the thirteenth century. Whereas inlaid tiles were made at many places, for many centuries the relief tiles were produced only in certain workshops. These workshops were clearly not in contact with one another. Kiln-wasters prove that relief-tiles found on the site of the early thirteenth-century Cistercian monastery at North Berwick were produced locally, as was the case at Butley Priory in Suffolk. Patterns on tiles of these series show that animals such as lions, gryphons and dragons from Sassanian or perhaps Alexandrian textiles were among the decorative prototypes; other patterns were heraldic symbols, and geometric designs,

49

also formal foliage which appears to be a late survival of the Romanesque style. They were glazed in olive-brown over high relief; signs of wear show that they were used for pavements. Lane drew attention to their resemblance to the twelfth-century German tiles of Schlettstadt type and conjectured that the technique was introduced into East Anglia from Germany via Holland.

In St. Albans in the thirteenth century attempts were made to produce a polychrome effect on relief tiles. Tiles which were found there and are now in the British Museum have raised motifs in light-grey clay coated with transparent glaze so that they stand out vividly against the dark-brown glazed background. Contrasts between dark and light-brown were also achieved. Relief tiles have been found all over England and were undoubtedly also made in Wales in the thirteenth century.

In the fourteenth century there was a workshop at Bawsey, near King's Lynn, Norfolk, which supplied East Anglia with small relief tiles mostly with monochrome green, yellow or, occasionally, brown glaze. The design is also sometimes sunk in the surface. The decorative repertory consists mainly, as one would expect of the period, of heraldic shields, the old motifs of animals and fabulous creatures; rosettes are less frequent. Related in style are two small brown-glazed tiles from Lilleshall Abbey in Shropshire with shields bearing a stag's head and the Instruments of the Passion respectively.

Tiles with impressed linear designs like those of the Rhineland, but glazed, have also been found in East Anglia, notably in Prior Crauden's chapel at Ely (1321–1341). In Devonshire and Cornwall, at least, the technique continued to be used in rustic potteries into the eighteenth century.

As the final variation, mention may be made of stoves with relief-tiles which may have been imported from Germany or were perhaps produced locally. This industry is of importance for the present book, which deals exclusively with tiles in their architectural setting, only in so far as cisterns were also made in this technique. They were often decorated with royal emblems or monograms, perhaps out of loyalty or perhaps as a modish touch of grace and elegance.

Early Tiles in France, Germany, the Netherlands and Switzerland

The European tiles of the so-called Dark Ages, like other forms of art, testify to contacts with the East and with antiquity. R. Lantier has published two interesting terracotta tomb-slabs.[1] One, from Grésin in the Auvergne (42×27×3 cm.) shows Christ triumphing over the serpent and the cockatrice; the other, smaller slab, found at Tours and now preserved in the museum there, shows Christ in prayer with the sun and moon as symbols. In view of the presence of the sun and moon, Lantier has pointed out, "In spite of the disinclination of Merovingian Gaul to portray the Saviour on the Cross, I venture to suggest that what we see on the terracotta slab from Tours is a representation of Christ crucified."

The Carolingian terracotta reliefs from Kellmünz and the former imperial palace of Ulm (55) are of particular importance. Alamannic slabs from a burial-place were found at Kellmünz and similar slabs must have been taken to Kirchdorf on the Iller. These pieces are fragments of four similar reliefs which show the upper part of a praying figure – on the analogy of the Grésin relief it may be assumed to be Christ – with his hands raised in front of him. Another fragment bears a round head with large eyes, surrounded by rays and a circle, which by reference to the tile from Tours, may be taken to be a symbol of the sun. Finds have also included stags' and cocks' heads. The tiles must come from a burial-place similar to the Roman tomb at Carnuntum, near Hainburg in Austria. The interlaced decoration suggests a date in the eighth century.

Twenty-six red clay tiles were excavated at the site of the Carolingian palace at Ulm (55); their measurements may be calculated from fragments to have been 52×39×2.5 cm. They carried impressed reliefs and were fired. The material is the same as that of the tiles found at Kellmünz, so that it is permissible to assume the existence of a local workshop. The motifs were a walking lion and a gryphon. The style of the lion is largely Byzantine, that of the gryphon wholly Sassanian. The fact that they are walking not towards one another but both in the same direction suggests that they may have been arranged as a frieze.[2]

Tile-mosaic floors imitating the Roman stone mosaic floors, were made in France, as has been said above, possibly even earlier than in England. The Chapel of Ste. Geneviève at St. Denis was paved in this manner in the second half of the twelfth century.

The technique of the inlaid tile was also known in the twelfth and thirteenth centuries; indeed, the pavement at St. Omer of inlaid stone slabs shows that by the beginning of the thirteenth century it had been fully mastered. Galloping knights against a dark-grey background, the details picked out in red, and stags with great antlers are arranged in large fields and bands. There is a well-known pavement of pottery with an inlaid decoration at St. Pierre-sur-Dives, which is perhaps to be dated to the twelfth century; it represents a rose-window but, in spite of its quality, it cannot stand comparison with the vivid details and careful drawing of Chertsey. Tiles of the thirteenth and fourteenth centuries at St. Etienne in Caen and in the cathedral at Troyes show great similarity to English work.

It was only in the second half of the fifteenth century that French inlaid tiles came to possess an independent national style. The motifs are usually dark against a light background and are freely and spontaneously drawn; they include centaurs, hunting scenes and jesters. Forrer[3] reproduces a lozenge-shaped tile on which there appears a fool running, wearing cap and bells and the inscription "prenez à grace la france," an allusion to the wretched state of the country during the Hundred Years' War. An interesting piece is the octagonal tile in the Vecht collection in Amsterdam with emblems of the phlegmatic temperament.[4] Coats-of-arms, monograms and makers' inscriptions were further popular variations. Some inlaid tiles have a green-flecked glaze.

The *sgraffiato* technique was also cultivated in France. At the time (1321–1341) when the chapel of Prior Crauden was being built at Ely, the potters of Molay in Normandy were making monumental tomb-slabs of tiles, on which the deceased appears under a canopy.

Relief tiles were rare in France. An exception is furnished by the roof-tiles connected with the Cluniac Order, of which the Boymans-van Beuningen Museum at Rotterdam possesses a group of high quality (62), consisting of grotesque heads derived from Sumerian symbolism of the waxing and waning moon and from the ancient Greek figures of Chronos and Argus. So it was that these archaic figures, now transformed into carnival masks and fair-ground apparitions, slipped into the solemn houses of the Order and the exhortations of Bernard of Clairvaux and the new austerity of the Cistercians were momentarily forgotten.

Lane dated to the sixteenth century a lion rampant and an angular leaf-pattern under an olive-brown glaze from a floor at Clermont-Ferrand. In the second half of the sixteenth century a factory in the neighbourhood of Neuchâtel-en-Bray in Normandy produced a series of square or hexagonal floor-tiles showing human heads in roundels amid stylised foliage. In many cases the olive-brown or blue glaze has worn away from the raised surface.

The development of tiles in the Netherlands took the same course as it did in France. Here again, the country acted as an intermediary: in the same way that the relief tiles from Germany found their way into East Anglia via the Netherlands, so, probably, did the idea of applying slip travel eastwards through the same countries. Of all the central European countries, it was only the Rhineland which produced slipware – and that relatively late. In Marburg in the eighteenth century, for example, Burkhard Keppler took over this old traditional local craft and developed it into a flourishing trade. The painting was done in brown and green slips directly on the clay or over a white slip ground; the outlines were engraved in *sgraffito*. In the Netherlands, in the choir of St. Lebuinus in Deventer, there is a handsome mosaic pavement which has the appearance of a series of oriental rugs laid out on the floor. Mention must also be made here of the objects found on the site of the Mariendaal convent near Utrecht, since these included a tile in the shape of a heraldic shield with inlaid coat-of-arms.[5]

In Germany the demand for tiles was met by relief-decorated wares. Alsace clearly took the lead. A miniature in the manuscript *Hortus deliciarum* of Herrad von Landsberg, written between 1175 and 1180 in the monastery of St. Odilia near Strasbourg, shows King Solomon enthroned before a wall faced with tiles decorated in relief. Here again, the style is derived from textile wall-hangings: the figures of animals betray their direct descent from Sassanian textiles or from those which were derived from them in Istanbul, Sicily, Spain or Germany itself.

Relief tiles have always been preferred in the German-speaking countries. The earliest known examples, designed for both wall and floor, were found in the Church of St. Fides at Schlettstadt, Alsace. They include hexagonal tiles with centaurs and long diamond-shaped tiles with fantastic two-headed birds; they probably date from the second half of the twelfth century.

The technique spread from Alsace to the Rhineland and Friesland and probably to England; in the opposite direction it extended to Switzerland. The monastery of St. Urban near Zofingen produced large, mostly unglazed, wall- and floor-tiles. The reliefs, which were applied by counter-sunk stamps show beasts and foliage in the Romanesque style which persisted long after the Gothic had become established in northern France and Germany (55). Often several small stamps were used for one tile. This type of tile continued to be made until 1350 and in places persisted into the fifteenth century.

Sites where they have been found include Frienisberg, Altbüro and Fraubrunnen.

In the cities of the Rhine during the same period small tiles became popular; they bore stamped linear patterns which were sometimes gone over by hand; motifs include heraldic devices, stags or a huntsman with hounds and quarry and are often vigorously drawn. The most important find was made in a house in Constance, which after 1565 was known, from the name of its tenant, the Domherr Kuonrat Freiherr von Stadion, as the "Domherrenhof". The tiles may be dated either to 1310 or 1346–1356, when the house was rebuilt. They are unglazed, of red or grey clay (55).

This simple but effective form of decoration was widespread in the Netherlands, Switzerland and Austria. It is often found in the Rhineland, as, for example, in Mainz, Worms, Bacharach and Cologne. It appears that red and grey tiles were laid alternately. The formal foliage gradually assumed a Gothic character. The technique, however, declined at an early date, became monotonous and increasingly restricted to ovals and simple tracery. By the sixteenth century it had completely degenerated into folk-art. It was now the general practice to apply lead-glaze. Under the glaze, particularly when it was coloured, slip was often applied, as has been mentioned before, in order to lighten the green or brownish colour.

Faience tiles were known in the Middle Ages on both sides of the Rhine and it is not surprising that they bear witness to the numerous contacts with the East which resulted from trade and the crusades and to those with Spain fostered by the pilgrimages to Santiago de Compostela. Knowledge of this technique derived from both these sources. Green and manganese are characteristic colours of the early European faience tiles. They pre-dominate in the products of Paterna near Valencia, which resemble Italian wares such as the vessels from Orvieto. Similar wares were made in southern and western France.

Faience tiles, mostly decorated with crude geometric patterns but sometimes with floral or animal motifs, were found in the Palace of the Popes at Avignon, at Toulouse and Narbonne and among the ruins of the Abbey of Escaladieu in the Pyrenees. Similar tiles with Gothic shields from St. Julien-de-Brioude, Haute-Loire, have come down to us. The "green-and-purple family" extended as far as Hamburg, where, from about 1320 to 1330 the tomb of Pope Benedict V in the cathedral was faced with faience slabs (60, 61) decorated with figures of knights and saints.[6] Some buildings in Utrecht contained floors of about 1375–1400, in which purple, green and yellow painted human heads, animals or foliage were set in pavements among plain coloured tiles (45). The monastery of St. Bertin at St. Omer had tiles of the same kind. And it must have been tiles of this kind which the Duke of Burgundy specified in a privilege of the year 1391 to be made for his castle at Hesdin by Jehan le Voleur and Jehan de Moustier after designs by the court painter Melchior Broederlam. Similar tiles were made at the end of the fourteenth century for the castle of the Duc de Berry at Poitiers. When we see tiles of this kind portrayed in the paintings of Broederlam or Van Eyck, we may take it that the artists had often looked longingly at the reality. In conclusion it should be mentioned that in the cathedral of Langres white faience tiles were found alongside inlaid tiles, showing that pavements in mixed techniques were being made as late as the sixteenth century.

Top: These clay slabs with representations of a gryphon and a lion were found in 1958 at the Weinhof in Ulm in the vicinity of the former Imperial Palace, thought to have been destroyed in the 14th century. Examination of the clay has proved Ulm to have been the place of manufacture, but the origin—possibly Byzantine—of the stamp used in production is uncertain, as is the exact date. Museum, Ulm. Middle row: In the region of the upper Rhine relief decoration on floor-tiles was usual. Middle row left: This design occurs in a miniature in the manuscript of Herrad von Landsberg's Hortus deliciarum written in the monastery of St. Odilia near Strasbourg in 1175–1180. Middle row right: A similar design on a larger scale extending over four tiles. Bottom left: A hunting scene with stag and hounds in the style of the pieces found at the Domherrenhof in Constance. Strasbourg, 14th century. Bottom right: A "St. Urban-type" tile from Freiburg im Breisgau for which several different stamps were used. 14th century. Victoria and Albert Museum, London.

Page 56, top: A stronger feeling for nature asserted itself in the technique of inlaid tiles in France in the 15th century. A dove, a cock, dogs and a dolphin in dark clay reserved on the lighter background. Bottom: In England the fantasy and stylisation of the Romanesque was not lost, as is demonstrated by the heraldic tiles here illustrated. They come from the floor in Thornbury Castle, the building of which was commissioned in 1511 by Edward, last Duke of Buckingham of the Stafford line, but which was still unfinished in 1521, when Henry VIII arrested the Duke. The tiles show heraldic badges: the chained antelope, the flaming hub of Buckingham and the chained swan of De Bohun. Victoria and Albert Museum, London.

Decorative Bricks on Fire-place Walls

The facing and surrounding of open fire-places with decorated bricks is a speciality of the Netherlands. They protect and adorn the wall behind the fire in an imaginative way. In the Middle Ages this protection of the wall was a plain necessity since most of the houses were still built of wood, thus making the presence of an open fire in the house a constant source of danger. In most towns there were regulations requiring that the wall behind the open fire should be made of stone or at least faced with stone.

In Flanders a kind of brick was produced which, thanks to its high measure of resistance to fire, was famous far beyond the Flemish borders. The methods evolved in Flanders were later imitated in other countries but these imitations still kept their name of "Flemish stones." In about the year 1400 bricks of this kind were in use in England but it is impossible to be certain whether they were imported or produced at home.[1] "Flemish stones" were also produced in Holland.

When, in the course of the fifteenth century, the middle classes grew more prosperous and the interiors of their houses were furnished with greater luxury, the fashion became general of decorating the fire-place bricks. These decorated bricks are by no means rare today and from this it may be assumed that they were widely used; nevertheless at the time they were undoubtedly considered to be a luxurious feature in the interior decoration of a house. They were certainly worth the expense for in their somewhat restrained way they awoke dark imaginings of brave thoughts, noble princes, heraldic panoply and evoked a nobler and better world.

In the less expensively furnished rooms, the fire-place bricks remained undecorated until well into the sixteenth century, as is proved by many of the paintings of Pieter Aertsen. In the seventeenth century cast-iron fire-backs and blackened smoke-hoods came into general use. So the decorated bricks which are still in existence must be relics from expensively furnished houses of a relatively short period.

From the end of the fifteenth century onwards the bricks were decorated by impressing a stamp into the soft clay. The makers naturally wanted a large surface for their decoration and therefore used the larger side of the brick, making it necessary—since the thickness had to be maintained in the interests of safety—to alter its original proportions. The earliest bricks measure about 13–15 cm. in length by 9–11 cm. in height by 7–10 cm. in depth. The stamps were at first much smaller than the surface of the bricks so that the designs were surrounded by a wide border. They were executed without much detail and mostly showed heraldic devices, such as the Flint and Steel of Burgundy, the lily, the eagle or the lion, single heads or even two heads facing one another.

Two important characteristics are noticeable: first of all, the clear grasp of material and function—motifs and ornaments are not lost in detail, for the effect of the open fire would have caused them to deteriorate too quickly; secondly, there is something rather solemn about these motifs and they are somewhat lacking in variety .This is particularly remarkable since the fire-place was the true focal point of the house, and it must have been by design that well-loved, conventional patterns were chosen in preference to novelties; though one would have thought that the fire-light would have stimulated the imagination as, in playing over the reliefs, it produced ever-changing effects.

It appears that the motifs were borrowed from furniture decoration or from stoneware jars, so that the choice was fairly limited; this is the more remarkable since the inlaid floor-tiles show a rich variety of designs. It is scarcely necessary to point out that these floor-tiles were not suitable for use as facings for fire-places since they were not heat-resistant. One may wonder whether colour contrast was essential to the people of the northern Netherlands for the full development of their artistic gifts. Did the glowing colours of the faience tiles perhaps provide the most propitious climate for the flowering of their imagination?

In about 1500 such biblical scenes or stories from the *Golden Legend* as did not present too many complications began to be portrayed. A series of different stamps were used. Prints, or, as before, furniture, provided the designs and by degrees more complicated detail came to be represented in a subtler, less bold, fashion. At the same time finer material began to be used and the fire-place bricks became thinner; this was possible because the houses were now built of brick or stone and the fire-place facing no longer served exclusively as a protection against fire. By about 1550 the size of the bricks had changed to these proportions: 13.5–15 × 9.5–11 × 5–8 cm. in thickness.

There were, of course, local deviations. In Liège thick bricks with broad borders and bold designs remained in use until about the middle of the eighteenth century. At this time the predominant motifs were still heraldic devices and fabulous creatures. The material used in Liège was a coarse-grained clay which turned yellow with a faint reddish tinge when it was fired. Highly detailed ornamentation began in Antwerp. As early as the first half of the sixteenth century a fine-grained clay was used here which turned red when it was fired. The motifs generally preferred were portraits of princes, series representing whole histories such as, for example, those of Samson (in a series of six bricks), David (four bricks), Esther, Judith, Susanna, St. George, St. Hubert, St. Martin, as well as pastoral scenes with *putti*. In the eighteenth century, when Roman antiquities became fashionable, it was thought that the Susanna bricks were of Roman origin and that they represented the revolt of the Batavi against Rome, the female figure being taken for the priestess Veleda. Engravings by Cornelis Matsijs were also frequently used as models.

In the second half of the sixteenth century another form of ornamentation came into use. The borders disappeared and the patterns themselves became larger. Often the pattern appeared twice on each brick, sometimes within ovals; or the decoration was taken right to the edge of the brick so that they appeared no longer to be separated from one another. The recurring patterns were placed side by side to form a large decorative field, giving, once again, the impression of woven fabric. The pattern which consisted of two lions within lozenges, the corners of which were decorated with rosettes, was highly popular. In order that the joins should not show, the edges of the bricks were rubbed down.

This elaborate arrangement shows that an illusion was intended, for it is not possible to tell at first glance that these are images pieced together from small parts. As this development proceeded, the thickness of the bricks decreased to 4 or 5 cm. The surface was divided into ovals, lozenges or circles in which were placed heads in profile, heraldic symbols, horsemen, stags, flower-vases, in short, all the motifs dear to the artists of the Renaissance.

Dates are also often found among the ornaments. J. Hollestelle[2] records the years 1561 and 1641 as the earliest and latest dates known to him on bricks with the design of the lion within the lozenge. Occasionally, fired bricks were also coated with lead-glaze, as, for example, was the case with the fire-place bricks of Nuremberg, for the manufacture of which a medieval procedure continued to be employed.

In order to give protection against an open fire, the bricks were arranged more or less in a triangle so that only the part of the back wall which was most severely exposed to the fire was covered; for it appears to have been extremely expensive to face the whole fire-place. The rest of the wall of the fire-place was faced with plain bricks, which were then plastered. It was probably the practice to blacken the triangle of decorated bricks with polish, for that would have looked better and cleaner than if the red bricks had become blackened with soot; had this happened, it would have been very difficult to keep them clean and they would have suffered from constant attempts to do so. It is also possible that the bricks were glazed in order to render them washable.

About fifty bricks were needed for a fire-place. We do not known the exact way in which they were arranged since only one fire-place has been preserved where we can be reasonably certain that the old arrangement has not been changed. It is in the Brouwershuis, the guild house of the brewers in Antwerp (71) and dates from the year 1666. This incomparably fine baroque fire-place is an extremely interesting work. The small half-bricks and the volutes which fill in the angles are rare. As far as is known, they were produced only to special order and the same applies to the many bricks the decorations of which have special reference to the brewers' guild.

For a commission as important as the facing with decorative bricks of a fire-place in a guild house, special stamps were made. As though to contradict what has been said above about the disappearance of borders, here in Antwerp in the seventeenth century, we find extremely wide borders round the motifs. A large brick in the shape of a triangular pediment surmounts the fire-place in the Brouwershuis; this was probably usual, although bricks in the shape of half-oval pediments are also known. Here again it is noticeable how poor in new ideas iconographic invention has become, for one would hardly expect to find in the place of honour in a guild house of the year 1666 the arms of the Emperor Charles V with the Pillars of Hercules.[3]

Religious unrest drove the brick-industry from Flanders to the northern Netherlands. The image of the "Dutch garden"[4] and the arms of Prince Maurice on tiles are purely Dutch motifs and prove that production of fire-place bricks was carried on in the northern Netherlands. A certain confusion has arisen from the fact that the old stamps were modernised. A later date, for example, would be substituted for an earlier one and the coat-of-arms of a city of the northern Netherlands was often added to the old design. In cases where the design has been altered a deeper relief is noticeable, but where something has simply been added there is often no difference in the depth of the relief.

Many contacts between the southern and northern Netherlands had already been established. In the southern part of the province of Zeeland and on the island of Zuid Beveland fire-places with decorated bricks have been found in peasants' houses, whereas farther north they have been found only in castles and the houses of the nobility. A few towns and districts such as Nijmegen and Brabant imported bricks by way of the great rivers Meuse and Waal, of which the former provided a direct link with Liège, the centre of brick-production. This explains the occurrence of Liègeois fire-place bricks in these parts. In the sixteenth century there was a factory in Utrecht which produced decorated bricks. Flemish immigrants probably worked there and the finer clay which was required to make the statuettes, and pottery produced at Utrecht must have been imported so that the desired mixture of materials could always be available.

It is impossible to say for certain whether fire-place bricks were regularly exported to England, where a great many bricks occur. It may be that the discerning English made a point of buying bricks and anything else that they needed to furnish their houses on the Continent. Precise clues regarding regular export to England are, however, not forthcoming. It is also quite possible that trade relations of this kind did exist, for in Scandinavia not only have decorated bricks from the Netherlands been found but also carved altars from Utrecht.

In the year 964 Pope Benedict V was banished by Emperor Otto I to Hamburg, where he died a year later. He was looked upon as the model of courageous opposition to overweening earthly power. In about the year 1320 a monument to him made of coloured faience slabs was erected in the former Cathedral of St. Mary in Hamburg and was destroyed when the cathedral was demolished in 1806. The sides of the tomb, here reproduced from an engraving of 1661, were faced with tiles representing knights and saints. The fragment illustrated opposite showing the head and shoulders of a saint is an example of the international medieval style of painting in green and purple. Museum für Hamburgische Geschichte, Hamburg.

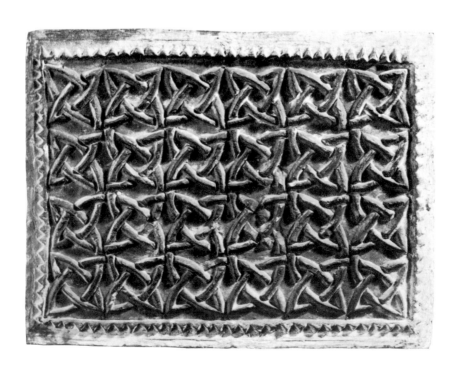

It has already been stated that faience tiles and cast-iron fire-backs took the place of decorated bricks, although bricks were still occasionally used for the centre of the fire-place wall, above the iron fire-back. They did, however, finally go out of fashion and the tradition persisted only in Liège. In the eighteenth century larger and thinner bricks were still being produced there and decorated in the style of Louis XIV and Louis XV; they usually covered the whole back wall of the fire-place. The same procedure was employed in the Dutch province of Limburg, which borders on the Liège region. More original ways of facing the fire-place were also adopted in Liège. These included borders with floral ornaments, half-bricks, quoins for surrounding an iron fire-back, and now no longer had to be specially commissioned. There were also many bricks with a transparent glaze, such as those of Tegelen, in Holland, or those of Utrecht.

This branch of the industry was thus able to keep going in Liège, whereas in many other places it had later to be artificially resuscitated. Under the influence of the Romantic spirit of the Gothic Revival as well as during the backward-looking phases of style which followed in the nineteenth century, the old tiles were brought into line with the taste of the day. They were imitated in terracotta using the old patterns and from the technical point of view, achieved the smooth and flawless perfection which was at that time the goal of all artistic handcraft.

Loseta *tiles surrounded by* alfardones. *Blue decoration. Valencia
1 5th century. From a pavement in the abbey of S. Domingo, with
the inscription :* Bon regiment–ap deligencia–e ap saviesa–da ap
sana pensa ; *which means, roughly,* "*Good government by diligence
and by wisdom and by sound understanding.*" *Boymans-van Beuningen Museum, Rotterdam.*

The arms of Castile and Leon. Blue roof-tile in lustre technique. 34 × 43 cm. Manises, first half of the 15th century. Boymans-van Beuningen Museum, Rotterdam.

The Tiles
of Spain and Portugal

The southern part of the Iberian peninsula was invaded by the Arabs under General Tarik in the year 711. It remained under Islamic domination and was thus subject to the artistic and technical influences both of the Near and Middle East and of the Mediterranean countries. These were the two sources from which ceramic tiles were introduced into Spain and Portugal, yet it is difficult to establish the chronological sequence and the exact course of the development.

SPAIN

Following the establishment of the independent caliphate in Córdoba in 929, a period of intense artistic activity began which attracted the Mozarabic workers —that is, Christians under Moorish rule—and Syrian and Moorish craftsmen, who built mosques and palaces, such as Medina Azhara, near Córdoba. Stucco, marble, wood-panelling and bricks were primarily used in the construction and decoration of the great buildings of the caliphs but, although decorated ceramics had long been popular, tiles as a form of room-decoration are rarely found. It was not until much later, at the time of the Almohádes (1146), who came to Spain from North Africa, and to a greater extent after the Christian reconquest following the victory over the Almohádes in 1212 and during the relatively peaceful period which ensued, that tile-mosaics began to be widely used. They were employed first for pavements and later for wall-facings. These compositions go back to geometric patterns of Persian origin and required from the workmen technical knowledge both of glazes—the following oxides were used: cobalt (blue), manganese (mauve and black), iron (green), copper (red and green), tin (white) or antimony (yellow)—and of the cutting of the individual pieces which were to form the pattern. There were *alicatados*, or mosaic panels, as early as the thirteenth

century, but it was not until they were used as decorations for the Alhambra (77) at Granada (1353–1391) and for the Alcazar of Seville that they reached perfection.

On the east coast and principally in the region of Valencia (77) and as far as Catalonia a ceramic-industry developed, the fame of which extended far outside the region. In the centres of Manises, Paterna and Teruel (Aragon) as well as in Barcelona itself decorated ceramic tiles were produced at an early date (65) which were cheaper than the Andalusian *alicatados* and came to replace these. They were called *losetas*—these were square tiles the sides of which measured about 10 cm. —and *alfardones*—long-shaped hexagonal tiles which were laid round the squares to form an octagonal unit (64). A famous example of this style is the pavement of the Aljafería at Saragossa. The tiles from the region of Barcelona, the *socarrats*, are different: they are long-shaped rectangular pieces coated with a thin lead-glaze and adorned with Gothic animals or, less commonly, with floral decorations of North African inspiration (65). It was not until the fourteenth century that the *azulejos* made their appearance and gradually ousted the *alicatados*. Their most important centres of production were

Red and black soccarat *ceiling-tile. Valencia or Paterna, second half of the 15th century. Victoria and Albert Museum, London.*

Cuerda seca *tile from a staircase. c. 1500. Boymans-van Beuningen Museum, Rotterdam.*

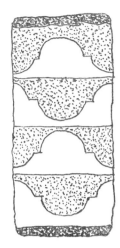

Cuenca *ceiling-tile. Seville, 16th century. Boymans-van Beuningen Museum, Rotterdam.*

Seville and Málaga in Andalusia. The word *azulejo* comes from the Arabic *al zulaich*, meaning "little stone". In North Africa it was used to denote the Roman mosaics which were found in the ruins of Leptis Magna, Volubilis, Caesarea and elsewhere. The word acquired currency and was soon used in Portugal as well as in Spain for the splendid ceramic tiles whose side-measurements vary between 12 and 14.5 cm. and whose surface is entirely covered with decoration. At first the *azulejos* reproduced on a single tile or on four juxtaposed tiles the geometric compositions of the *alicatados*. Oxides with a lead basis (litharge) were used for the glazes. During firing, however, these glazes tended to merge and run into one another. In order to preserve the outlines of the decoration special technical procedures were employed. One was known as "*de cuerda seca*", by which the design was engraved on the clay while it was still wet, producing furrows which were filled with a greasy substance; during the firing this *cuerda* (cord) prevented the coloured glazes running and at the same time produced the effect of a relief. The second process, which was called "*de cuenca*" or "*de arista*" might be described as a kind of negative version of *cuerda seca*. The place of the furrows was taken by sharp ridges which delimited the surfaces requiring to be glazed. These techniques (66, 67, 72) correspond to *cloisonné* and *champlevé* in the enamelling of metal.

Although the most important centre of production was Triana, on the outskirts of Seville, these processes also spread in the fifteenth century to more distant parts of Spain, where the potters did no more than copy Andalusian models. In Toledo, for example, during the sixteenth century, heraldic motifs or subjects relating to falconry, called *azulejos de cetreria*, were introduced. At the same centre, experiments were made in the use of lustre with metallic effect such as was used principally on the pottery of Valencia. All these techniques and processes were known by the term *mudejares*, from the fact that it was primarily craftsmen of Moslem origin who employed them, although the factory owners and the foremen had been Spaniards from an early date.

Such was the nature of ceramic decoration in the Iberian peninsula up to the beginning of the sixteenth century, in contrast to Italy, where, thanks to the use of colours in a glaze containing oxide of tin, ceramic art had achieved a new freedom. Although maiolica made its appearance in Italy, it is said to originate from the clay of the east coast of Spain.

The glowing, iridescent colours of the Andalusian *azulejos* and the exotic effect of their geometric patterns have caught the attention of connoisseurs and collectors; specimens of these beautiful tiles are to be found in most of the European museums. In their country of origin they have become rare although there are still a

Ornamental border composed of cuenca *tiles with a design of dragons. First half of the 16th century. Boymans-van Beuningen Museum, Rotterdam.*

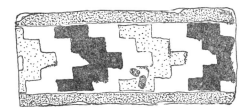

Cuenca *floor-tile in green, purple, ochre and white. Toledo or Seville. 16th century. Boymans-van Beuningen Museum, Rotterdam.*

Cuenca *tile with a representation of a mask, showing Italian influence. Part of a frieze. Toledo, 16th century. Boymans-van Beuningen Museum, Rotterdam.*

Cuenca *border-tile with bucranium motifs. 16th century. Boymans-van Beuningen Museum, Rotterdam.*

few fine examples *in situ*, notably at Seville (e. g. in the Casa de Pilatos).

The progress of Italian Renaissance art brought to Europe new aesthetic values and new technical processes. Spain, with her long tradition of ceramic production, and her distinctive artistic personality, opposed the new fashions. It took nearly half a century before *azulejos* with smooth surfaces won the acceptance of the public and overcame the prejudice of the *mudejar* craftsmen. In about the year 1500 an Italian maiolica maker from Pisa named Francesco Niculoso settled in Seville and began to work for their Catholic Majesties. In 1504 he made the altar for the chapel of the royal palace, the Alcazar, and signed it: *Niculoso Francisco Italiano me fecit.* This unique masterpiece of ceramic art demonstrates the perfect accomplishment of its creator both in technique and design. Niculoso also worked for the grandees, who were adherents of the Renaissance, and for monasteries: some of his compositions are hidden away in the church of Nuestra Señora de Tentudia in Estremadura, others are in the church of Santa Aña at Triana and in the monastery of Santa Paula at Seville. A tile-panel signed by Niculoso was found at Lisbon in the débris left by the earthquake of 1755 which destroyed the city. The panel belonged for a time to the prince-consort Dom Fernando and is today in the Rijksmuseum at Amsterdam. Francesco Niculoso was unable, however, to impose the new techniques on the craftsmen of Seville and after his death tiles began once again to be produced by the old processes of *de cuenca* and even *de cuerda seca*. They did, however, adopt the new idioms of the artistic language of the Renaissance which Niculoso had introduced. After 1510 the old patterns with geometric designs gave place to ornaments with leaves, bucrania, flowers and such-like. These motifs were used mainly at Toledo and at other centres of ceramic art which were more open to the acceptance of novelties.

With the exception of Niculoso's tile-panels and of a few panels made by his son Juan Batista (78), of which two are in the Gemeente Museum at The Hague, decoration using *azuelos* was confined to facings of the lower

Left: Cuenca *tile with design of centaur shooting with bow and arrow. Seville, first half of the 16th century. Boymans-van Beuningen Museum, Rotterdam.*

Right: Cuenca *tile with design of an acrobat running. Toledo, c. 1550. Boymans-van Beuningen Museum, Rotterdam.*

part of walls; the patterns on these tiles were repetitive and were sometimes surrounded by matching borders. *Azulejos* were also used for pavements but these were smaller and were called "*olambrillas*". For ceilings, double, that is to say, oblong, *azulejos* were used and were placed between the beams; these were called "*azulejos por tabla*" or "*tableros*".

About the middle of the sixteenth century, the political and economic relations between Spain and Flanders led artists to migrate from one country to the other and more than one Fleming felt drawn towards Spain. At the period of the great building enterprises at Toledo and Madrid during the reigns of Charles V and Philip II, architects and decorators were brought from Antwerp. Among the most celebrated of these was the Floris family. In 1563 Juan Florés, as he was called in Spain, was made "master tile-maker" to the king; we have him to thank for the decorations of the Prado palace. At the same period, a new centre of ceramic production came into being which was to become famous: Talavera de la Reina. The Flemish potters, who for the most part came from the workshop of Guido Andries, finally succeeded in introducing the maiolica technique into the peninsula and thereafter, in place of the *azulejos* made according to *mudejar* techniques, tiles with smooth surfaces were produced. These tiles were decorated with colours over a tin-oxide glaze which made it possible to paint and fix any pattern without the fear that it would run.

In Seville one of the most important makers of *azulejos*, Roque Hernandez, took into his service a certain Francisco Andrea, a "*flamenco*" who was to teach him to paint *azulejos* with the "colours of Pisa," that is to say, to apply colours in the Italian manner. This man was none other than a son of Guido Andries, who left his native land in about 1555. After his sojourn in Seville, the *azulejos* with smooth surfaces came to be called "*Pisanos*".

This change of technique dealt a death-blow to Seville and made Talavera (83, 85) the new production centre for tiles. In Seville Cristobal de Augusta (85), the son-in-law of Roque Hernandez, was the only one to profit by the teaching of Francisco Andrea: in 1577 he made the tiles for the salon named after Charles V in the Alcazar. Until the end of the century the wares of Seville made a poor showing by the side of the fine, modern *azulejos* from Talavera.

The efforts of Philip II, who lived in Madrid, to impose political centralisation on his country contributed to the development of Talavera. The *azulejos* painters were true artists, among them Hernando de Loayza, who made the tiles for the palace of the Infante at Guadalajara and for that of the dukes of Braganza at Vila Vicosa in Portugal, and an artist named Oliva, who signed the splendid ceramic decorations of the Generalidad of Valencia and of the monastery of the Descalzas Reales in Madrid. Although these works are

italianate in style, typically Spanish characteristics are already revealed in the brilliant colours enhanced by shadow.

The Flemings brought new designs with them from Antwerp and the old *azulejos* with the repetitive *mudejar* patterns disappeared. This explains why, both in Flanders and in Spain, in Holland (Middelburg) and in Portugal, the same decorative motifs are found.

The church of Nuestra Señora del Prado in Talavera is a veritable museum of *azulejos* where it is possible to follow the development of native production from the sixteenth to the eighteenth century. Further examples are to be found in the museums of Madrid (Museo Arqueológico Nacional) while the Boymans-van Beuningen Museum in Rotterdam possesses a fine collection. During the fifteenth and sixteenth centuries Seville was the great centre of tile production; in the seventeenth century it was Talavera and, in the eighteenth century, Barcelona. It is true that in the neighbourhood of Valencia the traditional workshops continued to produce pottery, but the production of tiles lapsed and did not come to life again until the middle of the seventeenth century in Catalonia. In the great Catalan port of Barcelona *azulejos* became more and more popular; citizens and guilds, the rich merchants and the nobility all gave commissions to the numerous workshops. The Vich Museum and the Museo Santacana de Martorell in Barcelona possess extremely comprehensive collections of Barcelona tiles, both panels and single tiles, of which the latter are particularly delightful.

The eighteenth century saw the decline of Spanish *azulejos*. Except for the wares of the last workshops of Valencia with their large rococo compositions in which the colours are too strong and the drawing somewhat weak, there were in Bourbon Spain only a few anecdotal tiles which have no decorative value but which are popular with tourists.

PORTUGAL

The Portuguese *azulejos* were derived from the Spanish yet their use was incomparably more widespread in Portugal than in the neighbouring country. Of all European countries, Portugal was the one in which walls were by far the most often decorated with tiles and is the one in which the greatest number may still be seen today. In 90% of Portuguese churches, chapels and monasteries, in 75% of the old mansions and pleasure-houses and on some thousands of façades – not only on the peninsula itself but also in the Azores and Madeira – the *azulejos* are preserved just as they were when they were placed in position centuries ago. Even today the art of making *azulejos* is one of the most highly regarded in Portugal and it seems as though the Portuguese are unable to do without them.

Since Portugal was less influenced than Spain by the Moors – it achieved its independence during the re-conquest of the peninsula by the Christians in the twelfth century – there is there no *mudejar* style such as influenced development in Andalusia. In fact there were no ceramic tiles at all in Portugal before the fifteenth century; the earliest – such as those in the royal palace at Sintra – date from the conquests of Dom Alfonso V on the Moroccan coast (1458–1471) or were imported from Valencia.

The great influx of wealth into Portugal during the course of the sixteenth century, the so-called Manoeline period, made it possible to import tiles of the *mudejar* style from Seville and Malaga. These tiles were widely used. In about 1510 the Bishop of Coimbra had the old Romanesque cathedral faced with tiles which were bought in Triana. King Emanuel I commissioned from this same Spanish centre of tile production *cuerda seca* tiles bearing his device, the armillary sphere, which were used when the royal palace at Sintra was newly decorated. Emanuel I fostered the use of tiles, especially for facing clock-towers – an example is that of the cathedral of Funchal (1514). Until the end of the century Seville continued to sell thousands of *azulejos* to Portugal, who was, in fact, her chief buyer. The Portuguese, however, took liberties with the arrangement of the tiles; they were not satisfied with the simple decorations formed by the repetition of a motif which were in general use in Spain, so they faced whole walls and gave a sense of lively movement to the compositions in which the individual tile was only a tiny part of a gigantic mosaic.

It was not until about 1550–1560 that the attempt was made to produce tiles in Lisbon, and even then it was Flemish artists who were responsible. The love of ceramic decoration became far more deeply rooted in Portugal than it had ever been in Spain and henceforth neither cultivated people nor the clergy wished to be without them. Thus Dom Diogo d'Eça, lord of the manor of Torres at Azeitão commissioned two large panels in maiolica tiles which were specially made in Fontana's workshop in Urbino. A certain Marçal de Matos, who had served his apprenticeship with the Flemish ceramist Phillip de Goes, made the fine *azulejos* in the manor of Bacalhôa also at Azeitão; one of these panels is dated 1565. There were other walls faced with *azulejos* which had been made in Lisbon in the churches and palaces of the city but they were all destroyed during the great earthquake of 1755. It was possible to save only the altar retable from the former church of St. Andrew and this is now preserved in the National Library at Lisbon. One work from the end of this period survives: the monumental wall-facing of the church of São Roque in Lisbon. It is signed by Francisco de Matos, probably a relation of the master of Bacalhôa (222).

One type of *azulejo* which was much used in Portugal and was undoubtedly produced there is the plain white, blue, green or yellowish tile. These were put together

69

to form chess-board patterns and were surprisingly effective (220).

During the reigns of the Spanish kings Philip II, Philip III and Philip IV, who ruled over Portugal also, an *azulejos* industry developed which was independent of the Spanish models. In particular, tiles for facing the walls of churches appeared in an enormous variety of patterns: finely harmonised designs in blue, yellow, green and manganese on a white background were cleverly combined and produced astonishing effects (221) in these otherwise dull temples. The altars were decorated with antependia made of tiles in which the influence of embroidery and chintz may be detected (224). In the course of the seventeenth century the factories of Lisbon and Oporto produced hundreds of thousands of *azulejos* which also found their way into the provinces and overseas to the Azores, Madeira and Brazil. A feeling for monumentality became universal; ceramic tiles were harmoniously combined with gilt panelling, called "*talha*", to form a decorative accessory to the architecture of the counter-reformation. In addition to the *azulejos* with polychrome patterns, pictures of religious figures (226), delightful battle-scenes, and even *singeries* (223) and caricatures were sometimes introduced. The nobility had a special liking for *azulejos* and it is difficult to imagine a villa or mansion which was not decorated with tiles, for these brought into the house and garden a breath of freshness, charm and gaiety. It is enough to name the palace of the Marquês de Fronteira at Benfica, Lisbon, to demonstrate the extraordinary decorative possibilities of *azulejos* (223). Towards the end of the seventeenth century the old polychrome tiles were forced by the influence of the pieces imported from Holland (see the chapter *The Influence of Dutch Tiles in Portugal*) to give way gradually to *azulejos* painted only in blue (222; 227). Between 1700 and the middle of the century the Portuguese workshops in Lisbon, Oporto and Coimbra (247)

increased their production many times over; they engaged artists of distinction or used prints and engravings, the subjects of which they altered as necessity demanded. Outstanding painters, such as Gabriel del Barco, António Pereira and, especially, António de Oliveira Bernardes (238, 231, 240) and his son Policarpo made it their business to rid the field of Dutch competition. They maintained the grandiose feeling for monumentality in huge wall-facings for churches and palaces, in which the decorations, stamped by the new predilection for the Italian baroque, harmonised with the features of contemporary Portuguese architecture (231). After 1725 no more was required of the pupils of these old masters (245) than to follow in the paths in which they had been taught and to execute the commissions of a steadily growing clientele whose riches had been further increased by the gold and diamonds of India and Brazil (225, 245). During the reign of John V, the so-called *belle époque*, everything was faced with tiles: staircases were decorated with large tile-pictures of liveried halberdiers who greeted the visitor upon arrival, while representations of bull-fights also formed part of the background of the pleasure-loving nobility (246). Although it is undoubtedly true that the artistic quality of the Portuguese *azulejos* of the eighteenth century was no longer what it had been before, they certainly possessed as much decorative value as stuccowork, mural paintings or tapestries (226, 247).

From 1750–1755 polychrome painting came into use again, at first for the rococo borders, then for whole panels. From this date, walls ceased to be entirely covered with tiles and the tile-pictures were now cut out round their outlines, a practice which produced extremely lively rhythms on the same aesthetic level as Borromini's architecture.

For less important rooms or in cases in which economy was necessary, single tiles were used. Their decorative

value is admittedly less but, even so, their naïve, popular motifs are delightful.

The workshops and their owners, the *azulejadores* as they were called, were always concerned to keep in step with fashion and style and it was, in fact, from the *azulejos* that the Portuguese learned of the changes in taste which were being introduced by way of the new collections of engravings and albums of drawings. The novelties of the rococo of the period of Louis XV, the *chinoiseries* of Pillement who himself worked in Portugal, the fantasies of Oppenord, Meissonier and Cuvilliés and the turn of English and French taste towards the neo-classic style at the end of century (248) were all splendidly reflected in the tile-paintings of Lisbon, notably those of the royal factory of Rato.

It was not until the occupation of Portugal by Napoleon, the ensuing flight of the royal family to Brazil in 1808 and the civil war of 1826–1834 that the tile-industry began to suffer and eventually came to a standstill. *Azulejos* survived in Brazil – in Rio de Janeiro, Bahia, Maranhão and Pará – where they had become indispensable; they were used to face façades as monumental as those of Portugal and these became a characteristic mark of Brazilian urban architecture of the nineteenth century. It was also the "Brazilians" who, when they returned to Portugal in about 1860, carried on the old traditions and ordered for their *nouveaux riches* homes romantic *azulejos* which were just as delightful as those of earlier centuries.

It is heartening to be able to affirm that this old national tradition is still alive today and that outstanding modern artists devote their energies to tile-making just as their predecessors did.

Catalan tile, from Palma, Majorca, c. 1800. Victoria and Albert Museum, London.

73

Renaissance and Humanism as Reflected in Italian Tiles

The fact that in the present survey of the tiles of the world the Italian floor-tiles are not counted among the outstanding expressions of this branch of ceramic art is due to the circumstance that floor-tiles of the finest quality have been rare in Italy and those which were made remained without influence. Were it possible, however, to regard tiles solely as works of art and not as objects of craftsmanship, one would be inclined to regard the Italian wares as some of the most expressive of all. The ceramic painter in Italy was the equal of great artists working in other fields; he was considered to be in no way inferior to the most celebrated maiolica painters of his time who used their special techniques to adorn dishes and vases with landscapes and figurative scenes which are imbued with imagination and feeling although in style they were only superficially related to the oil-painting of the time. Pavements like the one commissioned by Bartolomeo Lombardini for San Biagio at Forlì or the tiles of San Francesco at Deruta (89) illustrate the mastery of their creators. Humanistic learning is reflected in Italian tiles and the student is bewildered by the numbers of complicated allusions and symbols, recondite mythological subjects, Greek inscriptions, lyrical and inventive renderings of the thought of the subtlest minds of the age and the inexhaustible variety of ways of representing love.

The Renaissance style influenced the northern European countries in many spheres of art, yet the finest Italian tiles found no imitators. Floors and walls in Italy had for centuries been decorated with natural stone mosaics

Green and brown maiolica tiles from the exterior of the cathedral at Lucca. Similar designs also occur at Teruel in Spain.
Mid-14th century.

and with frescos, so that there was no need for glazed tiles like those found in Asia which sometimes glowed even more brightly than jewels. In the course of time, trade and the crusades increased Italian contacts with the East; relations with Spain also became closer. As a result of this, the exterior walls and the towers of churches began to be decorated with maiolica *bacini* or flat round bowls (76). In Lucca and Pisa there are still a few of these *bacini* in their original positions; in their bold, geometric patterns, mostly painted in green and manganese, they are delightful and worthy companions of the western European green and manganese maiolicas of the late Middle Ages which have been described in an earlier chapter.

Italian taste for maiolica decoration on outer walls persisted. In the fifteenth century it became the practice to use painted plaques or maiolica reliefs as house-signs. Faenza and Deruta were the main centres of production but they were undoubtedly made in many other places as well, although it is not always easy to distinguish them from the roundels made for the interiors of churches. It is almost impossible to visit Italy without seeing altar-fronts and pillars decorated with maiolica and fine examples of tiles of this kind are to be found at the Victoria and Albert Museum in London and at the Musée Cluny in Paris.

The finest of these devotional or protective panels were made in the workshop of the della Robbia family (95),

Bacini from the church of San Pierre a Grado near Pisa. Mid-14th century. Below: A cross-section in profile of these tiles.

where tiles were also made. Some of these have been preserved: we know of hexagons painted in brocade patterns in manganese, green and blue, showing elaborate, almost realistic bunches of flowers, in which the manganese was applied so thinly that the effect of pink roses could be achieved. The tomb of Bishop Benozzo Federighi in Santa Trinità in Florence (1455) is well known. Della Robbia tiles also still exist in the Bentivoglio chapel in San Giacomo Maggiore in Bologna (1486–1494). Luca della Robbia the younger made important tile-pavements for the Palazzo Vecchio in Florence, for San Silvestro al Quirinale and the Vatican in Rome.

The custom of composing pavements of maiolica tiles derived in the first place from Italian contacts with Spain. Blue and white lustred tiles were imported from Valencia, mainly by order of Alfonso V of Aragon, nicknamed *el Magnanimo*, to decorate the buildings which were being erected for him between 1446 and 1458 in his kingdom of Naples. In the year 1457 no fewer than two hundred thousand tiles were mentioned in connection with his palace. The favourite motifs of this prince, who was the spiritual heir of both the Middle Ages and the Renaissance, were ears of corn, an open book and scenes from King Arthur's Round Table. Another Italian prince of Spanish blood, the Borgia Pope Alexander VI, also ordered tiles from Valencia; they were used in 1494 to pave his apartments in the Vatican, where they may be admired to this day.

Some of the most important examples of Italian tile-decoration may be mentioned. The earliest surviving pavement was laid in the chapel built in 1427 in San Giovanni a Carbonara in Naples by order of the Grand Seneschal Ser Gianni Caracciolo. Ser Gianni was murdered in 1432 and the pavement must have been finished shortly after his death. Heads in profile, heraldic devices, animals and leaves decorate the oblong hexagonal tiles, which are arranged in the old manner round

a square. From the point of view of form and decoration these tiles derive from Valencian prototypes; the colours, however, –blackish-blue, green, yellow and manganese– are different, somewhat resembling Tuscan wares. It is quite possible that until the year 1488 there was no factory producing tiles in or near Naples; this surmise is borne out by a letter written in that year by Giuliano da Majano to his brother Benedetto in Florence asking him to order tiles.

Following this first example, a few other tile-pavements were laid in Naples during the fifteenth century. They frequently include a blue lion rampant on a yellow ground for this was the heraldic device of three great families, the Caracciolo, the Del Leone and the Aquaviva. It would be pointless to attempt a rigid geographical classification of the tiles, since the craftsmen travelled from one workshop to another taking the designs with them. Thus the Florentine style appears on Perugian tiles–in the form, for example, of a cupid with a scroll (79) painted blue and green, now in the

Small square tile. Perugia, late 15th century. Victoria and Albert Museum, London.

Victoria and Albert Museum. More is known about pottery vessels than about tiles and they provide clues to localisation. Blue, manganese, green and orange were, in the second half of the fifteenth century the characteristic colours of the regions of Florence and Faenza. One of the most important of Faventine works was the pavement for the Mazzatosta chapel in Santa Maria della Verità in Viterbo, executed in about 1470. This floor is made up of square and hexagonal tiles carrying Gothic lilies with curled and convoluted petals as well as other floral motifs, all with the shadows broadly painted in (86). The yellow stamens, themselves curving and full of movement, do much to diminish the somewhat sombre effect. The decoration gives an unusual three-dimensional effect which must have delighted the eye of contemporary mathematicians—for it is surely unnecessary to emphasise the religious significance which was at that time attached to the unchanging nature of arithmetic and mathematical fact.

Faenza was also the home of certain profile portraits (80), of which the finest are those of the convent of San Paolo in Parma; they were executed in 1471–1482 and

Portrait tile from the Convent of S. Paolo in Parma 1471–1482. Victoria and Albert Museum, London.

received additions in 1507. Those in the museum at Parma bear amorous inscriptions—somewhat remarkably in view of their provenance—while other tiles from the same convent carry representations of mythological love-scenes.

The variety of motifs to be found on Italian tiles has already been mentioned. Among these were inscriptions with mottoes and devices. Isabella d'Este in particular possessed a great liking for them. On the tiles for the Castello Vecchio at Mantua, together with the arms of her husband, Duke Gianfrancesco II Gonzaga, she had five motifs painted, of which four have a motto. Each of the mottoes is in a different one of the languages cultivated at her court (80, 81, 96). One of the tiles shows a white fawn with the motto *bider graft* which is the early German equivalent of "righteous power"; on another there is a bird on a smoking brand and the words *vrai amour ne se change*; the third shows a diamond on a crag surrounded by blazing faggots and has as its motto the Greek word ἀμυμων (blameless); the fourth represents a leashed hound, the fifth a glove with the Spanish motto *buena fe non es mudable* (good faith is unchangeable). Correspondence in the Gonzaga archives shows that in 1494 tiles were made in Pesaro, which may perhaps have been these.

These mottoes were doubtless the fruits of meditation. After the death of her husband, Isabella liked to use the motto *nec spe nec metu* (with neither hope nor fear). It occurs on her domestic table-ware, such as, for example, a dish by the splendid artist Nicolà Pellipario now in the Louvre which shows Abimilech observing Isaac and Rebecca.[1] The same motto is found on a series of octagonal tiles decorated in white, dark blue and brown, the colours typically used by Giovanni Maria of Castel Durante which have been described by L. Ozzola.[2] A group of these tiles is in the Boymans-van Beuningen Museum, Rotterdam (86). It is interesting to note the occurrence of the cipher XXVII, a cabbalistic sign for

courage and strength of character – it seems that Isabella sometimes liked to parade her erudition.

The decoration of the tiles of the fifteenth century is usually bold and detail is not obtrusive; colour-schemes are usually simple with blue predominating.

This would seem to be the place to describe three celebrated tile-pavements, which are the subject of much discussion. They are closely related to one another and Liverani convincingly argues that they are all products of the same workshop in Faenza.[3]

The earliest and the most beautiful from the point of view of execution is the pavement composed of hexagonal tiles dating from the year 1487 in the chapel of San Sebastiano in the church of San Petronio in Bologna. The chapel was built by the canon Donato Vasselli; the pavement which with its closely juxtaposed hexagonal tiles reminds one of a honeycomb, was made by Pietro Andrea. This artist, who has left a portrait of himself at work in front of his workshop, greatly enriched the iconography of the maiolica painters. In place of the usual uniform *famiglia floreale gotica* or peacock-feather motifs which still appear here and there, a great variety of inscriptions, animals, busts and implements made their appearance. More important than these were ornaments from classical architecture, including pearls, eggs, garlands, bucrania, grotesques, trophies and such-like. It is not, however, only these marks of humanistic learning which are of interest but also emblems which have their parallels in the inventions of the painters and architects of the time, such, for example, as geometric or stereometric compositions, the device of a pair of spectacles and a book, a claw ending in a wing on a book – probably a symbol for St. Mark – symbols of love, including flaming or pierced hearts as well as emblems of greater subtlety and refinement such as were found at the time among the decorations of the *piatelli amatori*, or lovers' dishes, of Faenza. Once again this work commissioned by a priest

shows that the Church was not entirely uninterested in secular life. The floating spheres and flourishes on tiles such as these indicate that these graceful decorations are the prototypes of the meagre "volutes" and "aigrettes" which we find in the northern Netherlands on the so-called Haarlem tiles. These pictorial conceits were not employed for compositional purposes but appear only in the form of isolated symbols. Yet they mark the moment at which the potter ceased to be a simple craftsman working to a prescribed plan and became a member of a group of cultivated artists. We shall have more to say about the consequences of this development.

There is no doubt that more modest undertakings must have preceded this pavement, for it would be hard to achieve mastery of this order at the first attempt. The colours of these tiles are extremely intense and it may have been because of this love of colour that ornamentation *alla porcellana*, that is, the blue and white decorations of Ming porcelain, held no appeal for Pietro Andrea. Blue and white decoration occurred in Faenza contemporaneously with the *floreale gotica* and the Persian palmettes, which had reached the stage of full development by 1470. *Alla persiana* decoration has nowhere, however, as far as is known, received more generous treatment than in Vasselli's chapel in San Petronio. It occurs on the altar-steps and in bands of rectangular tiles in the pavement. This type of ornament consists of rosettes and palmettes with pomegranates – Bode called the design the *Granatapfelmuster* or pomegranate pattern – between twisting stems and tendrils. The design was conceived in the East for textiles and soon began to appear on earthenware. The Italian potters probably became acquainted with it through Persian tapestries and also through the ceramics which came to Italy by way of Spain or the Arab world. The polychrome lustre decorations on ceramics of the thirteenth century from Kashan, Rayy and

Kerman were certainly of great consequence for the development of Faenza tiles.

Alla persiana decoration became a speciality of Faenza, where it was vigorously painted with a tendency to three-dimensionalism. From Faenza, it spread to Tuscany and Umbria[4] and is even found in Antwerp; but in all these places the effect is flatter and the motifs are painted with less tension than in Faenza. The feeling for colour shown by the artists of Faenza – it was particularly marked in this city because the flawless, glass-like glaze used there encouraged and facilitated nicety in the handling of colour-gradations – is apparent also in the Persian decorations. It is a far cry from these to the flat, monochrome blue designs found in other parts of Europe.

Giuseppe Liverani has analysed the important tile-pavements of Bologna.[5] He has come to the conclusion that the date on a tile in the Museo Civico at Turin from a now dispersed pavement which had long been accepted as 1511 should be read as 1501. If this is true, the pavement to which the tile belonged was not the third but the second of the series under discussion. Other fragments of the work are in the Museo Artistico Industriale in Rome, in the Victoria and Albert Museum and the British Museum in London, in the Turin Museum, the Louvre in Paris and the Museum für Angewandte Kunst in Vienna. Thirty-four tiles were discovered in the chapel of the Casa Cavassa, now a museum, in Saluzzo and have been published by Liverani.[6] A "bomb" device which appears in several of the rosettes has led to the attribution of the pavement to the Casa Pirota factory at Faenza (95). Other devices show animals and are much the same as those on the *piatelli amatori;* they include a rabbit symbolising fertility, a dog (faithfulness), a gazelle (grace), a unicorn (chastity). The animals sometimes look behind them as they stand still or run across a schematic landscape with conventionally drawn clouds and tufts of grass. In these landscapes strong shadows cut a tree clean in half. The pair of spectacles reappears and there are human beings: in the collection in Rome there is, for example, a priest preaching a sermon. In this same collection there is also a tile with a pure landscape subject showing a ship sailing out of harbour – doubtless a symbol of love. Among other less poetic symbols, mention may be made of a hand grasping a fish beside an hour-glass, a hand stretching up out of flames in the midst of hilly landscape, tools, such as a knife and a rule with a cut leather strap; this is probably also an emblem of love, the strap being intended to bind two people together. It is possible that it was sometimes intended to symbolise mystical or heavenly love where the emblem seems at first sight merely to suggest its earthly counterpart. Yet earthly love was at that time regarded with the greatest reverence since the humanists cultivated the personality of mortal beings. There are also many mathematical devices on this pavement. And the graceful movements of the *alla persiana* tendrils and of the figures are no less remarkable than the sure touch of the artist elegantly placing the strange symbols in the spaces reserved for them.

The tiles used for this pavement were no longer of hexagonal shape but were square, the decorations consisting of roundels with ornamental borders and trefoils in the corners. These roundels derive once again from those of Sassanian textiles. The same form of decoration, roundels and corner motifs on square tiles, is found in the chapel to the left of the high altar in the church of San Sebastiano in Venice.[7] The pavement there shows the arms of the Lando family, the date 1510 and the potter's monogram, apparently QVBLT. The ornaments are similar to those already described. Mathematical devices appear, emblems of love, birds, sometimes placed in fields of white irregularly outlined in blue, which remind one of the old decorative manner of Faenza. Another curious feature of these birds is

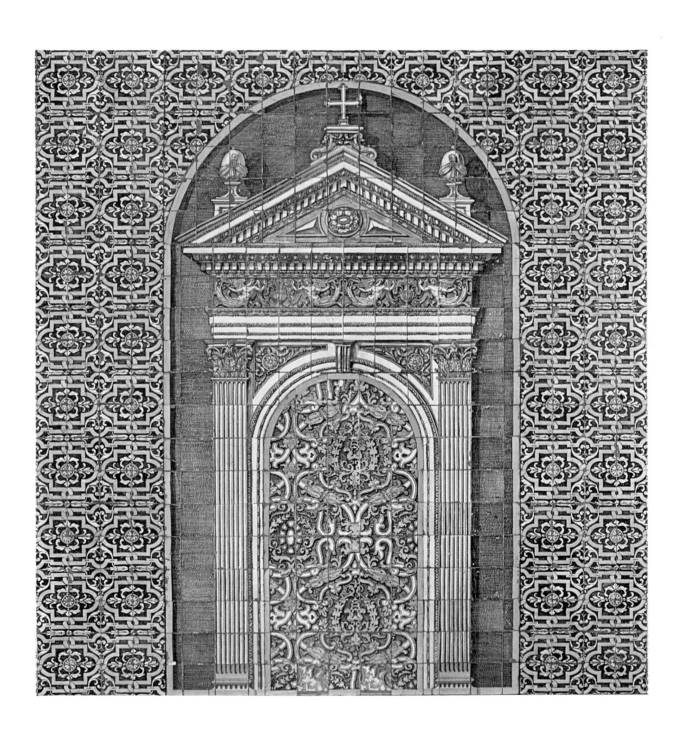

that their internal contours give the effect of a polygon with concave sides, a fact which suggests Eastern affinities.

Liverani shows that the same pounced pattern-sheets were used for a number of the tiles in all three pavements. Thus, for example, we find in all of them a grotesque with the head of a bearded man and a pair of spectacles; the lively drawing of the animals and the pattern of the borders is also common to all three. The Bologna pavement is the most sombre in appearance. The peacock-feather pattern and the Persian ornaments are reminiscent of the severe style of the *floreale gotica*. The tension of the Gothic line has been relaxed in Venice and the coloration has become lighter. In Saluzzo, however, blue still predominates and for this reason it is quite possible that the date on the tiles at Saluzzo should be read as 1501, as Liverani believes.

The effect of the three tile-pavements must already have seemed a little out of date at the time when they were completed, for the style of the sixteenth century was one of far greater subtlety than could be achieved with these plain roundels. The pavement commissioned by Bartolomeo Lombardini (1430–1512) for his chapel in the church of San Francesco at Forlì completed after his death—as can be seen from the dates 1513 and 1523 on the tiles—is an example of the unsurpassed beauty of certain Italian tiles. It consists of octagonal tiles surrounded by irregular polygonal ones. The octagonal tiles carry painted motifs of extreme delicacy on a yellow or orange-coloured background. The motifs include portraits, landscapes, animals, trophies, monsters, etc. Among the portraits there is a self-portrait of the maiolica painter Pietro Andrea, a portrait of the great painter Melozzo da Forlì and one of the organist Ugolino di Francesco Urbevetan, in fact, of a group of friends at Forlì. The technique of pouncing was used for the arabesques of the borders. The pavement must have been made, possibly in Forlì, by an artist from

Faenza with the initials P. F. Some of the panels are strongly reminiscent of the "Resurrection panel" in the Victoria and Albert Museum, the blue tones, the pale yellow or amber, the green, the amethyst shading to manganese of which reveal the talent of a man whom Rackham described as one of the most important of all maiolica painters. When the church was demolished, the pavement was relaid in a villa at Pievo a Quinto; most of the tiles are today in the Victoria and Albert Museum.

In Siena, a town with a very different tradition from that of Faenza, the refinement characteristic of the sixteenth century made its appearance earlier than it did in Faenza (86). This is of course not surprising, for the Gothic style and the sharp detail of Gothic art persisted long in Siena and the freedom of design which distinguished Faventine work of the fifteenth century never reached that city. Famous products of Siena are the tiles of the Palazzo Petrucci (1509) on which delicately drawn decorations appear against a black background. The Sienese black glaze, compared with the blacks used by ceramists of other countries and in other periods, must be regarded as the purest of all. The ornaments most often used in Siena were grotesques; they appear also against pale yellow or orange backgrounds. The variety of shapes of tiles is characteristic of Siena. Round, oblong and triangular pieces were combined in a way which is in itself a mark of the love of tradition which ruled there. Renaissance regularity found no encouragement in Siena.

An extremely fascinating and imposing composition of cruciform tiles and eight-pointed stars resembling old Persian forms was made locally for the church of Sant'Angelo at Deruta in 1524. The crosses are decorated with arabesques in white and yellow on a blue ground, the stars with half-length or full-length mythological figures, religious subjects or scenes, such as hawking, from the life of a nobleman. In the land-

scape there are plants and starfish unusually disposed in a kind of *semé*: they are out of keeping with their surroundings as regards both size and colour, for they are abstract in conception. The colours are strong in lyrical suggestiveness, with blue predominating; there are orange wings and hair, green horse-trappings, another detail glows yellow, like a flame in a world of blue, while the white tin-glaze of the figures and the sky is faintly tinged with pink from the clay beneath which has turned red in the firing.[8] The play of colours, so delightful in its abstract beauty, is equalled by the poetical quality of the figures. Once again one is surprised to discover how little these effects have in common with those of oil-painting. The pavement was

later transferred to the church of San Francesco in Deruta and most of it is now in the Museo Civico of that town (89).

Among the simpler and more everyday Italian wares, mention may first be made of the Sicilian tiles. Ceramic production had flourished in Caltagirone, the Faenza of Sicily, since the days of Arab domination. An industry developed in Sciacca also and in the second half of the fourteenth century maiolica began to be produced there. Sciacca was an international centre for traffic and commerce, where wares from Valencia and Savona, near Genoa, were those most frequently found. The Genoese, of whom there was a colony in Sciacca, commissioned a wall-decoration for their church of San Gior-

Part of a pavement from the Palazzo Petrucci, Siena. 1452–1512. Victoria and Albert Museum, London.

gio. The work was a large panel representing scenes from the Old Testament and is the best and most important work of the beginning of the sixteenth century. The tiles are now preserved in the local museum. A large slab was found in the same church with a self-portrait of the artist, M. Giuseppi Maxarato (1561–1624), as a sergeant of the town militia. These large wall-decorations, so reminiscent of the Spanish ones, found their way to Sicily by way of Genoa, Genoa having borrowed from Spain this very un-Italian practice of facing walls with tiles. Various panels representing San Calogero, the patron saint of Sciacca, have also been found in Sicily. The earliest dates from the year 1545 and is in the grotto of Monte Cronio, near Sciacca, where the saint is honoured. According to the records, two priests were even engaged in the Sicilian ceramic-industry.

In the Abruzzi, which was once part of the kingdom of Naples, the main centre of tile production was Castelli. The outstanding artists here were Oratio Pompei, Antonio Lolli and the Grue family, who began to produce tiles in the seventeenth century and in general kept to the old manner of Faenza, with its boldly drawn figures. In the small church of San Donato presso Castelli, however, there is a group of delightful ceiling-tiles (1615–1617) decorated in the *compendiario* style. This was a Faventine style involving a lively impressionistic manner of painting in which blue, yellow and orange were used on a white background, much of which remained unpainted. It constituted a reaction against very elaborate work and embraced only simple scenes made up of few units. Tito Pompei was probably the most important exponent of this style, in which busts, symbols and devices appear in cheerful confusion. It constitutes a complete contrast to the style of the Grue family, who remained loyal to the old traditions and painted detailed "pictures" portraying scenes from mythology and antiquity. In the course of time the quality of their work declined considerably until in the end they were producing only folk-art. The *verdi macerati* are well-known features of Abruzzi wares; they were greens mixed with yellow or covered by a second transparent layer of glaze containing comparatively few particles of yellow. Orange on yellow was also favoured.

There is no need, however, for these comments on the fine tiles of Italy to end with an account of a workshop in decline. No mention has yet been made of a room in the huge palace at Capodimonte which was entirely faced with porcelain of that royal Neapolitan manufacture. The enchanting *chinoiseries* of this virtuoso work display in incomparable form that sane and cheerful enjoyment of life and beauty which is the traditional and unfailing characteristic of Italian art.

It is perhaps a little surprising to learn that faience tiles enjoyed great popularity in France in the sixteenth century, and the fact that a number of important works were commissioned there calls for some explanation. As has already been stated, coloured tin-glazes are an Eastern phenomenon and played little part in Greco-Roman civilisation. At the time of the Renaissance, France seems to have adopted not only the classical elements of the new Italian mode of life and of decorative art but also the new attitude to colour – and this in spite of the fact that it disturbed the clearly defined architectural effects of classical taste. For all their reputed sobriety of taste and love of reason, the French welcomed the effect of tiles, which reminded them of tapestries; and these were not the only traces of the Gothic style which lived on in France at variance with current vogues. Whereas the Gothic style was international in character, the Renaissance laid stress on nationality, a result of the fact that interest had, to a large extent, turned away from the heavenly, towards the earthly, life. The faience tiles of Escaladieu (92) give as yet, certainly, no evidence of a typically French character, but in the new period a specifically French style is usually recognisable.

Five main groups may be distinguished in French tile manufacture. These are: (1) the beginning of the industry at Lyons and Nevers, under Italian influence; (2) the wares of Rouen, where Masséot Abaquesne produced works of art of outstanding quality; (3) the wares of Montpellier, which have a strong northern flavour; (4) the wares of Lille and Lisieux, of which the latter was later reduced to producing monotonous series of fireplace tiles; and (5) the floor-tiles dating from the middle of the sixteenth century which were made specially for the chapel of the Château d'Orion.

From the year 1512 onwards there was in Lyons a workshop which may perhaps be compared with those of Antwerp in as much as it was directed by Italian craftsmen. In Nevers, which had closer contacts with Italy – the Gonzagas were dukes of Mantua and Nevers – a workshop under the direction of the Conrade family of Albissola, near Savona in Liguria, was active from 1578 onwards. The work of the ceramists of Lyons and Nevers was at first very similar. In 1584 Jules Gambin went from Lyons to become the partner of Antoine Conrade in Nevers and in so doing established a further connection between the two centres. In both places engravings were the main sources of the decorations. As well as grotesques in the style current in Urbino, marine subjects were especially frequently represented at Nevers (98). At the same time, a French national style of decoration came into being at Nevers – characteristic of this being a yellow or, more rarely, a blue background. From 1600 to 1660 the Custode family worked in the workshop known as l'Autruche, principally in the Italian manner. From 1640 until 1789 Nicolas Estienne, Hallé and Ollivier worked with great success in the workshop named Ecce Homo, but it would be quite impossible to mistake their work for Italian maiolica. A characteristic manner of drawing foliage is recognisable in the Nevers wares, the copper-green running and making of each leaf a series of small spots. The coloration is somewhat paler than that of the majestic Italian ceramics; but in the indigenous productions we find a most unusual striped or wave-like mode of representing blue sea. The foliage is painted in a mottled manganese and a bluish copper-green. Although the branches are almost obscured by these, a firm structure is given to the leaves by a manganese-coloured outline.

Book-illustrations were of great importance at Nevers as models for the decoration of tiles. The Persian style shows itself in a blue or green background and in monochrome green painting. It is unimportant in the present context whether the blue background is of Venetian origin or whether it was taken straight from

Right: Faience tile from Escaladieu, Hautes-Pyrénées. Stylised floral motif, painted in green with purple outlines. 14th century. Victoria and Albert Museum, London.

Persian ceramics, which also had their influence upon Venetian faiences. What are certainly characteristic of Nevers are the undulating lines of the background. A fragment of a tile panel from the Château Gloriette, dating from the seventeenth century, now in the Musée Municipal at Nevers, is a typical product of Nevers. It carries representations of bluish-white Persian figures against a yellow background enlivened by green leaves and a few details in manganese. These are Persians seen through European eyes, having been taken from some of the engravings which were so popular at that time. The tones of the yellow background vary from dark to light, giving it a striped appearance. In the eighteenth century the ceramics of Rouen exerted a decisive influence on those of Nevers, where in 1755 there were still twelve workshops in production and output continued to be prolific.

The first tiles produced in France were influenced by Hispano-moresque or Italian models; later on, however, the Dutch style of decoration made itself felt. In Rouen some works showed Italian and others Dutch influence. Masséot Abaquesne, the outstanding representative of the Italian style, was active there from 1528 until about 1564, by which year it is known that he was dead. This artist distinguished himself particularly in the making of floor-tiles for chapels and châteaux; his speciality being archaising representations. He also made vessels, particularly for apothecaries. Abaquesne was associated with the court of François I and the School of Fontainebleau and was commissioned by the king to make tiles for the Château de Madrid with "antique" decorations after drawings by Girolamo della Robbia; of these, white entrelacs on a green ground and white bands from upper and lower borders have been preserved. One of his best works is the series of tiles for floor and walls executed for Anne de Montmorency's Château d'Ecouen (98, 103), of which one of the tiles bears the inscription "Rouen 1542". Pic-

tures showing Curius Dentatus, and Mucius Scaevola from the walls of this chateau are now in the Musée Condé at Chantilly. The work includes some wiry grotesques which were probably borrowed from the engravings of Ducerceau and his followers at Fontainebleau. At Polissy there was another pavement by this Rouen workshop. The Amoncourt Chapel in the cathedral at Langres is well known. A cross in the floor of Notre-Dame de Bondeville near Rouen is decorated with lilies and a cartouche, the effect of which in the somewhat sober aspect of the whole is more spectacular than the cross and the crown of thorns in the centre. In 1557 the workshop produced its last important work: this was an altar-front for the chapel of La Bastie d'Urfé, a château which was to serve the owner's grandson, Honoré d'Urfé, as background to his celebrated pastoral romance *L'Astrée* (93). The altar-front is now in the Louvre, while individual tiles have been dispersed among various provincial museums.

Abaquesne's outstanding abilities were demonstrated most clearly in his large pavements. Elsewhere his intentions were somewhat carelessly carried out. From the technical point of view there is a similarity between his work and Italian maiolica, blue outlines, brown shadows and a yellowish-green and brown occurring in both. The lead-glaze gives the white background an ivory-coloured bloom or else shades it with the palest grey. In other words, over the painting a second transparent, nearly colourless, glass-like layer, was applied as a *"kwaart"*. But however Italian his point of departure may have been, Abaquesne always adapted his designs to his personal intentions. In some respects he may be called the forerunner of Bérain. His compositions are light, ingenious, tautly and precisely drawn in a way that is wholly French. In these elegant grotesques much of the white background is left undecorated; the leaves growing out of their spindly branches are full of life and it is clear that a playful imagination

Indian grotesque with a design of tendrils. Tile-panel of 1557 by Masséot Abaquesne from the Château de la Bastie d'Urfé.
Musée du Louvre, Paris.

is at work; but in spite of this the composition as a whole reflects something of the detached spirit of its creator. The Musée des Beaux-Arts et de Céramique at Rouen possesses the major part of the extant work of Abaquesne; other interesting examples are in the Musée Condé at Chantilly and in the Musée Royal du Cinquantenaire in Brussels. It appears that after the death of Abaquesne no important works were produced at Rouen for some time. It was not until the middle of the seventeenth century, at the time of Poterat and of the fashion for Delft-ware that a trend began which was to develop into the "Rouen style", the *rayonnant* Louis XIV motifs of which are most delightful.

The tiles of Montpellier were obviously closely linked with the north: in the sixteenth century ornaments were being painted there which are reminiscent of the hexagons of Herckenrode (106) and from the seventeenth century onwards the wares of the northern Netherlands were imitated. It is usually, however, easy to distinguish the imitations from the originals. The corners are more compactly filled, while in the centre a white band surrounds a circular motif. Thuile[1] mentions a large pavement, which has now disappeared, which was painted mainly in blue and yellow, with some manganese and green forming a somewhat monotonous whole. It showed a crudely drawn peasant scene, more or less in the style of the painter Teniers.

The tile industry of Lille produced in the eighteenth century, among other works, a well-known tile-picture of the Holy Family, a polychrome work including much manganese, olive-green, a fine straw-yellow, a matt red painted on the glaze after the main firing and a slate-blue less deep than those of Delft or Rouen. At Lisieux tin-enamel and *cuerda seca* techniques were used in the production of tiles. From the second half of the fifteenth century these had been decorated with geometric designs as well as with rosettes and lilies in blue and yellow. These tiles were used for fire-places

Top right: Faience console from the workshop of the Della Robbia family showing a nest of pelicans flanked by cornucopias. 15th century. Breadth 60 cm. Gemeente Museum, The Hague. Bottom left: Part of a pavement, the tiles of which are today in museums in Saluzzo, London, Rome and elsewhere. Alla persiana decoration, geometric figures, emblems of the dead fish and the hourglass symbolising the link between love and death, birds, hares and dogs, symbolising fertility and fidelity, against a schematic landscape. Probably 1501. From the Casa Pirota workshop, Faenza. Victoria and Albert Museum, London. Bottom right: Part of a pavement from the chapel of Castracani family at Scagli. In the foreground are grotesques including winged horses and Moors' heads. The central rectangle shows putti and more grotesques. Not shown on this detail-photograph are the representations of dogs with the Castracani arms or the mark of the Fontana workshop in Urbino. Mid-16th century. Musée Royal du Cinquantenaire, Brussels.

Page 96, top left: Gazelle with scroll bearing motto "Bider Graft" (righteous power), tile from a floor in the palace of Isabella d'Este at Mantua, on which are symbols with mottoes in the four fashionable languages of the day. Pesaro, 1494? 24×24 cm. Gemeente Museum, The Hague. Top right: Bird against a background irregularly framed in blue in the manner of Spanish and Sicilian models. Archaising painting in blue and green. Faenza, c. 1500. Boymans-van Beuningen Museum, Rotterdam. Middle row left: Small tile 7×7 cm. showing the head of a girl in profile. Siena, 15th century. Gemeente Museum, The Hague. Middle row right: Naked angel riding on a gryphon; the beast is spotted in blue, ochre and manganese in the oriental tradition. The form of the tufts of grass is unusual; the whole design is surrounded by a blue border. Faenza, 1550–1570. Boymans-van Beuningen Museum, Rotterdam. Bottom: Tiles showing roundels with cable borders, trefoils in the corners. Left: A rabbit as an emblem of fruitfulness, a favourite symbol of love. Strongly schematic tree and landscape. Faenza, c. 1510. Gemeente Museum, The Hague. Right: A stag in the roundel, probably intended as a symbol of grace, as on the piatelli amatori. Blue is still the predominant colour. Faenza, 1500–1510. Boymans-van Beuningen Museum, Rotterdam.

Page 97, top: Cain slaying Abel. Coloured plaque from the workshop of the Grue family in Castelli. c. 1700. 20×26 cm. Gemeente Museum, The Hague. Bottom: This chinoiserie finely drawn in blue with a misty background is related to Augsburg engravings. From Augsburg, 1720. Victoria and Albert Museum, London.

94

and were sold to a distinguished clientele which included the king at Versailles.

The extremely interesting tiles which were made for the Château d'Oiron (98) are mentioned last since they have no connection with any other workshop, except that in style they resemble the ware of Saint-Porchaire. No faience was made at Saint-Porchaire, where, instead, extremely delicate inlaid work in white clay was produced which may be regarded as a continuation of medieval techniques. The factory does not, however, come within the purview of this book since no tiles from it are known. However, in about 1550 Claude Gouffier had floor-tiles made for the chapel of the Château d'Oiron bearing the same unusual decoration only executed in maiolica. His motto *Hic terminus hacret* (Here ends my work) may be read in capital letters on juxtaposed tiles. In addition to these we find the monograms of Henry II and Catherine de Médicis, the crescent moon of Diane de Poitiers as well as the arms of Gouffier and his wife, Hélène de Hangest. It was probably Hélène de Hangest who sponsored the work. We know that she was highly regarded by talented friends; her circle, which included Clouet, Dumoustier and even the king, lives on in the letters of Marot to Rabelais and in those of Ronsard to Montaigne. Among the decorations of the tiles at the Château d'Oiron there are realistic representations of dolphins, lizards and geese which may be regarded as forerunners of the figures on the ornamental dishes of Bernard Palissy. The colours are dull and bubbled and much inferior to those of the Rouen wares. Here and there the work shows a certain refinement, but it was of small consequence for the future of the tile-industry of France.

99

Antwerp occupies a key position in the history of ceramics. The beautiful faiences which were made there in the sixteenth century, the golden age of the great city, provided the link between the faiences of southern Europe and Asia, and those of the north. The result of this was a vast extension of ceramic production reaching as far as the northern Netherlands and beyond.

There is no doubt that faiences from abroad were known in the Netherlands even before the sixteenth century. In the pavements of the Middle Ages use had already been made of tiles with coloured tin-glazes of Spanish inspiration. In documents relating to the household of the Duke of Burgundy *Valenschwerc* (Valencian work) is mentioned. As early as the beginning of the fifteenth century large tiles for pavements were being produced in Andalusia, at Manises, Paterna and Valencia; for the citizens who knew only the small tiles this no doubt represented a spectacular innovation. They alternated in use with lead-glazed and inlaid tiles.

It is possible that the considerable imports from Spain during the fifteenth century prepared the way for the great success of the Antwerp pavements of the sixteenth century made under Italian influence. Spanish maiolicas[1] were also copied at an early date: by 1442 the *geleymakers* were already working in Antwerp. In these early years, however, faience was still exceptional and was generally regarded as a luxury product. With the arrival in Antwerp of Guido di Savini[2] from Castel Durante and the setting up of his workshop, which was already in production by 1508, a new chapter opened in the history of ceramics. The people of the Netherlands enthusiastically assimilated the new style into their own culture. Cipriano Piccolpasso, describing in 1548 the spread of ceramic production from Castel Durante, wrote, "In Flanders they work quarried clay *(terra di cava)* I mean in Antwerp, where a man from this town, Guido di Savino, introduced the art [of maiolica] and his sons still practise it to this day." Guido, who died before November 1541, lived from 1513 in Den Grooten Arendt op de Eiermarkt and from 1520 onwards in Den Salm in the Kammenstraat, or more correctly, the Cammerstraat, the brewers' street. He had pupils in Antwerp and was also associated with the ceramists of Venice[3]. One of his fellow-craftsmen was Pierre-Frans van Venedigen, who is known from the pavement which he made for the Abbey of Herckenrode, and in 1526 Guido was in contact with the Venetian ceramist Giacomo da Pesaro[4]. There were certainly numerous Italian motifs in his decorative repertoire: Piccolpasso mentions *"trofei, grotesche, quartiere, candeliere, istoriati"* (trophies, grotesques, rim panels, candelabra motifs, figure-subjects).

Philippen[5] and Nicaise have gathered details concerning Guido's life in Antwerp and his house by the Kammerpoort and have pointed out that in the Antwerp archives he was always called Andries, presumably after his father-in-law. Seven children were born of his marriage; his widow, who married another *geleybakker*, sold the workshop to one of her sons.

Philippen has recounted the history of Antwerp's period of great artistic activity, which lasted for only half a century and barely exceeded the period from 1520 to 1570. He was the first to analyse the typical qualities of Antwerp faience and laid the foundations of informed appreciation of its special character. We shall see how necessary this was after the indifference with which this old pottery was treated in the nineteenth century. Philippen further describes how the Italians settled in Antwerp and enumerates their five pigments: blue, orange, yellow, green and rarely, especially in the early years, purple (manganese). The orange may sometimes be almost red. Half-tones and blended colours are rare. The outlines were drawn in blue but it is the vivid yellow which first leaps to the eye. The clay mass is lighter in tone than the tawny colour common in Italy and is sometimes of a pale straw-yellow. The white tin-enamel is similar to the Italian. The palette was less strong than either the Italian or that of the later faiences of the northern Netherlands. By way of explanation, one might describe the Italian colours as resonant and those of Antwerp as, on the whole, vivid. Antwerp differs from the Netherlands in its lack of bluish-black and of a strong orange-brown.

A link with Italy was the lead-glaze, *coperta* or *kwaart* which, during Antwerp's golden age, was applied to tiles as well as to other wares. In general, however, the wares remained less refined than the Italian. In that country the ceramists were very closely associated with the painters. This was not the case in Antwerp, where decoration took its cue to a greater extent from the given form of a vessel or a tile. This explains the fact that in Antwerp colours were often used to achieve highly plastic effects which meant that the total appearance was extremely powerful. It should be remembered that in Antwerp, except for the tiles, few luxurious wares or decorative pieces were made in faience. The jar in the Musée du Cinquantenaire in Brussels by Jan Bogaert and signed and dated 1562 is quite exceptional. Faience plaques did not come into use until the second half of the sixteenth century. The Antwerp industry was conditioned by the fact that it was not difficult to import luxurious jars or vessels, while difficulties were encountered in ordering tiles from abroad and having them sent to Antwerp. In the early years the Antwerp style was related to that of Faenza, where the Hispano-moresque was a strong influence, and later to that of Venice. As a consequence of this change, the designs became less refined: busts began to show less detail, foliate decoration acquired highly conventional shadows while outsized fruits and leaves began to grow on slender twigs. In the second half of the sixteenth century the influence of Urbino made itself felt and showed most obviously in the use of roundels containing biblical or mythological scenes. The two most important Italian schools – Faenza, with Siena and Venice, and Castel Durante and Urbino – both set their stamp on the faiences of Antwerp. Further elements are to be found in the Antwerp decorations which belong to no definite region of Italy but which may be summed up by the name of Raphael; they include grotesques, candelabra, and trophies and were in Flanders adapted to ironwork or *ferronnerie* in the Floris style. There were many engravers working in Antwerp and their style had a great effect upon decoration. Pieter Coecke van Aelst (1502–1550) specialised in *ferronnerie* and Cornelis Floris (1514–1575) made strap-work ornaments of such strikingly three-dimensional effect that they appear to start out of the decorated surface.

Antwerp was also creative in the sphere of figure compositions. The Chamber of Rhetoric known as De Blauwe Schuit (the blue barge) provided the ceramists with indigenous subjects which replaced the Eastern busts from Venice and the mythological and historical scenes from Faenza. Later on costumes also assumed a Hispano-Flemish character.

The wares of the Antwerp tile-makers reveal the relations of the city with southern Europe in a special light. Influenced as they were by Italy, the Antwerp ceramists naturally turned in the first place to the production of pavements. They were made largely for chapels, both at home and abroad, examples of which are The Vyne, Herckenrode, Rameyen and Brou (106, 107, 108). The shape, square or hexagonal, of these floor-tiles is Italian or, more precisely, Faventine. The numerous contacts with Spain, however, which resulted from the political union between the two countries, led also to the facing of walls with tiles.[6] Closely

DIT·ĪS·IN·ROY·ROS·B ^{LO}

INS·TAN·NA

related to the wall-tiles were the house-signs and panels, for which a lively demand soon developed. Panels carrying large and elaborate pictures, however, are again Italian in spirit and were modelled on Italian engravings. The tile-picture, *The Conversion of Paul*, (112) is such a work.

Following upon these general observations, it will be well to discuss some of the best known works. The earliest known pavement of this series is the one commissioned for the mansion The Vyne near Basingstoke in Hampshire (107, 108). It was Bernard Rackham who first examined this pavement and demonstrated its Antwerp origin. Rackham's pioneer work was carried out under unusually difficult conditions. The pavement had been relaid in the nineteenth century and it was almost impossible to judge the colours since the stained glass windows of the chapel allowed only a rather dim light to penetrate. Rackham showed that the floor-tiles come from the earliest Antwerp manufacture and dated them to about 1520; they are thus more than ten years earlier than those of Herckenrode (106), which was executed in 1532. Rackham further established that the floor at The Vyne, compared with

that at Herckenrode, is clumsier, simpler and the product of a less cultivated imagination. As against this, Nicaise suggested that this is the result of the increasing independence of Italian models shown by the Antwerp tile-makers and believed that there was little difference of date between the two. When, however, the deed ordering the floors for the abbey of Herckenrode was discovered at Averbode, it was found that Rackham was right: The Vyne is earlier. Yet Nicaise's theories are extremely illuminating and should not be dismissed. The subjects represented at The Vyne are in many cases the same as those at Herckenrode; and the composition—a square tile surrounded by hexagonal tiles—which was previously unknown in the Netherlands, is the same.

Rackham found that some of the motifs were taken from mythology, among these being Hercules and Venus; some from Roman history, including Lucretia and Divus Julius, in honour of the great Caesar; some from contemporary life, such as Montefeltro, always recognisable by his broken nose, as well as other figures and symbols—among them a crane—some of which must have come from the plays and popular festivities

Floor-tiles from the English country-house, The Vyne, near Basingstoke in Hampshire. By Guido Andries, Antwerp, c. 1520.

Floor-tiles from the English country-house, The Vyne, near Basingstoke in Hampshire. Antwerp, probably by Guido Andries. c. 1520.

of the Chambers of Rhetoric. We also find Lancelot, "Lans", from the romance of Lancelot's unhappy love for Sandrin which was extremely popular in Flanders at the time. On a banderol similar to those which were carried in processions the inscription *Amor* occurs as do Dutch names such as Aert, Jannet, Jasper and Lisebet, which Rackham regarded as proof of the Dutch origin of this faience. Further proof is provided by the occurrence detected by Rackham's observant and practised eye, of the Dutch word *sotge*, meaning "buffoon". The *sotge* came, of course, from the world of the Chambers of Rhetoric.

The work contains many marks of Italian influence, including the blue background and the monochrome blue arabesque which are related to tiles from the Casa Bettini in Faenza of the years 1486–87; but these are always counter balanced by more original, Netherlandish, features. In his *Sources*, Nicaise eloquently describes the picturesque qualities of the busts, which are common to the whole Antwerp tile-industry.

Margaret of Austria (1480–1530), the aunt of Charles V, had lost her second husband, Philibert II, Duke of Savoy, in 1504 and from 1507 had been regent of the Netherlands. She mourned her husband deeply and ordered that a chapel in his honour, in which she herself would also be buried, should be built at Brou, near Bourges-en-Bresse. She divided her commissions principally between Flemish artists, including Lodewyk van Bochem, and Conrad Meyt (1480–1551), a native of Germany, who between 1525 and 1531 executed both tombs. In 1526 she commissioned a pavement for the choir, which was destroyed at the end of the nineteenth century (106, 109, 114). A few of the surviving tiles are to be found at the base of Margaret's tomb, a few in the Louvre and others are scattered in various places. Chompret was the first to analyse the work as a whole. The tiles are arranged in the same way – a square surrounded by a hexagon – as those of The Vyne

and of Herckenrode. The basic conception of the composition, and therefore its realisation, is, however, completely different. The design apparently included a genealogical tree, in the branches of which appeared members of the princely houses as well as historical and oriental potentates. Reconstructions suggest that a death's head occupied the centre, marking the unyielding power of death, and that there was a little rabbit to embody the fertility to which all the persons portrayed on the pavement owed their earthly life. The portraits were meticulously executed and there were none of the bold, and somewhat crudely drawn heads like those at The Vyne. Pious mottoes testify to the princess's striving after a state of resignation.

These tiles have been the subject of numerous controversies and will, presumably, continue so until documents are found which provide the missing information. The extremely delicate execution and decoration of the hexagons have led some authorities to ascribe them to Italian tile-makers, while others have linked them with the work of Masséot Abaquesne. I consider these opinions to be without ground. The painted branches of trees on the hexagons, which distinguish the pavement so clearly from those at The Vyne and Herckenrode, derive from the underlying conception of the Brou pavement. They demonstrate the characteristic quality of the Antwerp shading, which is related to *ferronnerie*, a material which has lost contact with living nature. The hesitant execution of the branches, with their air of having been copied, produces a somewhat stiff effect. It lacks, as do so many Antwerp decorations, the spontaneity usually found in Italy. The style of the branch decorations of the tiles is close to the work on the sculptured tombs; it is not very different from that of the tiles with interlocking circles and even less so from the garlands at The Vyne, though these are more crudely drawn. There is no evidence of the style of Abaquesne. There was a greater concentra-

One of the Antwerp tiles made in
1526 for the memorial chapel of
Philibert of Savoy at Brou.

tion of fantasy in the products of his workshop and the composition was at once more playful and more controlled. One final point may be added to this long discussion of a problem of somewhat specialised interest: although the basic idea of the tree with the portraits was presumably to portray members of the family, Romans, oriental potentates and others were often painted in the spaces provided for the family portraits. In other words, figures were used which were current in Antwerp and originated from numerous sources. When, in 1867, N. Rodot[7] first saw the pavement, he wrote that the figures, of which as many were taken from antiquity as from modern times, were facing one another, a position which in Italy would have been unthinkable.

A deed which Nicaise discovered at Averbode and immediately published, although it refuted his theories, shows that Mathilda de Lexhey, Abbess of Herckenrode near Hasselt, commissioned a tiled floor for her refectory. She gave the commission on the 5 May 1532 to Pierre Frans van Venedigen, who had been working since 1531 in the Kammerpoortstraat in Antwerp. As early as 1922 Laurent demonstrated the Antwerp origin of the pavement.[8] Philippen mentions a similar pavement in the infirmary.[9] The Abbey was dissolved during the French Revolution and its possessions sold. What remained became the property of the Claes family, who, in 1856, passed the stained glass windows to Lichfield Cathedral. The greater part of the pavement – 505 tiles – has been since 1888 in the Musée Royal du Cinquantenaire in Brussels; further pieces are in various other collections.

The composition is the traditional one of oblong hexagons surrounding a square. The squares are decorated with busts, animals, birds, floral motifs and rosettes. The busts include a few nobly idealised heads, such as are frequently to be found in Italy; they are not portraits and their function is merely decorative, similar to that of masks on pieces of furniture. Other busts, however, are portraits of contemporary princes, such as Mathias Corvinus and Montefeltro. King Mathias Hunyadi Corvinus was portrayed because he had married Beatrice of Naples and Aragon and was a much valued patron of the arts in Italy; he was a celebrated book-collector and his books are known from the device on the bindings as "Corvines". Federigo of Montefeltro was that colourful duke who kindled imaginations in the region of Castel Durante which lay so near to his palace at Urbino. In addition to these, we find the portraits of Burgundian princes, including Maximilian, Philip the Fair and Charles V. They were undoubtedly drawn by a Flemish artist. This fact is proved by the landscape backgrounds with the parallel clouds typical of Antwerp work.

Here again the activity of the Chambers of Rhetoric made itself felt[10]. We find a buffoon with his following, Eve, other figures from the romances of chivalry, such as the *History of Saladin*, the heroes of which are the Sultan and his adversary, Richard Lion-Heart, clad in a lion-skin. Richard Lion-Heart was portrayed as he was on his tomb at Fontrevault; it was well-known that he had orange-coloured hair and this fact has been faithfully recorded on the tile. There are also many animals on these tiles. Hares call to mind numerous predecessors in Faenza and are related to the East and to Hispano-moresque models. Dogs and foxes, as well as the swan and the stag, were taken over from Italy. As companions to these animals there are others of the same species within different borders, elegantly placed in a summarily suggested world comprising a blue ground with small green tufts of grass beneath a sky in which short strokes stand for clouds. A strange cock and another bird belong to this second class. A boar quietly moving across a grassy plane, restricted by no roundel but with the entire surface of the tile at his disposal belongs to yet another class of decoration. He recalls The Vyne rather than Italy.

Opposite top: St. Anthony with the pig. House-sign in two parts in the Mannerist style. Antwerp, 1560. Gemeente Museum, The Hague. Middle: Round house-sign in the Mannerist style. Het Vleeschhuis Museum, Antwerp. Bottom left: The eye is an age-old decorative motif. Henry III of Nassau, a patron of the arts, commissioned a tile-pavement with representations of eyes for his castle at Breda. It is possible that memories of Egyptian representations of eyes on obelisks had something to do with this design, which was frequently imitated in other places. c. 1550. Gemeente Museum, The Hague. Bottom right: Tile with geometric checker decoration. Early 17th century. The same ornament occurs in Faenza as early as the end of the 15th century. Boymans-van Beuningen Museum, Rotterdam.

Page 112 top left: The famous tile-picture of the Conversion of Paul *(1547) after a painting by Enea Vico is of great importance not only for the animated Italian composition and lighting of the picture itself but also for the borders. These show typical Antwerp ferronnerie decoration. Three different tones of green, two tones of blue and two purples are used. From Guido Andries's house in Antwerp. Het Vleeschhuis Museum, Antwerp. Bottom: Two tiles from the Abbey of Aduard. They show the family and ecclesiastical arms of Abbot Reekamp. Antwerp, 1547. Museum voor Stad en Lande, Groningen. P. 113 bottom left: This tile from Gorhambury showing a wild boar was perhaps exported as a pattern from Antwerp to England. c. 1560. Victoria and Albert Museum, London.*

Part of a tile-pavement from the castle of Henry III of Orange at Breda. Tiles of this irregular form are known also from Genoa and in works by Abaquesne, evidence of relationships which were possibly established by the School of Fontainebleau. Antwerp, before 1538.

designs found in the church of San Petronio in Bologna, the pavement of which is Faenza work, and were, indeed, in general use in Faenza and Castel Durante during the fifteenth century. Conventional floral motifs, which are mostly Eastern in origin and came to Antwerp in a roundabout fashion by way of Italy, are found in countless varieties.

A second group of hexagonal tiles is decorated with blue arabesques on a white ground. The strongly conventional, symmetrically arranged floral motifs recall wrought ironwork. Laurent conjectured that these tiles were ordered from Spain to replace worn decorations. But blue and white decoration was known in Faenza from the end of the fifteenth century.

The models for the pavements at Herckenrode were engravings of arabesques which had been made fashionable by the Venetians and were highly regarded in France and the Netherlands during the first half of the sixteenth century. The surprising effect of these blue and white arabesques in the polychrome pavement in no way sanctions the inference that they are of different origin from the coloured tiles. Confirmation of their common origin is the fact that three such arabesques are also to be found at The Vyne and that the Victoria and Albert Museum possesses a hexagonal tile from Herckenrode with polychrome tendril decoration in the style of Faenza, on the back of which is a black and white drawing of an arabesque of this kind.

In conclusion, I should like to say of the Herckenrode tiles that they are incontestably of Antwerp origin. They are closely related to the wares of Faenza but are different since in Italy the white enamel is of a clearer white and therefore gleams less strongly. The colours at Herckenrode are less strong but more harmoniously assorted. The popular figures and landscapes possess a primitive realism, while the Chambers of Rhetoric provided specifically Netherlandish subjects. A clear distinction is to be found in the drawing of the portrait-

Carefully drawn floral ornaments appear frequently in wellbalanced compositions. They call to mind the *protomi floreali* of Faenza in the second half of the fifteenth century. When they are not surrounded by a square border they are more vivid in colour and bolder in composition. The same may be said of the busts and animals, but we must bear in mind the possibility that these may perhaps look fresher because they are less worn. Some of these compositions are to be found on plates and vessels throughout the sixteenth century in both the southern and the northern Netherlands. The hexagonal tiles are usually decorated with rosettes, palmettes and conventional flowers which grow on tendrils and curving stems. They are similar to the

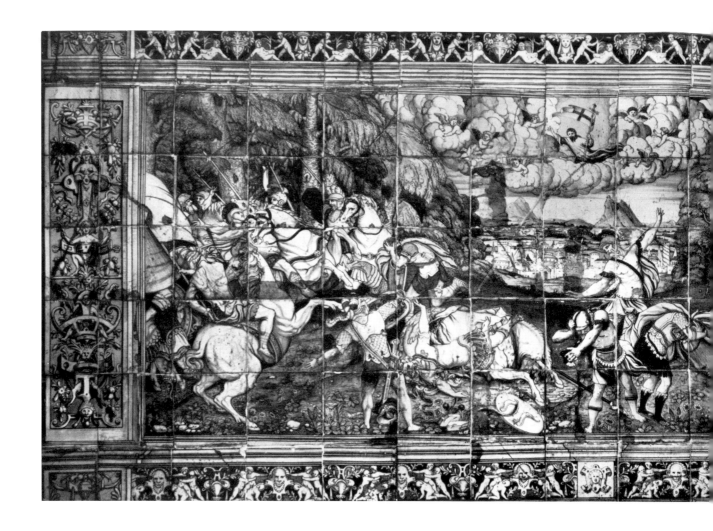

busts: the effect of the Antwerp tiles is somewhat awkward compared with the sure hand of the Italians. Another important product of the Antwerp workshops is the large tile-picture showing the *Conversion of St. Paul* (112) which was made after an engraving by Enea Vico (1523–1567), an Italian Mannerist who worked in the style of Raimondi and Agostino Veneziani. The picture was found on the site of the house of Guido Andries in the potters' quarter of Antwerp. Until now we have had cause to refer most often to the ceramics of Faenza, but in considering this work we have to recall the style of Nicolà Pellipario of Castel Durante. The relationship is apparent in the bold blue strokes of the background, the blue outlines and the shaded modelling, in the lemon-yellow and the thick spiral-shaped clouds which look like shells. As usual, the green shows a tendency to run. Apart from these technical points, the picture is of great importance for the ambitious nature of the undertaking. Some of its features put one in mind of battle-paintings while its dramatic coloration makes it powerfully effective.

The borders of canary-yellow and blue in the style of Pieter Coecke[11] and Jan Floris[12] are highly characteristic of Antwerp. The picture is framed in the antique manner. Two pilasters, decorated with grotesques and resting on a base, support a cornice. The impossible proportions of the pilasters and architrave make it clear that a number of rows of tiles are missing. At the bottom we must presumably imagine a row of tiles, probably with a marbled design, and at the top a cornice, a tympanum or even a pediment. The picture may therefore originally have been nine or ten tiles high. The upper frieze is undamaged. In the bottom row, the eight, ninth and tenth tiles were probably taken from a similar picture. The eleventh and twelfth tiles belong to one another, but not to the tenth and thirteenth. The masks in the bottom frieze and the baskets in the top frieze do not fit in with the tile

borders. There is no central motif. That large parts are missing may be seen from the second tile from the left at the bottom, where only the upper part of the figure is shown. The architecural features are treated not according to the laws of perspective but as though they were seen from directly in front. This analysis, which agrees in part with Van Herck's observations, gives a hint as to how scattered tiles may be recognised as having come from borders of similar pictures. Borders like the one described were used for pictures of historical events; examples as late as 1607 are known. Nicaise published a series of such fragments[13] although he still had doubts as to whether they came from the northern Netherlands or from Antwerp. But the researches of Van Herck have made it clear that they were being copied from the prototype, the picture of St. Paul, continuously for sixty years. The need for architectural features in the borders probably diminished later and these were replaced by borders with grotesques which call to mind the engravings of Balthasar Sylvius.[14]

The artist responsible for the picture of St. Paul is still unidentified. The execution of the work is technically excellent. The first potter to have been registered as a master in the Guild of St. Luke was Hans Floris in the year 1550. The picture, however, shows evidence of long practical experience and dates, moreover, from two years earlier.

The picture of St. Paul was the starting-point for many developments. The friezes persisted in countless variations of *putti* playing in flowery meadows. The background is usually yellow, sometimes orange or manganese, rarely white. The background to the ornaments on the pilasters is sometimes blue, although more often yellow. The fragments showing *putti* which were originally placed at the corners of pediments are extremely picturesque. The same picture was also the source of the tile-decorations which were produced according to Spanish or even Italian practice and used for façades. It should always be remembered that the connection between the Antwerp ceramics and Spanish models was extremely close, in spite of the fact that the work of their Italian predecessors, such as Guido di Savini and his colleagues, usually comes first to mind. The reserved ornament, such as we find on tiles with cartouches, masks, etc. is undoubtedly of Spanish origin.

The house-signs were handsome panels, larger than they ever were in later periods in the northern Netherlands (105), where the tile-makers confined themselves to tiles of normal size or composed pictures from several such tiles.[15] The earliest known house-sign is a representation of the story of the fox and the stork; it is similar in style to the Italian woodcuts and is presumably taken from an illustrated edition of Aesop's *Fables*. The *Red Rose* and the *Elephant* are of a slightly later date. Two large tiles 16.5 × 16.5 cm. decorated the refectory wall of the Abbey at Aduard. They are dated 1547 and the perspectives of the Floris style are recognisable both in the border of the shield and in the mask. The subject is the coat-of-arms of Rekamp, showing a stag or *ree*. Both tiles were probably produced in the workshop of Guido Andries. The background is blue, in accordance with the tradition of the Casa Bettini. The tiles showing the mask of a lion with deeply indented oak-leaves revealing its relationship with Castel Durante also illustrate the persistence of the style of the St. Paul picture. The date 1554 occurs in connection with these designs.

The tile-makers responsible for all these works remained in contact with Italy and Spain, the countries where the foundations of their craft had been laid. Jan Floris of Antwerp was summoned to Spain by Philip II and worked there for twenty-seven years; he received the title of master of the *azulejos*. In this way, features of Antwerp work became incorporated in the Talavera tiles. Rackham was of the opinion that in the early period a contemporary of Guido di Savini travelled to Italy but that he made no tiles, only vessels, there. The Netherlands also became the home of tile-makers from Antwerp. In 1534–36 Jos Wijts introduced the art of maiolica into Bruges. Hans Guldens, who in 1558 was a pupil of Joris Andries, went to Italy, tried his luck in Hamburg and finally settled in Bruges. In 1572 Christiaen van Abeele of Antwerp was in Bruges, but in 1584 we find him in Amsterdam. Philippen made a survey of those tile-makers who moved northwards. Nouts went to Delft; in 1564 Joris Andries moved to Middelburg; in 1572 Adriaen Bogaert went to Haarlem, where, in 1598, he bought a house. In 1606 we find in Haarlem the monogram of Hans Bernaert Vierleger, whose tile-pictures are in the Rijksmuseum in Amsterdam. S. de Molenaer moved to Amsterdam after Christiaen van Abeele, mentioned above. It is probable that many of these potters were adherents of the Reformation and together with countless other Flemish Protestants fled to the northern Netherlands. Jasper Andries and Jacob Janson also went northwards and settled in Norwich, England.

The hey-day of the Antwerp ceramic industry was of short duration. We find no potter's name in the register of the guild of *liggeren* or shopkeepers until 1550, although it had been obligatory since 1453 in Antwerp for *geleyers* to be members of the Guild of St. Luke. We must conclude from this fact that in the intervening hundred years there was no potter who could be compelled to join the guild or who was acceptable. By the middle of the sixteenth century at least fifty potters can be identified from the registers but many of these probably did not make tiles. By 1565 the zenith had already been passed. In 1626/27 we find the last name, that of Adriaen van Houten; in 1636/37 Vincent Montaly's widow paid her dead husband's debts; and that was the end.

We may regard the Brussels industry, which began in 1647 with a tile-picture, as an offshoot of that of Antwerp. In his *Céramique bruxelloise*,[16] Helbig described this picture of a flower-vase which undoubtedly derives from Antwerp. But its copper-green and manganese already reveal the colours which were to come into general use in the Brussels industry. The clay turned reddish when it was fired. In the Musée du Cinquantenaire in Brussels there are several tiles which are probably of Brussels manufacture.

But it would be more appropriate to see as the final phase of the glory of the southern Netherlands and of Antwerp in particular another tile-picture preserved in the Musée du Cinquantenaire. High above the clouds, the Virgin stands in heaven; yet she is still surrounded by such earthly beauties as a balustrade and two fine flowering plants in vases reminiscent of the thank-offerings of ancient times. This work serves to remind us of the love of plastic values, of richness and colour, which were the great delights of the artists of Antwerp (213).

Although the early tiles of the northern Netherlands are often indistinguishable from those of Antwerp, the stronger colours are usually a mark of the more northerly origin. Dark blackish-blue was, for example, not used in Antwerp. Top left: A stylised heraldic eagle in an Italian roundel. Top right: A dolphin in a similar roundel. Middle and bottom: In Spanish lozenge-shaped frames a bird perched on a tree-stump, a group of buildings, an owl and a rabbit. The landscape, clouds, trees and bushes are stylised as in Italy. The spotted coat of the rabbit is another indication of Italian inspiration, which itself derives from the East. c.1600. Lambert van Meerten Museum, Delft.

Page 120 top: Arion on the dolphin's back and a castle in flooded country. Rotterdam, c.1600. Lambert van Meerten Museum, Delft. Bottom: Two representations of Venus or Fortuna in the shell on the sea. On the left she is sitting shaded by a parasol and drawn by a turtle; on the right, she stands in the shell holding a sail and is drawn by a dolphin. Rotterdam, early 17th century. Historisch Museum der Stad, Rotterdam.

The Iconography of Dutch Tiles

The beginnings in the sixteenth century of the great tile-industry which was to develop in the northern Netherlands marked a third peak in the history of tiles. As Persia and the Near East and the Iberian peninsula had done, so now the Netherlands created a whole new world of tiles. Our consideration of the character of this new world may well begin with its iconography. The charm of the tiles of the Netherlands is generally held to be due to their realism and the humour of their scenes. In my view, this opinion is open to question. The high point of tile-production in the Netherlands began to be reached at the time of the Renaissance, at a period, that is, when great attention was paid to the fleeting moments of everyday life. It is true that everyday life had often been represented before: we have seen the Persians with their beautiful women in gardens, the medieval knights on horseback; indeed, no artist has ever represented anything which had not some physical or mental reality for him. In the new period, the histories related by tiles certainly acquired greater actuality, although this development made slow progress. In Antwerp the portrait of a duke was painted on a floor-tile, but he also embodied a legend and a symbol. On another floor-tile we find a buffoon, but he came from the plays of the Dutch Chambers of Rhetoric, which had a strong tendency towards didacticism. It is noteworthy, however, that this development soon came to an end. No true realism was ever achieved in the decoration of tiles, not even during the period when the realistic style in painting was at its zenith. One might have expected that painted tiles would come nearer to the realism of the great masters than the products of any other branch of decorative art. This lack of realism may perhaps be partly explained by the fact that only a limited palette was used for the decoration of tiles; it was splendidly brilliant, certainly, but it possessed no great range.

One of the reasons for the fascination of Netherlandish tiles lies in this very fact. If we look at them as though we were seeing them for the first time, we shall, if we are not entirely insensitive, recognise how strange these lively accompaniments of our existence really are. They appear to be homely but their very brilliance endows their unassuming subjects with a quality of unreality which becomes almost oppressive. Colour and brilliance have, so to speak, cast a spell upon the motions of life and petrified them.

This quality is often in tune with the general trend of the time. Mannerist grace and startling beauty extended to all branches of art in the first half of the seventeenth century. On the tiles of the time, however, we find warriors and flowers which have lost all semblance of life. But we must not forget that in the sphere of tiles painting from life is extremely rare. For the most part, drawings or engravings served as models, and the use of pounced patterns soon simplified the work to such an extent that creative talent was no longer required. This meant that although the works lost a great deal in the way of realism, a skilful and tolerably gifted tile-decorator could always find a way of embodying his ideas and his love of nature.

In the seventeenth century the scenes were set against a broad white background, which often produced an impression of emptiness. Diminutive landscapes are reproduced with all perspective details apparently highly realistic, yet the disproportionately large white fields surrounding them sever their whole connection with cosmic reality. This may have been the artist's intention. At all events, the effect must have pleased him; and the usual explanation based on the baroque dislike of clearly outlined colour contrasts, leaves open many possibilities for the decorator of tiles. The white fields surrounding the motifs are either peaceful in effect or they suggest dramatic solitude; either way, they give the work a certain unreality.

Ornamental design covering groups of four tiles. Holland, c. 1600. Boymans-van Beuningen Museum, Rotterdam.

The landscapes themselves are conventional. Only Cornelis Boumeester (1652?–1733)–who often worked from engravings, including those of Romeyn de Hooghe – suggests atmospheric values, creating the effect of wind, cloudy sky and rough sea (180, 181). The blue and white colour-scheme also invests his scenes with an unreal quality, a kind of lyrical dreaminess. Boumeester reminds one to some extent of his fellow-artist F. van Frijtom, who was able to create an enchanted world of blue on his decorative panels and yet not lose contact with nature. The other decorators, however, drew their landscapes in routine fashion with the help of pounced patterns. What is true of landscape is equally true of other motifs. Actuality was rarely represented. We find portrayals of unusual events, such as children watching the comet of 1664 or jugglers on a tight-rope; but such things did not belong to daily life and daily life is the extreme of realism. Children playing embody play in general; people going about their business or seeking their distractions are images of human types and their occupations. The use of pounced patterns made it almost impossible to vary the presentation, but the fact that this style of decoration was universally appreciated speaks for itself. The variety of subjects is not as overwhelming as may at first appear. The patterns were used in different combinations, which makes it easy to over-estimate the number of subjects. Representation of the greatest possible number of aspects of everyday life cannot, therefore, have been the aim of the maker of tiles.

But so much for general principles. In the early days of Dutch tiles the geometric compositions of Spain and Antwerp were used and there were even chess-board designs, but these are so rare that they cannot have been produced in great numbers. The small scale of their design cannot have made them very effective as wall-decoration. The geometric designs most frequently encountered in the Netherlands are the well-known intricate strap-work ornaments, moresques and arabesques (129) from Antwerp. We find circular compositions from Italy, diamond-shaped compositions from Spain and often the Persian stars and crosses which at this time were still in use in Asia. Quadrilobes were also popular (122). The Italian circles and circular forms had by now lost all real connection with Sassanian textiles. The Spanish lozenges which were at first cut through by the tile-edges were technically improved and at the same time so arranged that one of the lozenges was reserved to form the centre of the decoration. In these later centuries tiles often preserved the appearance of textile hangings. But the material in which they imitated them was a cold one and that is one of the reasons why tiles are basically unsuited to northern climates.

Life is complex, and in order to understand anything which man has created it is necessary to take into consideration a succession of ephemeral events and complex circumstances. One such set of circumstances may be mentioned here. In the Netherlands, which had been annexed by treaty to Burgundy and had then fallen to the Spanish crown, Spanish domination was felt as an intolerable burden. But during the war of liberation, which brought a Spanish army to the Low Countries, the northerners came into closer contact with Spanish civilisation. The adoption of tiled wall-facings was one of the consequences. No Guido di Savini or follower of his making pavements, house-signs and decorating tiles would ever have opened up such possibilities for tiles. The Netherlandish tiles, however, soon lost their Spanish character. Purely geometric or ornamental compositions, such as we find in Moorish work, was not to Netherlandish taste. The ornamental designs disappeared, at least from the centre of the tiles. They persisted longer in the corners, perhaps because they were found less unpleasing when their geometric character was interrupted by the separating lines of the

So-called Portuguese design. Holland, 16th century. Boymans-van Beuningen Museum, Rotterdam.

Tile design reminiscent of the gilded lilies on the round inlaid tiles of the Duke of Burgundy of about 1390. Holland, late 16th century. Lambert van Meerten Museum, Delft.

Dutch tile. Early 17th century. Boymans van Beuningen Museum, Rotterdam.

tile-edges. The centres of the tiles were decorated with animals, busts in various forms of dress, often with high collars, and flower-vases or fruit. The Moorish inspiration was replaced by the Chinese fashion. Designs from Wan-Li porcelain began to appear, at first occupying the centre as well as the corners and the whole painted in Chinese blue. Soon, however, the artists freed themselves once again from foreign influences and put the motifs we know from other tiles (135, 142) such as birds, flowers and insects, into the medallions; these were not simply presented in the form of round discs but were executed in the Chinese manner with scalloped outlines and were usually polychrome though sometimes plain blue. In a short time the white and blue corner motif which was derived from a Chinese meander came into common use as ornament for filling up the corners and almost ceased to be recognisable as a meander. It may be mentioned that the monochrome blue and white palette occurs at the same period as the sombre Spanish colours, which in the first half of the seventeenth century gave its character to Spanish fashion, where black and white were almost the sole colours used. In the eighteenth century the coloration was altered to suit the rococo taste, the blue giving place to manganese. The fact that a single colour is much easier to use than many was, of course, also an element decisively in favour of this use of monochrome.

The earlier quadrilobes and moresques were in many instances replaced by scallops and meanders but the Italian element in Dutch tile-decoration did not die out. A well-known design shows the head of a cherub floating in a medallion surrounded by strongly coloured blue and white leaves, which Piccolpasso calls "Venetian leaves". A similar colour effect is found in the blue and white lilies which soon became a favourite corner motif. The corners of tiles long continued to be decorated, even during periods when the baroque spirit no longer required each separate tile to make an individual effect. The repetitive corner decoration emphasises the wall as such while the small motifs within large, white fields tend to break down the architectonic boundaries. When lilies came to be regarded as too heavy a motif, the *ossekop* or ox's head, a double volute which suggests the horns of an ox, was evolved from them (124, 188, 189, etc.). Later came the even smaller *spinnetje* or small spider (190, etc.). Heavily shaded oak-leaves were also used. In the eighteenth century, at a time when the desire for exact delimitations had re-awakened and a pretentious archaism was in favour, carnations were selected for corner-motifs. These emphasised the wall itself once again. Other motifs which isolated the individual tiles and emphasised the wall included gates and candelabra.

Abstract designs persisted but were not much used. A variety of marbled tiles was made in the seventeenth century. In the eighteenth century the marbling was simply painted on to the tile, whereas in the older tiles the effect was produced by combing, stippling and blurring the colours. Simple geometric compositions, such as checker-board designs or diagonal partitioning appear in provincial work. These designs came from Friesian factories which also made plain white and blue tiles which could be assembled to form wall-facings in checker-board design.

In the course of the eighteenth century a world of discrete forms again appeared on tiles and may be compared with the ornaments of the sixteenth century. They were now put together to form designs which embraced four tiles. Their derivation from leaves remains recognisable and they are known by fine-sounding names of feathers; thus the acanthus was transformed into "ostrich-feathers", palmettes into "Jerusalem-feathers"; there were in addition "African birds", "imperial feathers", as well as a completely abstract buckle motif.

Flower-vases, which had appeared on tiles at a very

123

Figures of animals with "ox-heads" in the corners. Holland, 17th century. Het Houten Huis, de Rijp.

early date, were presented in a uniformly conventional manner. They came originally from Italy but are found within square Spanish frames as well as within Italian medallions. The vase is always of greater importance than the flowers it holds. At first these were daisies but they were later succeeded by the newly imported tulips (135, 136). The same process of "naturalisation" may be seen in the case of fruit: the pomegranates of the south become oranges, and are promoted in Holland to the status of a national emblem since they allude, as do marigolds, to the princely house of Orange. Fruit and flowers may be arranged in quadrilobes, but when they are in a vase or on a dish, the vessels are always the most important element. The composition of the bunches of flowers is so conventional, so completely lacking in imagination or originality that it became the habit to call a vase-tile a *"drie-tulp"* or "three-tulip".

Manganese-coloured ornamental tiles. Holland, 18th century.

The decorations based on flowers and fruit are at their most beautiful in the compositions consisting of lilies, oranges or pomegranates, grapes and perhaps tulips and when the outstanding feature is not the flowers and fruit but the wonderfully balanced arrangement cleverly centred on a corner-motif and unfolding in magnificient harmonies of blue, green and orange. The tiles decorated with flowers after book-illustrations are quite different. Franz Hals' pupil, Judith Leyster, made drawings for tulip catalogues which inspired the tile-decorators to create a special type of floral decoration which brought into the house a life-like, lasting image of these precious blooms. These tiles are painted well and with care and must have been comparatively expensive. They remained polychrome throughout the period when blue and white decoration was generally in favour. From this point of view, we may compare them with the tiles which carry polychrome compositions of birds and flowers, mostly within blue borders. Almost the only realistic feature here is that the grass and leaves are green, but it appears that at least a faint reflection of the brilliant colours of nature was required before the tile could give satisfaction. The prints of C. van der Pas (1560–1637) were often used as models for floral designs, the choice of colours being left to the imagination and habits of the ceramic painter.

Bunches of flowers, though much favoured, were rare on single tiles; they achieved their full glory in tile pictures. Naturally not all the flowers portrayed bloomed at the same time; the bunches were as much a creation of the human imagination as were those in the oil-paintings of the period, which, in their turn, were copied by the decorators. In the eighteenth century special attention was paid to roses which were portrayed sometimes in a simplified, sometimes in an elaborate manner. Later again, flower-designs lost all contact with nature and were rendered in an archaising style. The designs were given names such as *starrebloem* or star-flower, *rozenster* or star of roses. In other words, flower-painting, once so highly refined, declined to a provincial craft.

Animals – as it were, a legacy from Italy or even from Persia – appear only in the squares or medallions. One theme was the great hunt (135). Which animals were represented, whether they were wild or tame, exotic or indigenous, depended entirely upon what models were used (124, 126). As has already been pointed out, birds (125) formed an accompaniment to the carefully painted flowers. It was, indeed, customary to alternate birds with flowers on wall-facings. The finest representations of birds are the *spijkers tegels*, in which the birds are perched upon nails (136). About the middle of the century small blue animals, drawn with spirit and in great variety, were highly popular. They were placed within the wide borders resembling a great white

no-man's-land which were described earlier in the chapter.

Portraits were painted only rarely but there are certain renderings of famous personalities both past and present for which prints were again the models. Portraits occurred more often in tile-pictures than on single tiles. Members of the house of Orange, particularly, were often portrayed in this way and continued to decorate the houses of the people up to the beginning of the nineteenth century (142). The features of the so-called portraits of citizens, or their wives or portraits of married couples were less individualised. The works of Willem Buytewegh the Younger, Frans Hals, A. Pala-medesz and other artists of this school provided models for the tile-decorators, which were accessible to them in the form of prints.

Human occupations taken from the popular books issued

Tiles carrying representations of birds, debased lily-motifs in the corners. Mid-17th century. Lambert van Meerten Museum, Delft.

Dutch tile. Early 17th century. Boymans-van Beuningen Museum, Rotterdam.

during the sixteenth century appeared on tiles in numerous variations, at first within borders and later with ever smaller corner-motifs. Colours were in general confined to blue, though there were a few polychrome representations. Everyday as well as more unusual occupations were portrayed and both were conventionally painted, though sometimes in a lively style which gives a superficial impression of realism. These subjects were extremely popular.

The most important of them are the soldiers after the engravings by J. de Gheyn. The most splendid pieces are to be found in the Château de Beauregard, near Blois, where they form a pavement. Prince Maurice of Orange had seized the popular imagination by his re-organisation of the army training exercises and it is not surprising that this should have been reflected in tiles. These figures are naturally not individuals but types (155). The rare, large tiles with polychrome representations of Saracens and Christians may be regarded as the rich relations of these soldiers; this was a popular subject in Europe, Islam having only recently advanced to the very gates of Vienna. These tiles show horsemen in headlong action, their coats romantically flying in the wind. It is possible that studies by Sebastian Vrancy, Essaias van de Velde or Wouwerman were the sources of inspiration for the figures, which are so diverse that they could be put together to form a battle-picture. Documentary evidence shows that these works were in existence as early as 1637. The polychrome versions were of early date; in general the horsemen were painted blue and only their sashes and the fire from their pistols touched with red. Duels between a Polish and a Turkish horseman are usually references to the Battle of Khotin, which Sobieski made famous in 1673. These motifs persisted well into the nineteenth century and may have been copied from German prints. Scenes from riding-schools and figures of Amazons are also known.

Representations of children at their games were extremely popular at this time (149) and there are tiles showing either one child on its own or two children playing. Their universal popularity was probably due to the verses of Jacob Cats, which were widely read. Pieter Brueghel had already done paintings of these games, as had Jan and Caspar Luyken after him and the subject persisted until deep into the nineteenth century – showing that although games may be timeless, the same is not true of fashions in children's dress. An extremely rare series which once decorated the fire-place in the burgomaster's room at Haarlem portrayed the daily life of the people of China (142); the scenes – of a China viewed through European eyes – were painted in a deep cobalt blue.

Harders or shepherds appeared with great frequency on the tiles of the eighteenth century in varying degrees of realism and pastoral fantasy (127); their air of graceful nostalgia, which was so strong an element in the culture of the day and which even influenced Marie-Antoinette and found its way into the dairy at Hampton Court and the kitchen at Nymphenburg, never assumed the character of elegy. The painters also represented theatrical subjects and love-scenes, though these can hardly be called idyllic. The best of them are the two-figure tiles of Utrecht.

In the later eighteenth century a decadent form of realism led to the representation of less conventional subjects. One of the earliest of these works (214), shows the potter's workshop at the Bolsward factory; other pieces show a ship, a peasant's cottage, a cow, a horse (219), a dog (267), a cat (202) and a canary in a cage. These were regarded as portrayals of personal belongings but were, in fact, painted with the help of pounced patterns. Biblical scenes were produced more often in the eighteenth than in the seventeenth century. Here also prints served as models, particularly those of Romeyn de Hooghe (1645–1708). At least two hundred

126

Man sitting on a bench in a roundel with a foliate border. Holland, c.1600. Boymans van Beuningen Museum, Rotterdam.

Tile showing a landscape. Holland, late 17th century. Lambert van Meerten Museum, Delft.

Tile showing a landscape. Holland, late 17th century. Lambert van Meerten Museum, Delft.

and fifty biblical subjects are known, with or without inscriptions – which, indeed, often refer to a passage other than the one portrayed. These tiles are usually somewhat lacking in refinement for the subjects were too complicated for swift handling (203); yet there is sometimes an attractive quality in their very simplicity. Saints and apostles painted after Flemish prints occur occasionally (192).

Secular subjects were less common than biblical ones. There are, however, representations from Ovid, scenes of courtship or tea-parties in parks and on terraces, the latter often surrounded by a balustrade.

Ships were copied from paintings or prints and, since the same models were always used, the types of ship found on tiles long remained unchanged (179). Thus convention rather than realism reigned in this sphere also.

Four tiles showing pastoral scenes in blue and manganese, within roundels, carnations at corners. Late 18th century.

Surprisingly enough, landscapes are limited to about forty subjects (127). They are still closely related to the traditional manner of representing nature in series of pictures of the months or seasons or in topographical illustrations. Van Goyen was a great source of inspiration here, but it was principally the so-called minor masters who were imitated. The best works are fairly true to nature. They were carried out with the help of pounced patterns, but clouds and such like were painted free-hand. The motifs are often placed within roundels though sometimes they fill the whole surface of the tile.

Tiles showing heraldic devices were extremely rare in the Netherlands. There is one, dating from 1619, in the museum at Leeuwarden; a series showing the papal arms is known, as are tiles with the arms of Orange-Nassau. The later elegant series of coat-of-arms of towns in manganese (202) were regarded as suitably discreet. Lions and eagles in heraldic attitudes also occur.

Although the Dutch tiles are not distinguished by realism, they nevertheless provide much scope for popular imagination. They are sometimes unctuously didactic, often humorous or even ironical. Cupids and angels of Italo-Flemish descent sometimes turn to human occupations in scenes which may extend over several tiles; thus, for example, we see a cupid flying down to earth on one tile and coming nearer to his goal on a second. They have no weightier purpose than to express playful fancies or an occasional ironic comment on humanity.

The tile-makers sometimes entertained their clients with mythological scenes. A flying Chronos, a satyr and other creatures may be more picturesque than meaningful, yet they are noteworthy examples of the imaginative quality sometimes to be found in Dutch tile-decoration. Sea-monsters in particular, after prints by anonymous Mannerist engravers, continued to appear until well into the eighteenth century (188, 189). They are painted in bold strokes with considerable imagination. They were often placed before a horizon to form a *zee jacht* or marine hunt and were sometimes given the quaintly inappropriate attributes of a pipe or a hat. These expressive monsters indicate a development which was apparent in certain tile-decorations which showed nightmare phantoms and terrifying creatures, symbols, perhaps, of primitive fears which continued to haunt the soul of mankind and even troubled the simple hearts of the tile-decorators. It may be that these Mannerist monsters, denizens of land or sea, whose effect is often due simply to distortion, derived their quality of strangeness from the painter's lack of skill. But they appear so frequently that they must have been appreciated at the time. Terrifying, staring, weird faces, repulsive naked figures with heads that are too small, flowers and insects of menacing size against a diminutive landscape combine to form a strange, grotesque, often frightening, world.

Individual Dutch Tiles

It is incorrect to consider the Dutch tiles of the early period solely as an offshoot of the Italian tiles. Our attention should be concentrated not on the imperfections and shortcomings which are so clearly apparent in comparison with the ceramics of Italy, but rather on the features which are characteristic of Dutch tiles. To be sure, everything we find is more or less artless and the roundels which were so popular on these tiles are little more than plain circles. The Dutch tiles are rather an expression of a middle-class people, its folklore, its sentiments and, often, its sense of humour.

In the early Dutch tiles, however, the Italian influence is unmistakable. In the last years of the fifteenth century Italian square tiles became fashionable and they reappear in the early Dutch maiolicas. The thick Dutch bluish-black pigment, the orange-brown, yellow and manganese are comparable with the palette of Faenza. The Italian influence found its way into the Netherlands by way of Antwerp. During the course of close investigation of this subject, tiles have been found which were imported into the Netherlands from Antwerp.[1] The names of Antwerp potters who emigrated to the Netherlands have already been given (132). Middelburg and Rotterdam soon became centres of ceramic art. Maiolica was produced in many towns including, probably, some of whose ceramic-industry we know nothing.

After the Netherlands came under Spanish domination, tiles continued to be produced only for wall-facings. Practically no tile-pavements dating from after 1550 have been found.

Much has been published on Dutch ceramics. Some of the earliest authors have retained their reputation. Hudig, who, among other things, edited the illustrated volumes of Vis and de Geus[2], may be regarded as the foremost authority. It is thanks to the flourishing tile-industry that pioneer works such as that of Hoynck van Papendrecht, *Rotterdamsche Plateel-en Tegelbak-*

kers, have been issued. In 1947 C. H. de Jonge published a comprehensive work, which, like that of Hudig, deals with the whole of the Netherlands and soon became one of the most important works of reference. In recent years Dingeman Korf has made a name for himself with informative analyses of surviving tile variants.

Between 1609 and 1629 many new maiolica workshops were opened: six in Rotterdam, five in Delft, three in Haarlem, others in Amsterdam, Gorinchem, Gouda, Leiden, Hoorn, Enkhuizen and probably also in Dordrecht and Leeuwarden. No new workshops were set up in Delft or Haarlem—where vessels of the finest quality were produced—after 1629. After 1650 tiles were no longer made in the old factories but at establishments set up exclusively for the purpose.

It is often difficult to ascertain the origin of an individual tile. The manner in which clouds or waves are painted and the habit of representing trees by hatching may be important and informative in this connection. These are the parts of the decoration not executed by means of pounced patterns and may thus reveal the features of an individual style. But even so the results of numerous investigations continue to be the object of controversy. Tiles which were usually considered to have been manufactured in Haarlem have been discovered in large numbers in Zeeland, while others, believed to have originated in the western provinces, have been found in Friesland.

Until the beginning of the seventeenth century, Dutch tiles were scarcely distinguishable from those of Antwerp. Only in the representation of shadows, which, in the former, are arbitrarily placed and without real effect, did they differ from one another. The reddish Rotterdam clay gave a warm tinge to the white; in Delft the clay was softer and yellower so that the effect of the glaze was clearer and whiter. The colours of Friesian tiles are harder.

After 1625, when the Antwerp industry had passed its

131

zenith, the northern Netherlands looked to Italy for their models – especially to the Patanazzi workshop in Urbino, which created outstanding grotesques – to the Wan-Li imports from China and to indigenous prints or paintings, such as the engravings of soldiers after de Gheyn which had been issued as early as 1608.

The import of Chinese porcelain into the Netherlands increased in volume after 1557 when Portugal established an agency at Macao near Canton. The first Dutch auction was organised to dispose of the cargo of an impounded Portuguese ship. After the beginning of the seventeenth century importation was no longer by way of Portugal but through the newly founded Dutch East India Company.

Of the tiles with regional characteristics, mention should be made of those attributed to Haarlem manufacture; these tiles are carefully drawn and carry an unimaginative ornamentation in blue, orange or brown, occasionally with a touch of yellow or green. Plant motifs were debased and became geometric patterns, among which many spirals are found. Rotterdam made impressive compositions of sea-monsters. Utrecht early became known for its pastoral scenes, although its products were comparatively expensive. In 1663 pastoral scenes began to appear in Rotterdam also, but these tiles were probably cheaper; for the best *harders* were considered to be those from Utrecht and cost between 20 and 37.50 guilders a thousand. This is a fairly high price. Tiles with landscapes or figures as subjects were very expensive because they required careful workmanship. In 1664 landscapes cost nearly 70 guilders a thousand; first-class historical scenes cost 100 guilders a thousand, while scenes with a single figure sold for no more than 33 guilders.[3] The cupids which we find so amusing today were the cheapest. "Pillars" used at the back of the fire cost two guilders a pair. These figures are quoted only to underline the fact that the more or less ordinary tiles were regarded as in no sense objects of value. For an account of the appearance of the tiles, reference may be made to the chapter on their iconography and to the illustrations. A few rarities must, however, be mentioned. From 1700 onwards in Utrecht and Limburg, lustre decoration was used, strangely enough on tiles with geometric patterns or rustic motifs and not on those which showed the highest degree of technical and artistic accomplishment. Marbling was painted on to the raw clay; lead-glaze or *kwaart* was added but, as in the case of lustre, this is not found on the more expensive tiles, though the most expensive of all were an exception to this.

The provincial art of Limburg, which was related to the products of the Lower Rhine, often produced tiles (219) with *ringeloor* or poured slip decoration.[4]

Mention must here be made of a derivative of the Dutch faiences, the tiles of the *Habaner*, or followers of Jakob Huter, Anabaptists who had settled in Slovakia and Transylvania.[5] When two of their number visited the Netherlands in 1655, they took back from there a type of blue and white decoration in the Chinese style, as well as Dutch animal and architectural motifs. The castles, trees, the mountain-houses of their homeland, the conventionally portrayed lilies-of-the-valley and the pictures of the Turks whom they always felt to menace them lend their simple products a picturesque air. Their faiences are often covered with a marbled glaze flecked with blue and white. Decoration may have been painted on to the lighter parts.

Mention should at this point be made of the export of Dutch tiles. The finest specimens, which came in the main from Rotterdam or Amsterdam, went to Spain and Portugal. Export to the countries of the North Sea and the Baltic also assumed very large proportions. An important part in this trade was played by the wares of Harlingen, Makkum and Bolsward, to which a separate chapter will be devoted.

Christ at the well. Coloured tile by Joris Andries of Antwerp. Crude but extremely rare product of the early days of the Middelburg manufacture when it was still dependent upon Antwerp. The manganese of the tunic has been spoilt by excessive firing. Although the colours are reminiscent of Faenza, direct Italian influence is unlikely. Last quarter of the 16th century. Lambert van Meerten Museum, Delft.

If we consider the whole range of Dutch tiles, we shall find that certain wall-decorations – the fine "pictures" illustrating given themes – make a special appeal. The largest and finest of these works are to be found among the many treasures of the Iberian peninsula. Yet there are Dutch tile-pictures elsewhere which claim our attention by virtue of their beauty or the curious presentation of their subject. These will therefore be discussed in a separate chapter. Tile-pictures are not purely architectural decorations but pictures executed by means different from those usually employed. The element of virtuosity is stronger here than in the case of the more ordinary tile wall-facings. Sometimes the effect of the tile-pictures is almost that of *trompe l'œil*.

As far as can be ascertained, individual tiles were used without much regard to cost – they were, in fact, not very expensive. In some tiled rooms, the tiles were simply cut through as necessity demanded without regard to the motif. The aim of tile-facings was always a large-scale decorative effect; this was achieved, for example, by alternating white tiles with landscape tiles or even by placing a large landscape picture in the centre of a wall decorated with single landscape tiles. No great importance was attached to proportions: a "vine-tendril pillar" may be found hard up against a small landscape the size of the vine-leaves, the pillar looking as though it had been set in place by a giant.

Chronologically the earliest and certainly pre-eminent in point of artistic value is a highly impressive picture which was placed in 1594 on the wall of a house in the Grote Markt in Rotterdam[1] and is today preserved in the Historisch Museum at Rotterdam. It is known by the name of *In Duysent Vreesen* (The House of the Thousand Terrors) but this designation is misleading (139). Traces of its great Antwerp prototype, the *Conversion of Paul*, are readily discernible in the picture, not only because this work too is a decoration

for a façade but also in respect of its colour-composition. It shows a lamb surrounded by wild beasts and warriors and bears the inscription in Dutch *In duysent vreesen*, meaning "a thousand fears". G. de Goederen[2] has argued that the lamb is not, as had long mistakenly been thought, the symbol of the young republic, and that the other figures do not portray its protectors, Prince Maurice of Orange and the Dutch lion; nor, he maintains, does the oriental figure embody the countless dangers which threaten the lamb. Rather, according to De Goederen, are we dealing with an image of the Lamb of God. The fire in the background symbolises God, who spoke out of the burning thorn-bush, as well as the fire on Mount Sinai, and God who is the fire which consumes sinners. The lamb, therefore, is the symbol of Christ, who is the way to God and so stands before the fire. The stream is the river of the water of life which flows from the throne of God and the Lamb. On the left of the stream is the "tree of life, which bare twelve manner of fruits, and yielded her fruit every month: and the leaves of the tree were for the healing of the nations" (*Revelation* 22, 2). Two warriors stand for "the glory and honour of the nations" (*Revelation* 21, 6), the oriental wearing a turban, the European a helmet. The men and animals living at peace with one another with the lamb in their midst illustrate *Isaiah* 11, 6–9. The inscription "*In duysent vreesen*" on the bottom row of tiles was not originally composed for this picture. Incongruities and lack of proportion may be found in the decoration and in the placing, as, for example in the framing of the inscription, which is incomplete and does not harmonise with the picture itself.

Proceeding chronologically, we come next to two small pictures after the Haarlem painter Maarten van Heemskerck (1498–1574). They are signed and dated 1606 HVB or HBV; this was probably Hans Barnaert Vierlegger, whom we have already encountered as an emigrant from Amsterdam who settled in Haarlem. Fragments of a tile-picture of the Prodigal Son, now in the Lambert van Meerten Museum at Delft, carry the date 1570 and the initials IB; these stand for Jan Bogaert the Younger, an Antwerp ceramist. The picture may date from the beginning of the seventeenth century and have been copied from an engraving dated 1570. Their character suggests that these tile-pictures are Antwerp rather than Dutch work.

A few other house-signs have been preserved, among them *De drie blompotten* from Gorinchem, which formerly decorated the façade of the house of a seed-merchant and is today preserved in the Victoria and Albert Museum. The three flower-vases are similar to those we know from single tiles, although the arrangement of the flowers is somewhat less conventional. A horseman from a potter's house in Rotterdam, 't Graefschap van Buijren, is now in the Rijksmuseum; the house-sign of the Amsterdam potter Haye Esdré now belongs to the Koninklijk Oudheidkundig Genootschap (Royal Archaeological Society). Also in the Rijksmuseum is a large picture after an engraving by C. Visscher; it is painted mainly in blue and represents the Battle of the Downs off Gravelines in 1639 at which Admiral Tromp was victorious over the Spanish fleet.

This is the earliest series of tile-pictures intended for outdoor decoration, a type always rare in the northern Netherlands. Tile-pictures inside the house began to proliferate as soon as the fire-place acquired its new form. In about 1620, in place of the old triangular arrangements of decorated bricks, black smoke hoods came into fashion. They were protected at the bottom by an iron fire-plate and flanked by ornamental tiles. These tiles were usually singletons but sometimes there were also small tile-pictures or even large ones showing life-sized portraits of warriors such as Hannibal, Scipio or the Princes Maurice and Frederick Henry. These figures doubtless derived from the sandstone caryatids which in the sixteenth century supported the fire-place hoods. The conception of a supporting function for the figures gradually disappeared.

As early as the beginning of the seventeenth century there was yet another type of tile-picture. These were the specimen-pieces which demonstrated the capabilities of a given workshop. The Historisch Museum at Rotterdam possesses a tile-picture of this kind which shows Julius Caesar on horseback under an arch (141). It was painted in blue and is dated 1640. This picture was formerly in the Opport, a street in Rotterdam, on the back wall of a house near the tile-factory of Jan Pieterz Valkhoff (d. 1649), but the numbering on the back of the tiles indicates that the picture must originally have been somewhere else.

Similar specimen-pieces[3] were found in the workshop De Swaen in Gouda, which from 1621 was under the direction of two potters from Rotterdam. One of the directors, who took the name Willem Verswaen or "William of the Swan", had in his yard four pictures on walls hung with white tiles. The first showed two female allegorical figures in manganese (199), the second a polychrome cockerel (161), both now in the De Moriaen Museum at Gouda, the third a personification of hope in blue, and the fourth another polychrome cockerel, both these now at the Boymans-van Beuningen Museum at Rotterdam. The four works were undoubtedly showpieces used as samples for work for sale.

The output of Willem Verswaen was considerable. He appears to have been given the use of the drawings representing freedom of conscience which J. Utewael prepared in 1599 for the window of the church of St. Jan at Gouda. Both the female figures from his courtyard are direct copies of these drawings and also resemble the half of a fine tile-picture, now in the Victoria and Albert Museum, showing the same four figures who, on the church-window, draw the chariot

In duysent vreesen. *This tile-picture from the façade of a house in Rotterdam shows figures which are still harmoniously coloured separated by areas in which only the ground of white glaze appears. The sky shows the characteristic painting of the clouds in horizontal lines, which, like the brown colour, ceases to occur at a later date. Historisches Museum, Rotterdam.*

139

of freedom. Willem Verswaen used a putto from the church-window to recreate a tile-picture which is to-day in the Lambert van Meerten Museum in Delft. The figure appears in reverse so that the drawing must have been traced and the tracing then pounced to serve as a pattern – it would, of course, have been possible to reverse the sheet, as was often done with pounced patterns. The word "re-create" has been used advisedly, because this putto in dark blue, manganese and yellow shows that Verswaen derived great pleasure from the colour and the light striking through the window and rendered his perceptions in a splendid fashion.

This survey of tile-pictures will now be continued in chronological or geographical order. In Rotterdam, under the influence of contemporary painting, flower-pieces began to be produced at a very early date. The style of R. Savery (1576–1639) is most readily discernible here. Rotterdam was an important centre of tile-production, particularly of tile-pictures. Cornelis Boumeester (1625?–1733) had his workshop on the Delfste Vaart. As has already been stated, he emulated the achievement of his fellow-painter Frijtom. Marine subjects, harbours, landscapes and parks were his favourite themes. He was much imitated and we may regard him as the inspiration of a delightful picture of whaling, in spite of the fact that stylistically this version is more reminiscent of Salm (193).

Another Rotterdam workshop, known as De Bloempott or "the flower-pot", was under the management of the Aalmis family. The masterly works executed in this workshop for the castles of Brühl and Falkenlust and for the Amalienburg will be discussed in the chapter on rooms decorated with tiles.[4] Aalmis often used Italian or French engravings as models. His workshop produced pictures of biblical scenes for the orphanage in Rotterdam and the interior facings for a smithy; these are now in the Gemeentemuseum at The Hague.

Works, now in Bremen, after engravings by Amigoni showing allegories of astronomy, music and architecture must also be mentioned here. The luxurious villas of the Amsterdam merchants were a great source of admiration at the time and it is therefore not at all surprising that a series of engravings recording their beauty should have found an echo in the products of the Aalmis workshop: the house Zijdebalen near Utrecht was one so commemorated.

The Amsterdam workshop which may be compared with that of the Aalmis family in Rotterdam belonged to the Van der Cloet family. The most important works of this atelier were commissions from abroad. Indeed, there is in Holland only one tile-picture by the Van der Cloets; now in the Rijksmuseum, it is dated 1707 and represents a dinner-party on a garden-terrace. J. M. dos Santos Simões has published a study of the connections between Holland and Spain which contains an account of the activity and significance of this workshop.[5] Its products are distinguished by the powerful expression given to the painter's imagination and the boldness of the effects attempted; its style is primarily pictorial; magnificent effects are achieved by long, flowing lines. However, the polychrome of the Aalmis atelier is of far greater brilliance, the Van der Cloets usually even working in blue monochrome.

Rotterdam was not the only source of flower-pieces. The blue picture of J. van Oort of Utrecht is extremely unusual; it is dated 1697 and was placed in the orphanage at Sommelsdijk in a position where the hood of a fire-place would normally be found; it is now in the Rijksmuseum. The workshop known as De Roos in Delft produced for important commissions tile-pictures portraying large vases filled with all kinds of flowers (163). Thirteen of these masterpieces have been preserved: three of these are in the kitchen of the Amalienburg at Munich (164), but many errors have been made in reconstructing them and these

C. IVLIVS. CÆSAR

impair the effect of the whole: it is, for example, a disappointing experience to look closely at the vertical rows in the centre. Of the other extant examples, four are in the Château de Rambouillet, one in the Musée de Sèvres, two in the Nicollier collection in Paris, two in the Rijksmuseum in Amsterdam, one in Copenhagen and one in the Victoria and Albert Museum, which, in spite of the fact that it lacks its border, still preserves a compelling elegance (168). These tile-pictures reveal clearly the great difference between painting and ceramics. They express full awareness of the artistic qualities of the material; only in faience is it possible to set bold, vivid colours against a background of gleaming white and to achieve in the process a smooth surface with an effect of coolness.

It must surely be true that the finest Dutch tile-pictures known are those which came from Delft. They represent a form of *chinoiserie* and are painted in a manner very seldom found on tiles. The figures and animals have the expressive power of drawings but the total effect, nevertheless, is entirely appropriate to ceramics. The pictures in this series are to be found today in the Amalienburg, in the Musée Royal du Cinquantenaire in Brussels, and in the Rijksmuseum in Amsterdam; there are a few more fragments in other places. The Tapuya Indians which are found in these compositions, together with Chinese elements, undoubtedly derive from the paintings or drawings of Albert Eeckhout who had visited Brazil (169). The pictures, therefore, cannot have been made before 1690–1725.

North of Amsterdam the houses and farm-houses were often decorated with less pretentious tile-pictures. They were often substitutes for paintings and were sometimes even valued as optical illusions. The game went so far that the "pictures" usually "hung" on the tiled wall from cords which were painted on the tiles. Works of this type were produced principally in the Friesian factories of Makkum and Harlingen.

One final group, also coming close to provincial art, embraces pictures with portraits of the members, both male and female, of the House of Orange. The many symbolic allusions, such as the orange-tree, are in full accord with the popular character of these works. They continued to be produced until well into the nineteenth century.[6] Even portraits of King William (1772–1843) and Queen Wilhelmina (1774–1837) appeared on tiles painted from prints by W. Senus after E. Maaskamp. A comparison of the tile-portrait of the king with C. Hodges' sketch for a portrait discloses the curious fact that the heroic head has become on the tile the effigy of a friendly but not unduly intelligent country gentleman in officer's uniform.

*Flower-panel from the side of a
fire-place. c. 1700.*

144

Dutch Tiles as Decorations for Walls and Fire-places

The subject of this chapter is the decoration of walls with tiles covering areas larger than those of the pictures and for purposes not exclusively ornamental. Fire-places may be taken first.

Until the end of the seventeenth century the wall behind the fireplace was very large and the smoke-hood was placed at a considerable height. This meant that the decorations of this wall were very much in evidence. Tiled walls such as have already been described were commissioned for these fire-places.

PILAERTJES

A characteristic element of these decorations were the *pilaertjes* or pillars (194). They were undoubtedly derived from the old sandstone pillars which supported the smoke-hood in the houses of the early seventeenth century. It is noteworthy that the same transition to two-dimensionalism took place here as in the tile-pictures of standing figures evolved from the earlier sandstone caryatids and in those of flower-vases such as the picture from Sommelsdijk, now in the Rijks-museum.

The *pilaertjes* may be of various types. They are named in documents as ordinary pillars, twisted pillars, "vine-tendril" pillars – *pylaar wijnrank* in Dutch – and so on. A feature common to them all is that they have lost all architectural significance: they cannot be used as supports nor do they even look as though this were their function. Their capitals are unattached and it is particularly noticeable that their bases do not touch the ground. They seem to float in mid-air and awaken a need for some architectural element which is felt to be missing.

In about the year 1700 the style of the fire-place changed. The smoke-hood was lowered to a height of about one metre from floor-level, so that the fire-place

itself no longer offered any great scope for decoration. From this time onwards, simpler tiles were used in this position and in many places, particularly in lower rooms, it was decided to face the whole smoke-hood with tiles.

SMUIGERS

Smuigers[1] is the Dutch word for fire-places the smoke-hood of which as well as the wall behind the fire is faced with tiles. The appearance of such structures is most striking: the effect of so many tiles in such small, dark rooms is surprising: they appear so incongruous in such surroundings that their brilliance and colour have an almost barbaric effect. They were valued for their cleanliness though not for this alone: *smuigers* provided the opportunity of assembling many different scenes which stimulated the dreams and flights of fancy which have always been a pleasure of the Dutch. Constructions of this kind would be unthinkable in Italy or Spain. Sociologically speaking, the *smuigers* belong to the houses of the citizens of the small towns. They are not found in the houses of the nobility though they were installed in those of well-to-do citizens and in municipal buildings. Examples are principally to be found in the region of the river Zaan, north of Amsterdam, in Koog, Assendelft, Wormer (212), De Rijp and elsewhere.

These new features of interior decoration were entirely baroque in nature. There were no clear architectural combinations in the classical sense; that is to say that the effect of pillars and beams, of supporting and supported elements, is completely lacking. The whole complex consists of protruding and receding features and the top thrusts forward in a powerful curve. This strange form was undoubtedly derived from the slope of the beams supporting the roof. In small houses, such as those in which *smuigers* are found, the beams begin at the ground-floor and it was in fact an obvious solution to fill the space between them. The peculiar shape which resulted determined the whole form of the *smuigers* (211).

The *smuigers* of the region a little farther north than that under discussion are simpler in form; the overmantel does not curve forwards at the top (212). In the course of time the *smuigers* began to lose much of their overladen baroque effect. In place of the masses of blue or manganese-coloured tiles, a fire-place of white tiles framing various small pictures appeared. These might include a dog or a cat sitting facing the fire, a picture of a bird-cage placed at about the height at which a real one would hang, and other motifs from everyday life. These fire-places were an expression of the Age of Enlightenment, embodying the factual aspects of life in a rational manner.

Less well known than the *smuigers* was a form of fire-place which occurred in the Catholic region of Zeeuws Vlaanderen and Brabant. These express the religious allegiance of the householder: crosses in blue appeared in the centre of the wall behind the fire while the sides were decorated with New Testament scenes.

RECESSES

Some mention must here be made of other parts of the house for which tile-decoration was used. The walls behind the beds were often hung with tiles, sometimes even with composite tile-pictures. Winding staircases provided another opportunity to face walls with tiles. It should be remembered that the Dutch used tiles to protect themselves from the whitewashed walls as well as to keep the walls clean. The wall-facings of the staircases are extremely attractive; tile-pictures were not used, simply combinations of graceful designs.

There were also tiled niches. The border-tiles which were needed were decorated and glazed on their edges. The West-Friesch Museum at Hoorn possesses a large slab with a horseman in manganese and a blue decoration on the side, which was presumably used as the floor of a niche. A large square tile of the same type in private ownership was undoubtedly made for the same purpose and is even more interesting since it shows in what a carefree manner the artists set about presenting biblical scenes (190). In the museum at Gouda there is a tile showing a *Crucifixion* which served as the cover of a foot-warmer. For further examples the reader is referred to the illustrations.

One very strange phenomenon is found in the Netherlands and nowhere else in Europe. It is difficult to decide whether it should be regarded as an oriental element haunting the human mind like an archetype or as the work of some fairy whose magic wand can reach everywhere; there is, quite simply, no explanation for what gave the people of Hinlopen in Friesland the idea of facing their window-frames and cross-bars with faience. In seeking an explanation one can only recall the numerous oriental elements in Dutch popular art.

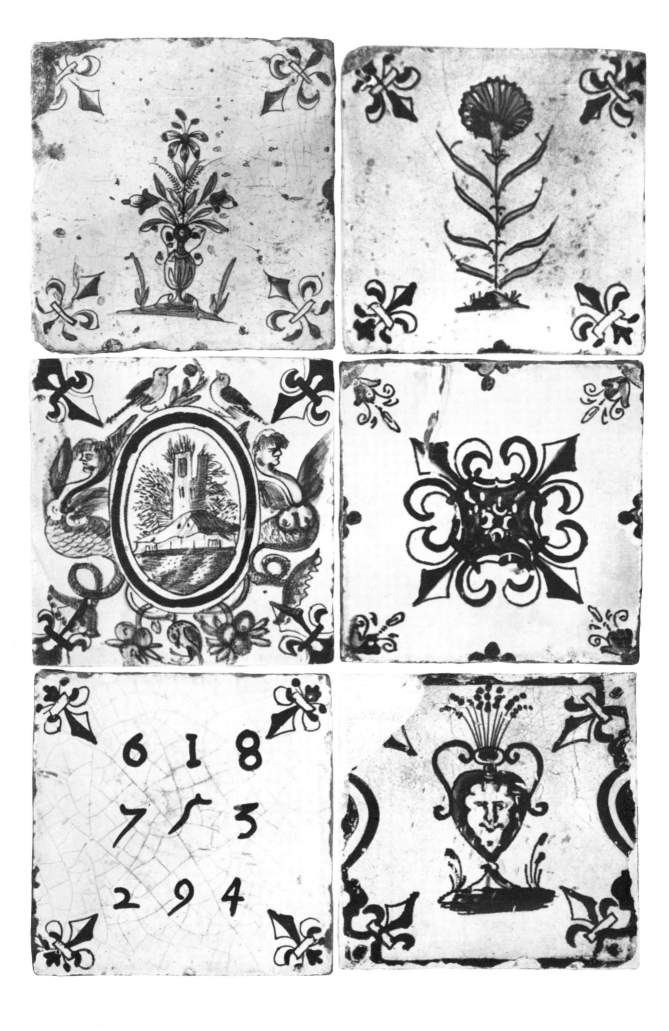

Although they were not created for this purpose, we ought not to omit those tiles which in 1630 were commissioned for the gallery of the Château de Beauregard near Blois and which form a most unusual pavement. Each tile carries the picture of a soldier. C. H. de Jonge has published this extremely decorative composition[2], in which the predominantly military atmosphere of the floor harmonises perfectly with the portraits of celebrated personalities of French history on the walls. Further research by C. H. de Jonge, the results of which have so far not been published, has disclosed documentary evidence relating to the unusual use of these tiles.

Walls of kitchens, cellars and passage-ways wholly or partly faced with tiles need no further explanation. They are to be found in countless gentlemens' houses in Holland, and exist solely for purposes of cleanliness. Although attractive tiles were occasionally used, these situations did not call for works of art.

151

Rooms lined with Dutch Tiles

It was thanks to the reputation of the fine ceramics of Delft that foreign princes and builders became interested in the tiles of the northern Netherlands. The most important commissions came from the Iberian peninsula and from the Spanish and Portuguese colonies, all countries in which tiles as a form of decoration had long been appreciated.[1] The tiles also went, however, to France and Germany, Poland and Russia and even as far as India, where, in the palace of Udaipur[2], a small private room belonging to the prince was lined with tiles. In all these countries princely apartments were totally lined with tiles. The international reputation and high quality of the Dutch tiles were maintained until the last quarter of the eighteenth century.

FRANCE

The initial impulse to the spread of Dutch tiles overseas was occasioned by an order for Dutch tiles for the Trianon de Porcelaine which was being built in the park at Versailles. This commission was given at a time during the reign of Louis XIV when court-life derived its character from Madame de Montespan, then *maîtresse en titre*. Royal festivities were held at this Trianon, however, only during the period 1670–1687, after which it was pulled down, since it was found that the material, particularly that on the outside walls, would not withstand the weather. The Comte de Toulouse, son of Louis XIV and Madame de Montespan, saved many of the tiles and later used them at his palace, the Château de Rambouillet (1715–1730).[3]

The accounts for the royal buildings show that the tiles for the Trianon were supplied by workshops at Nevers, Rouen, Lisieux and in Holland. Payment for the Dutch tiles was made to Claude Révérend, a Paris merchant, who, from 1662 onwards if not before,

bought faiences in Delft, chiefly from the workshop De Paeuw (the Peacock), for export to France. Claude Révérend had devoted long and careful study to the tile-manufacture of Delft for he wished to found a factory of his own in France to produce wares of similar quality. Shortly after 1665 he returned to France and, with his brother François, established workshops at Saint-Cloud and in Paris, whither he managed to attract potters from Rotterdam and Delft.[4]

In any case, in about 1665, tiles were ordered in the Netherlands for a large project in France in which whole walls of princely apartments were to be faced. R. Danis's book supplies more detail about the Trianon.[5]

The tiles now to be found at the Château de Rambouillet are the ordinary Dutch wares and were not specially commissioned with a given décor in mind. The borders to the flower-vase pictures were made from tiles from Révérend's workshop which came from the Trianon. The flower-vase pictures themselves, however, were not ordered for the Trianon. They must be dated to the year 1730.[6]

HAMPTON COURT AND ROZENDAAL

The courts of Europe clearly followed French fashion in this sphere as in so many others, so that throughout Europe there arose a desire for tiled rooms and the demand for Dutch tiles increased considerably. Daniel Marot, an *émigré* Huguenot (b. Paris 1663, d. The Hague 1752), who became court architect to William III of Orange, King of England and Stadholder of the Netherlands, and his wife Mary Stuart, introduced the style of his native land into Hampton Court. He designed complete tile-decorations for a "Delft Ware

153

Top: Very rare tiles after engraved portraits. First row: Henry of Brederode, King Stephen of Poland, Archduke Ernst of Austria, Stadholder of the southern Netherlands, Henri II of France, François Valdez. Second row: Duke of Alba, Emperor Matthias, Emanuel-Philibert of Savoy, Stadholder of the southern Netherlands, Charles IX of France, the Earl of Leicester. Musée Royal du Cinquantenaire, Brussels. Bottom: The engravings of de Gheyn representing the training-exercises introduced by Prince Maurice of Orange often served as models for painted tiles. c. 1640. Tönder Museum.

Closett" for the Old Water Gallery and for the dairy in the Gallery in the grounds (174). In the year 1695 Adriaen Kocks of the Grieske A or "Greek A," the best-known and presumably also the largest workshop in Delft at that time, produced large tiles 62 × 62 cm. painted after Marot's designs and forming a series of panels 248 × 62 cm. in size. Thus we see that even Louis XIV's enemy, William III, was pleased to follow the French fashion of tile-decoration. The surviving tiles from Hampton Court are today divided among several collections, the majority being in the Rijksmuseum in Amsterdam and the Victoria and Albert Museum in London.[7]

It is interesting to note that in Holland also certain outside walls were decorated with tiles in the manner of the Trianon de Porcelaine. These were at the castle of Rozendaal near Arnheim, the country residence of Lubbert Adolf Torck, one of the favourites of William III. Rozendaal was built from designs by Marot and the tile-decorations probably came from the workshop of Cornelis Boumeester in Rotterdam (200, 201). The execution is not nearly as refined as that of the Hampton Court tiles, which are blue whereas those of Rozendaal are manganese-coloured. The surviving tile-pictures from Rozendaal are in the Cooper Union Museum in New York.[8]

POLAND AND RUSSIA

It is possible to trace numerous connections in the last decade of the seventeenth century between Holland and the countries of eastern Europe. In the year 1697 the Czar Peter the Great visited the Netherlands and opened up important possibilities of extending the Dutch export trade. These may have included tiles. The connection with Poland can be established with greater precision. Francastel[9] maintains that the bath-

ing pavilion known as the Lazienki (baths) in the Ujazdów park in Warsaw, originally built at the end of the seventeenth century for Prince Lubomirski, was the work of the Dutch architect, Tylman van Gameren, who is known to have been in the prince's employment in about 1690. The walls of the Lazienki are faced with blue-painted tiles. There are only a few different types, yet the designs have been extremely skilfully arranged. They show landscapes within roundels and ox-heads in the corners.

GERMANY

The tiled rooms in the princely palaces of Germany were designed by French architects. We have to do here principally with garden-rooms, staircases, dining-rooms, pavilions and swimming pools, these last being in large halls frequently surrounded by a gallery. The walls were completely faced with tiles. The example was set by Max Emanuel, Elector of Bavaria, when, in the year 1702, he began to alter and enlarge the palace and park of Nymphenburg, near Munich, which had been begun by his mother. The Elector had lived from 1691 to 1702 as stadholder in the southern Netherlands and, even if he did not see the Dutch tiles during his stay in Brussels, he must certainly have seen and liked them when he visited the northern Netherlands in 1691. From 1702–1704, during the War of the Spanish Succession, he was exiled to France because of his pro-French leanings. From 1704–1714 he was in the Netherlands again and thereafter lived for a few years at Saint-Cloud. The Trianon at Versailles, however, no longer existed at this period and the tiled room at Rambouillet had not yet been built. Yet the Elector must have been well informed regarding tile-decoration, for immediately after his return to Munich

he began the alterations to Nymphenburg. He engaged for this purpose in Paris the Bavarian architect Joseph Effner (Dachau 1687–Munich 1745). Between 1716 and 1719 Effner built the Pagodenburg based on the design of a Chinese pagoda. The ground floor is an octagonal tea *salon* with a small room opening off four of its sides, one of which houses the staircase. The tea *salon*, the staircase and the room on the east side have tiled walls (164). The colours of the stucco-work, *boiseries* and furniture harmonise with the blue and white of the tiles. This blue and white colour-scheme, at once distinguished and unassuming, was fashionable during the whole of the period from 1640 to 1725 and was influenced by the porcelain imported from China.

Some thousand tiles were used for the Pagodenburg. The wonderful landscapes appear in the east room and on the lower part of the staircase. The colour here is a deep sapphire blue and more than one variety of tile has been used; in the *Salettl*, the blue verges towards purple. It is certain that more than one painter was at work in the Pagodenburg and it is possible that the tiles came from several different workshops. Tiles of the type found in the *Salettl* were produced at the Bloempot in Rotterdam. A horseman which occurs here was also found in Lisbon as part of a consignment from Rotterdam and a pounced pattern for this design exists in the City Archives of Rotterdam, all of which leads to the conclusion that the tiles are of Rotterdam origin. The still-lifes and peacocks in the foreground of the tile-pictures of the staircase are further indications of Rotterdam origin.

The Badenburg was also built in the park at Nymphenburg between the years 1718 and 1721 from plans by Joseph Effner. The swimming pool measuring 8.70 × 6.10 m. with a depth of 1.45 m. exceeded in size the pool at Versailles, regarded as a highly fashionable novelty, which measured only 3 m. in diameter and was less than 1 m. deep. Compared with the Lazienki of Prince Lubomirski the landscape tiles above the swimming pool are extremely monotonous and are not so skilfully arranged, the appearance being spoilt by a diagonal effect carrying on from one tile to another. Dr. de Jonge describes these tiles as "mediocre products of one of many workshops which probably combined to produce tens of thousands of tiles for delivery to all the principal countries."[10]

After the Badenburg, no further buildings containing tile-decoration were erected in Munich for some time. Joseph Clemens, however, the Elector of Cologne and a brother of Max Emanuel, who had also lived in exile in France during the War of the Spanish Succession, began on his return to the Rhineland to build at Brühl a counterpart to his brother's palace in the French taste. To this end, he set about altering the castle of Augustusburg. Building was undertaken at first according to designs by Robert de Cotte (Paris 1656–1735). The final result, however, is the work of the Elector Clemens August (1700–1761), third son of Max Emanuel of Bavaria who, in 1725 at the age of only twenty-five, took over direction of the work. J. K. Schlaun and Joseph Roth were both employed by him but he soon entrusted the assignment to the architect François Cuvilliés. Cuvilliés had also worked in Munich for Max Emanuel and, after his death, for the Elector Carl Albrecht, elder brother of Clemens August.

One of the favourite haunts of Clemens August, who was very rich and set great store by the pleasures of life, was Falkenlust, a little hunting-lodge in the park, which was used for a form of hawking which was very popular at the time. A heron and two falcons were released simultaneously, a fight ensued and one or other of the falcons usually succeeded in bringing down the heron alive. The heron was ringed and released again. Falkenlust was built between the years 1729 and 1737 and is one of Cuvilliés's masterpieces. The tiles were delivered in 1731 (187). They represent hawking scenes, a theme excellently suited to decorative purposes, and show the courtiers riding to the hunt, the ladies looking on, the servants with the falcons and herons on perches, the suspense of the falcons waiting to be released, herons and falcons fighting or at liberty on a nest in a tree—nature itself could not have painted these scenes better. The pictures at Falkenlust are on walls entirely faced with tiles, and are interspersed with the blue and white lozenges of the arms of Bavaria. The tile-pictures were undoubtedly designed by a French master and we may suppose that this was Cuvilliés himself. They were actually made in Rotterdam, in the De Bloempot workshop, which, from 1674–1705, was directed by Jan Aalmis the elder. Aalmis has created decorations of great artistic merit, in a pale blue which harmonises beautifully with the graceful rococo motifs. Pounced patterns for these tiles also are in the city archives.

As a result of the success of Falkenlust a commission was given for a suite of five rooms on the ground-floor of Schloss Brühl. These apartments, a masterpiece of Cuvilliés and the French garden-architect Girard, had been begun in the year 1732 under Roth but the work was interrupted, probably because, in 1735, Cuvilliés returned to Munich; it was still not complete in 1740. The great new artist at Brühl was Balthasar Neumann (1687–1753) who, between 1743 and 1748, built a new staircase and a dining-room on the site of the old staircase.

A commission for six hundred tiles for Schloss Brühl was received by the Bloempot, which by this time was probably under the direction of Jan Aalmis the younger. Water-colour drawings for these decorations have been preserved in the Rotterdam City Archives. These tiles are unfortunately considerably inferior to those of Falkenlust, carrying no graceful French figures, only geometric and plant motifs in few variations. The blue and white colour-scheme is, however, the same. The only attractions are the alternation of white and blue for the backgrounds and the clever combination of tiles of the same pattern to form different designs. In the dining-room there are tile-pictures after paintings by Teniers, twenty-six flower-vases of only three different types and little pictures of *commedia dell'arte* figures. The execution shows little imagination. Neither Cuvilliés nor Neumann can have had any part in these decorations. It was probably Michel Leveilly, who took over the supervision of the work after Cuvilliés's departure, who was responsible for them. Everything points to a diminution of interest on the part of those in authority; for example, remains of old tiles were used. But by this time the art of tile-making had passed its zenith in Holland also.

To return to Munich, where, after the return of Cuvilliés, tile-decoration flourished once more. The Elector had a small hunting-lodge, the Amalienburg, built for his wife Maria Amalia in the park at Nymphenburg (164). He had commissioned Cuvilliés to do this in 1734 before Cuvilliés returned to Munich and the little pavillion was completed in 1739. It contained a whole kitchen faced with tiles. It was not, however, a kitchen in the usual sense of the word but a room in which the princess and her guests could pass the time in cooking and other rural pastimes. It is characteristic of this period with its cry of "back to nature" that the idea arose of installing kitchens for the use of the elegant world: others of the kind were the dairy at Hampton Court and Marie-Antoinette's Hameau. The kitchen in the Amalienburg is divided in two by a wall supported by pillars; in one half are the cooking-stoves while the other half of the room was designed as a place for the ladies to consume the delicacies they had prepared. This part is especially richly decorated. The tile-pictures and tile-pilasters have been described (on pages 143 and 145).

Another circumstance which furthered the spread of Dutch tiles to Germany was the relationship between the houses of Brandenburg and Orange. The first result of this was to be found at the palace of Oranienbaum, near Anhalt, where, in 1662, Henriette Catharine of Orange (1637–1708), wife of Johann Georg von Anhalt-Dessau, had a porcelain cabinet installed. Cabinets of this type would be filled with porcelain of all kinds, mostly Chinese, which had often been purchased through Dutch intermediaries. The example of Henriette Catharine was followed in many of the palaces of the Hohenzollern-Brandenburg princes where porcelain was collected and displayed in a special room or cabinet. There are also accounts of porcelain kitchens in most of these palaces and Dutch tiles are sometimes mentioned, though no such kitchen has been preserved. It is probable that only the part round the stove was tiled and that on the walls Chinese plates were ranged on long shelves. To select one example from many, the decorations at Schloss Schwedt on the Oder may be mentioned. These were the work of Albert van der Eeckhout who in the year 1637 had followed Prince Johan Mauritz of Nassau-Siegen to Brazil and who specialised in painting exotic birds and landscapes. He also decorated the *Vögelsaal* at Hoflössnitz and designed the splendid tile-pictures discussed (on p. 143).

Surveying all these enchanting rooms in France, Germany and England, we are bound to recognise that their significance does not equal that of the tiled buildings of the Iberian peninsula; for whereas these were rooms intended simply as places in which to pass the time elegantly or in pleasant diversions, those of Spain and Portugal were places of devotion and spiritual meditation, usually churches and monasteries.

One may wonder whether these orders for large and important buildings abroad stimulated the Dutch to emulation. At all events, larger undertakings were carried out in the Netherlands than had earlier been the case. Or should we see here the workings of a secret longing for the unknown, for distant Persia perhaps? There has so far been no explanation of the fact that every so often oriental features made an unheralded appearance in the countries of northern Europe. Examples of this were the seventeenth-century window-frames of Ebersbach and Hinlopen and the popular decorations of blue palms on a red background also found in the village of Hinlopen. To explain the phenomenon as a result of chance is not entirely satisfactory.

In the Netherlands as well as in northern Germany, Denmark and the Baltic countries, tiled rooms occurred in farmhouses and in other provincial buildings. In the Friesch Museum at Leeuwarden there is a reconstruction of a room from the Tichelaar factory at Makkum made in 1779 for a house at Workum (212). The whole room is inspired by French engravings and is thus in this respect another foreign element. Rooms such as the tap-room at the inn De Prins in Makkum, where there are six tile-pictures of ships on a wall faced with white tiles, accord better with the Dutch character and way of life. This same wish to portray the owner's possessions finds expression in many tiled kitchens and living-rooms not only in the Netherlands. We find, for example, a dog or cat staring into the fire, a canary in its cage, a horse, a cow, a farm or a ship (212, 219, 265, 267). These tiles were not, of course, individually made but were executed in the ceramic factories from pounced patterns which were used many times over, although they were often taken to be personal and unique representations. Farmyards and ships are often to some extent realistically portrayed but in general the representations were symbolic. It was the attitude towards them that was important. The pictorial tiles which surrounded the inmates of the houses day after day bred a sense of intimacy which pleased them and must surely have made them feel at home in the glistening cleanliness and exotic charm of their rooms.

Tile-picture of a cock. A specimen picture by Willem Verswaen who was active in Gouda from 1621 onwards. Second tile from the left in the top row does not belong. Boymans-van Beuningen Museum, Rotterdam.

Page 162: Top: Wall-niche painted in blue and manganese. Below the niche is a representation of Neptune in a triumphal chariot; he appears to be receiving from above gifts of the earth in the form of fruit and flowers. Inside the niche are single tiles carrying representations of whales, with spinnetjes *in the corners. Second half of the 17th century. De Moriaen Museum, Gouda. Bottom: Niche of quadrilobe tiles. The flanking flower-tiles are later additions. The visible narrow sides of the tiles on the edge of the niche are painted and glazed. Early 17th century. St. Pieters Hofje, Hoorn.*

Page 163: Tile-picture of a large flower-vase. One of the thirteen known large polychrome flower-pictures from De Roos in Delft after engravings or paintings by Huysum or Rachel Ruysch. Outstanding drawing in powerful colours and a masterpiece of Dutch tile-making. c. 1700. It is possible that a tile-picture of the same subject in blue monochrome of the year 1697, from Sommersdijk and now in the Rijksmuseum, Amsterdam, is a little earlier than this polychrome painting. Victoria and Albert Museum, London.

Page 164: Top: Kitchen of the Amalienburg pavilion in the park of Schloss Nymphenburg near Munich, built 1734–1739 by François Cuvilliés. The kitchen was installed as a pastime for the court-ladies. A wall supported by pillars separates the kitchen from the chimney under which the stove stands. The flower-pictures on the fire-place wall come from the De Roos workshop at Delft, the pictures of the four quarters of the globe (Europe, Asia, Africa and America) on the side-walls probably also come from Delft. Bottom: The Salettl on the ground-floor of the pleasure-palace, Pagodenburg, in the park at Nymphenburg. Built 1716–1719 by Josef Effner after a Chinese pagoda. Stucco-work, wood-panelling and furniture are in the same white and blue colour-scheme as the tiles, which come from the De Bloempot workshop in Rotterdam.

German Tiles from the Renaissance to the 18th century

The history of ceramics in Germany falls into four main periods: the Middle Ages, the Renaissance, the period of importation of Dutch faience and, lastly, the period of indigenous manufacture of porcelain and pottery, during which Dutch influence remained decisive.

The Renaissance, in this connection, was significant only as a period of transition. In the new era, the artistic crafts of the Middle Ages, which had atrophied and degenerated into conventionality, gained a new impetus. There was no revolutionary innovation, but new forms of the old ornaments were produced with fresh embellishments. Circles were transformed into laurel-wreaths, ebullient tracery patterns were given a more regular form and became tapering ovals; symmetrical scroll-work, arabesques and intricate cartouches were favoured.

Opaque tin-glazes came into general use. They lacked the brilliance of the Spanish, Italian and Dutch maiolica, however, in spite of the fact that in the year 1520 an Italian potter was active in Nuremberg, while another Italian master, Guido di Savini, was working in Antwerp. The faience manufactured in Germany and in the other mid-European countries during this period is distinguished by matt colour contrasting with a great deal of black. Another sign of the dawn of a new period was the standardisation of sizes. Very small tiles disappeared altogether; extremely large ones became rare. It is also interesting to note that two categories of tiles persisted in Germany throughout all these periods; these were, on the one hand, the peasant tiles and, on the other, the products of those factories which catered for more pretentious and sophisticated tastes. This became even more noticeable in the second half of the eighteenth century. It was then that the contributory influence of the porcelain factories, which had become so active in Germany, began to be felt. Now, for the first time, importation of Dutch tiles declined noticeably, while indigenous production increased. Many German princes made a hobby of founding and maintaining ceramic factories, thereby continuing the tradition of the *dilettanti* of the Italian Renaissance. Many of these factories also produced tiles for princely apartments.

So much for German tiles in general. At the time of the Renaissance many regional styles emerged. Mention may first be made of the inlaid tiles. These were decorated with white or red linear ornamentation on a red or dark-grey background; this background was obtained by reduced firing, that is to say, the final phase of the firing process was prolonged by producing smoke in the kiln. This particular type of tile was produced in the Stuttgart region. Quite a different type was produced at Nuremberg. Here the old tradition of using glazed relief tiles for stoves and sometimes also for walls persisted. These tiles were made in various colours and the glazes often ran into one another. In the seventeenth century they began to be produced in green or yellow monochrome. In Racren, salt-glazed tiles were produced in the same way as the well-known jugs which are decorated in stamped relief. The Krefeld tiles, used mainly for stoves but also encountered as wall-decoration, and the so-called St. Tönisberg tiles, are decorated with old-fashioned Gothic tracery patterns. This technique persisted until deep into the eighteenth century. Rosettes, a shimmering glaze of black, green, light yellow and brown, and the narrow stripes of the background are all characteristic.

In Switzerland and Austria the production of ceramics was, in the main, restricted to stoves, which do not come within the scope of this book. Glazed stove-tiles with decoration in relief came on to the market in such numbers that they were often used for floors as well. The same is true of the painted faience tiles. In the sixteenth century it became usual to compose designs for floors out of unglazed tiles or bricks, in a baroque desire to subordinate the parts to the whole.

A new golden age of tiles dawned when the so-called Delft-ware – which, in fact, came from different parts of Holland – became fashionable and was used to decorate many of the mansions of the nobility and houses of the middle classes. These have been discussed in the chapter on Dutch tiled rooms. Tiles were used in the houses of north Germany just as they were in the Netherlands. Certain tiles from Franconia, dating from about 1720, now in the Victoria and Albert Museum, comprise a curious category of their own. They are painted blue, as had become the practice not only in Holland but in all other countries, and their quality is far superior to the usual German products. This refinement may point to a connection with the Netherlands and this is the more probable since Chinese figures dominate the decoration; but the supposition cannot be further verified. The only works which recall these strange landscapes are certain engravings by Augsburg artists.

The final phase, during which native production expanded to full activity, began in about 1757. As will be seen in a later chapter, close relations with the Netherlands persisted into this period. Thus, for example, it is by no means unusual to find among the employees of the German factories workmen from the Netherlands, usually from Delft, who, even if they were not natives of Delft, were at least trained there. The designs of the Dutch tiles were retained but the execution was stiff and the colours harsh and somewhat tasteless. Subtle shading and artistic organisation are rare and this is the more surprising since, in other spheres, German rococo and classicism produced outstanding works of art. It can be said that in general Chinese ceramics were less well known in Germany than in Holland. The Germans did not achieve an intellectual mastery of this Far Eastern art. Neither did *chinoiserie* gain a footing in Germany, for the Germans did not succeed in adapting the Asiatic style to native conditions: it remained an imitation of Dutch prototypes.

It may come as a surprise to learn that Delft, which was not, indeed, the principal centre of the Dutch tile-industry, had so great an influence on the production of tiles in Germany. There is, however, a simple explanation for this, namely that the Dutch workmen were masters of their own craft and for this reason their assistance was extremely welcome in Germany. Moreover, tiles were never more in Germany than a by-product of the ceramic industry.

English Tiles
from the 16th to the 18th century

If we compare the tiles of the sixteenth century in England with those of Germany, we find that the general situation was similar but that the results were very different. The traditions of the Middle Ages persisted for a long time in both countries. In view of the historical development of Europe, it is, however, in no way surprising that the English tile-makers responded to the Renaissance quite differently from their German fellows. The new era was not proclaimed in England, as it was in Germany, by the appearance of a maiolica lacking in brilliance; that would have been out of keeping with the England of the Tudors. At a very early date tiles began to be imported from Antwerp, introducing to the light of the north the Italian designs in a somewhat coarsened form and the Italian colours in shades even brighter than those of their native land. The pavement which was laid in about 1520 in the chapel of the Tudor country-house, The Vyne, near Basingstoke in Hampshire, and which was made in the workshop of Guido di Savini has already been discussed in relation to the maiolica of Antwerp. Lane[1] mentions finds in London, in Tunstall near Sittingbourne in Kent, at Titchfield Abbey near Portsmouth and references from the time of Henry VIII to "Fleymshe pavynge tiles, of greene and youllow" which had been ordered for the halls at Hampton Court and Christ Church, Oxford. The predominant colours, as in all Antwerp tiles, are indeed yellow and green, with some blue and yellowish-brown. The success of these tile-pavements was so great that Jasper Andries and Jacob Janson of Antwerp founded a workshop in Norwich in about 1567. A tile showing a boar within a roundel and the arms of the Bacon and Whaplode families in the corners, inscribed "Mediocria firma N.B.", is reputed to have come from Gorhambury, the house built for Sir Nicholas Bacon, father of Francis, Lord Verulam, between 1563 and 1568 near St. Albans. Only one other tile from this source is known. Both may have been

samples for a pavement which was never executed.[2] In fact very little is yet known about the activity of the Antwerp potters in England. It may be assumed that they were highly successful, for it has been established that in the year 1571 Janson, with four other Flemish workers, was active at Aldgate in London. It is clear that in the seventeenth and early eighteenth centuries there were numerous connections with the Netherlands, especially, of course, with the northern Netherlands. This was true of nearly all branches of culture. Mention need only be made of the chairs, particularly those of the reign of William III of Orange, and his English wife, Queen Mary, which are impossible to assign as between English or Dutch makers. In the sphere of ceramics Dutch fashion found such approval that the designation "Delft-ware" was extended to cover the whole species.

Work in England followed the same directions as that of the Netherlands. Important factories existed in London (Lambeth), Bristol and Liverpool and their wares show how polychrome painting gave place to the blue and white style of decoration inspired by imported Chinese porcelain. In the year 1671 a patent was granted to another Dutch potter, Jan Ariens van Hamme. Conversely, English craftsmen also worked in the Netherlands[3] and it is difficult to say what the craftsmen of one country learned from those of the other. In the eighteenth century, however, English pottery in many cases acquired a clearly distinguishable national style. As an example of this, mention may be made of the loving care reflected in the decoration of the tiles of this date, for mass-produciton and routine painting were not congenial to the English temperament.

Tiles were made in the three large centres, London, Bristol and Liverpool, in the first two of which production had continued since the seventeenth century. It is often impossible to say in which of the three centres a given tile was made. A number of clues have been found in the kiln waste-heaps but by no means all the problems involved can be explained in this way.

The production of tiles was restricted to a few centres. In this respect also the situation in England was entirely different from that in Germany, where the factories normally enjoyed the protection of a princely family; in England, on the contrary, there were a small number of large private enterprises which had to be run at a profit.

Tile-pictures were made in both London and Bristol; there are examples of these in the Victoria and Albert Museum and at the Guildhall in London. Some of them are so much like the Dutch tile-pictures that it is impossible to say whether they were imported or made by a Dutch immigrant. Two tile-pictures in the museum at Saffron Walden, however, are unmistakably English in origin. They came from the local Old Swan Inn. Busts of Oliver Cromwell and an "Edwardus Pri(nceps)" accentuate the Englishness of the landscape backgrounds with their ruins evoking the romanticism which made so early an appearance in England. These pictures are signed with the initials W.E. and dated 1739, the date presumably referring to the birth of Edward Augustus, Duke of York (1739–1767), grandson of George II. Other tile-pictures are known, including some which were made in about 1749 from engravings after Hogarth.

These pictures, as well as tiles in the *famille verte* style with a strong red pigment, probably came from the Lambeth factory, but a carefully and elegantly drawn tile-picture, unfortunately damaged, which shows the church of St. Mary Redcliffe in Bristol was probably made by Taylor of Redcliffe Street in that city and the date 1737–1750 may be inferred from the arms of Bishop Butler in the lower margin. The picture was formerly set into the wall of a local shop. Tiles of Bristol manufacture, decorated in blue by John Bowen, are extremely attractive. The same designs are found on

Detail of a wall-decoration, probably after Albert Eeckhout, who was in Brazil in 1637 and specialised in painting exotic animals and landscapes. The Chinese and South American elements – a group of Tapuya Indians is clearly shown – lead one to suppose that this was a picture of the quarters of the globe, similar to those in the kitchen in the Amalienburg, with which it has much in common. This picture also probably comes from Delft. c. 1700. Musée Royal du Cinquantenaire, Brussels.

Page 170: Flower-piece. The refined enamel technique was in Holland only rarely used for tiles; these are in the famille rose *style. Delft, 18th century. Lambert van Meerten Museum, Delft.*

Page 171: Park at the Delftschen Vaart, Rotterdam. The grounds adjoined the property of the tile-kiln in which Cornelis Boumeester worked from 1676 onwards. The picture, which is completely in tune with the international heroic style of the time, gives a particularly good impression of Boumeester's fine atmospheric style of painting. The picture was found over a kitchen-sink. Historisch Museum, Rotterdam.

Page 172: The country seats on the Vecht of the patrician families of Amsterdam were often portrayed in copper-plate engravings. This view of the Villa Zijdebaelen, the property of the Utrecht merchant David van Mollem (1670–1746) very probably also derives from one of the highly popular engravings of the time.
Symmetrical gardens with orange-trees surround the pool. Ladies and gentlemen stroll among the buildings and garden-architecture of this miniature Versailles. Prototypes of these groups of figures can also be found in the engravings of the time. From the De Bloempot workshop, where much work was done from engravings. Centraal Museum, Utrecht.

Page 173 top: Scenes showing acrobats were made fashionable by the celebrated family of artists named Marginot. The idea of using such illustrations for tiles suggests a provenance in the De Bloempot workshop of the Aalmis family. The borders still reflect the Chinese scalloped form. Visch and de Geus Museum. Bottom: Scenes from the life of the great world were also illustrated on tiles, here carelessly executed in two pairs of ill-fitting tiles. Trees, architecture and foreground are conveyed in stereotyped manner. Early 18th century. De Moriaen Museum, Gouda.

Bristol pottery vessels. A feathery tree in the foreground serves as a foil usually to a waterscape in the middle distance, behind which appears a slight evocation of a landscape. The painting is highly poetic. Other tiles, not by Bowen but also very delicately drawn in light blue or manganese, show small figures in a landscape; these too are delightful. They are sometimes decorated with a characteristic slight sprig design in the corners with a roundel in the middle. Other highly esteemed Bristol products are the polychrome birds on a light blue ground within a *bianco sopra bianco* border (253). Another speciality of this factory was probably the manganese-coloured tiles showing a goat and a kind of otter. To sum up, it may be said that the Bristol tiles are distinguished by their extremely sensitive and refined execution. The tiles made in Kellinghusen for Dr. Grauer's room are only a pale reflection of the Bristol wares.

The significance of the Liverpool manufacture was quite different (253, 254). European or Chinese figures were presented in such summarily rendered surroundings that one is sometimes put in mind of a stage set. The Liverpool tiles with birds and flowers in polychrome or manganese, surrounded by an octagonal border or in an ogival medallion, which recalls its Chinese origin, and enriched by corner decorations, are much simpler than the Bristol tiles but still testify to devoted and keen workmanship: a decoration painted in crude, insensitive strokes is a rarity. Attributions to a given factory are largely based upon comparison with vessels which bear the same kind of decoration and the provenance of which is known. It is by this means that we know that some fairly elaborate polychrome representations of flower-vases on tiles came from Liverpool. The best-known of the Liverpool wares are designs made by John Sadler and Guy Green from transfer-prints (253, 254). These methods appear to have been used between 1753 and 1756 at the Battersea enamel factory. A pattern in black, red, brown or purple enamel was transferred from an engraved copper plate to a sheet of paper. This sheet was applied, face downwards, to the tile, which had already been fired, and was then removed, leaving the transferred image to be fixed by a second firing. By the year 1756 seven years of experimentation had given Sadler and Green such mastery of their technique that they were able to decorate twelve hundred tiles in six hours.

In the years 1756/57 the decorations were still being printed from wood-blocks, usually in manganese, sometimes in several colours. Engravings by J. E. Nilsson of Augsburg were used as models. A relatively large number of these rare tiles printed from wood-blocks have been preserved in America, as, for example in the Longfellow House, Cambridge, Mass., which was built in 1759 and in many fire-places in other old houses. This is due to the fact that tiles decorated by transfer-printing were appreciated at an early date in America.

From 1757 to 1761 the printing was done from engraved copper-plates. From this time on, the tiles, with the exception of the series showing actors, have only a single border pattern. In the year 1770 Sadler retired, but Green carried on the business until his death in 1789.

More than 150 designs of these Liverpool printed tiles are known. Lane mentions Chinese motifs after Jean Pillement, portraits of actors in their parts, Aesop's fables, scenes of courtship and gallantry, satirical subjects, representations of sports and pastimes, landscapes, ships and mythological motifs.[4] In addition to these, there were classical figures or groups in medallions and classical vases, printed in black with a wash of transparent green enamel. These show the influence of Josiah Wedgwood (253), and, indeed, tiles of this type are mentioned in a letter of 1776 from Green to Wedgwood.

The delightful designs and excellent workmanship make these transfer tiles most pleasing objects; they were, moreover, extremely cheap, costing four or five shillings a dozen. The English character of these unpretentious tiles is unmistakable—they are civilised and full of genuine charm.

The influence of Dutch Tiles in Portugal and Brazil

Earlier chapters have already dealt with the development of ceramic tiles in the Iberian peninsula, their decorative significance in Spain and Portugal and the part played by the workshops of Antwerp in the development of the art of tile-making in the Netherlands. The attention of the reader was drawn to the contacts and exchanges between Italian and Flemish ceramists as well as to the spread of the new maiolica techniques from Flanders.

It is well known that the *azulejos* were highly regarded in Spain and, especially, in Portugal and that in both countries the ceramic workshops found a very large market. It will be recalled that it was mainly from the end of the sixteenth century that the liking for decorations with glazed tiles came into being and quickly established itself.

PORTUGAL

The political and economic development of the Netherlands after the beginning of the seventeenth century and the commercial, cosmopolitan ideas of the people led to the establishment of real art industries, among which ceramics assumed an important position. The Dutch trading-ships facilitated the marketing of the wares since they touched at Spanish and Portuguese ports, especially Lisbon, Setúbal and Cádiz. The Dutch, with their practical sense, had discovered the potential market for ceramic tiles in these two countries, whose indigenous workshops were no longer able to satisfy the demand.

The ship-owners of Middelburg, Rotterdam, Amsterdam and even those of the Zuider Zee ports could offer, through their agents in Lisbon and Cádiz, the *tegels* manufactured in Holland which were so different from those of Spain or Portugal. They must, indeed, have been less expensive since they were made in series, were thinner and therefore lighter. In addition to this, they were more attractive because they were more up-to-date and were better painted. It was the *enkeletegels*, the single tiles, of which every piece bore a design of its own in blue or manganese, which were principally exported.

By about the middle of the seventeenth century, the manufacture of *azulejos* in Spain had already passed its peak and the tiles never again achieved the fine quality of the old specimens from Seville or Talavera. In Portugal, where tile-decoration was at the height of its popularity, the decorators simply repeated motifs with polychrome patterns and took little trouble to improve the artistic quality which could no longer satisfy even the least demanding of clients. It was natural, therefore, both that the Lisbon merchants should have welcomed the *azulejos do norte*, the tiles from the north, and that the native ceramists should have tried to imitate them.

It is surprising to discover from a study of the development of the Portuguese *azulejos* that, from the year 1660 onwards, polychrome tile-designs were reproduced in only two tones of cobalt-blue. This preference for monochrome grew and in the course of a few years the polychrome designs disappeared altogether after two-hundred years of popularity. This technical and aesthetic change can be explained by the influence of the blue painting of the ceramics of southern China, which were brought to Europe by the newly established India companies. In Holland and in England the effect of this influence was undoubtedly decisive, but was scarcely so in Portugal, where Chinese porcelain had been known since the beginning of the sixteenth century. It is more probable that in Portugal it was the direct influence of the Dutch ceramics, which imitated oriental porcelain but cost less, which stimulated the new fashion for monochrome blue decoration, a fashion which was not confined to Portugal but extended to all the European centres of ceramic production.

As in Holland, the manufacture of tiles in Portugal was entirely independent of the production of pottery and although blue and white tin-glazed pottery vessels had long been made in Lisbon, the *azulejos* workshops persisted in making their polychrome tiles. The first Dutch tiles appeared in Portugal in about 1660 and a little later in Cádiz, where tiles dated 1660, 1671 and 1679 are found in the Armenian chapel of the church of Santa Maria. These, however, are only *enkeletegels* which are painted in manganese and some of which bear Armenian inscriptions – an indication that they were specially commissioned. That the importation of Dutch tiles into Lisbon was, by 1687, already very extensive, is proved by a decree of the head of the customs authority forbidding the continuation of the import of pottery and *azulejos de Holanda*. This decree proceeded from the royal council and was doubtless the result of protests from the Portuguese makers of *azulejos*, who felt their position to be threatened by foreign competition. However that may have been, the prohibition was rescinded in 1698 whereupon Holland began to export more tiles to Portugal than she had done before.

From 1670 onwards, however, Portuguese customers ceased to be content with single tiles which offered only limited decorative possibilities and no longer kept pace with the demands of the great surfaces which it was now customary to face with tiles. The Dutch had to suit their products to the demands of their new clientele and began to paint tile-pictures for the houses and Catholic churches of Portugal, in so doing setting their commercial interests above their religious and iconoclastic convictions.

The famous panelling in the Fronteira palace at Benfica, Lisbon, which was made between 1670 and 1678, is the earliest example of tile-facing of this kind. In spite of the prohibition of 1687, after 1690 Dutch tiles were again reaching Portugal and in about 1698 Jan van Oort of Amsterdam made the tiles for the new church of Cardais, Lisbon, which is among the finest of all examples of Dutch ceramic art. The importation of Dutch tiles reached its peak at the beginning of the eighteenth century. The splendid tile-pictures in the church of the Madre de Deus in Lisbon and in that of Nazaré to the north of Lisbon have survived to this day. Other tile-pictures have disappeared or have been scattered, as, for example, the *azulejos* of the Galvão Mexia palace signed by Willem van der Kloet of Amsterdam, those of the Quinta Nova do Miranda at Sacavem illustrating the triumphs of Alexander and others which we know by repute only. These works – similar ones also existed in Cádiz and were produced to order for use in a given position – were always figural panels. The splendid views of harbours – Antwerp, Rotterdam, Middelburg, Hamburg, Venice, London, Cologne and Constantinople – in the former Palacio Saldanha at Junqueira, Lisbon, which may be ascribed to Cornelis Boumeester of Rotterdam were made a little later, in about 1715.

There was a demand for single tiles as well as for tile-pictures and these were used in many places, although, from the point of view of the quantity and the quality of the specimens, the collection of the Casa do Paço at Figueira da Foz is unique.

The Dutch tiles were popular, however, not only in continental Portugal; before there were any in Lisbon, Dutch tiles were known in outlying territories such as Terceira and Fayal in the Azores, the island of São Thomé in the Gulf of Guinea and Pernambuco in Brazil. Dutch tiles probably reached Brazil at the time of the occupation of the northern coast of the country by Prince John Maurice of Nassau, nicknamed "the Brazilian". But in the Azores it was undoubtedly Portuguese who bought the tiles, most probably in Rotterdam. However that may be, at all events the Portuguese decorators used these small single tiles to create effective compositions

178

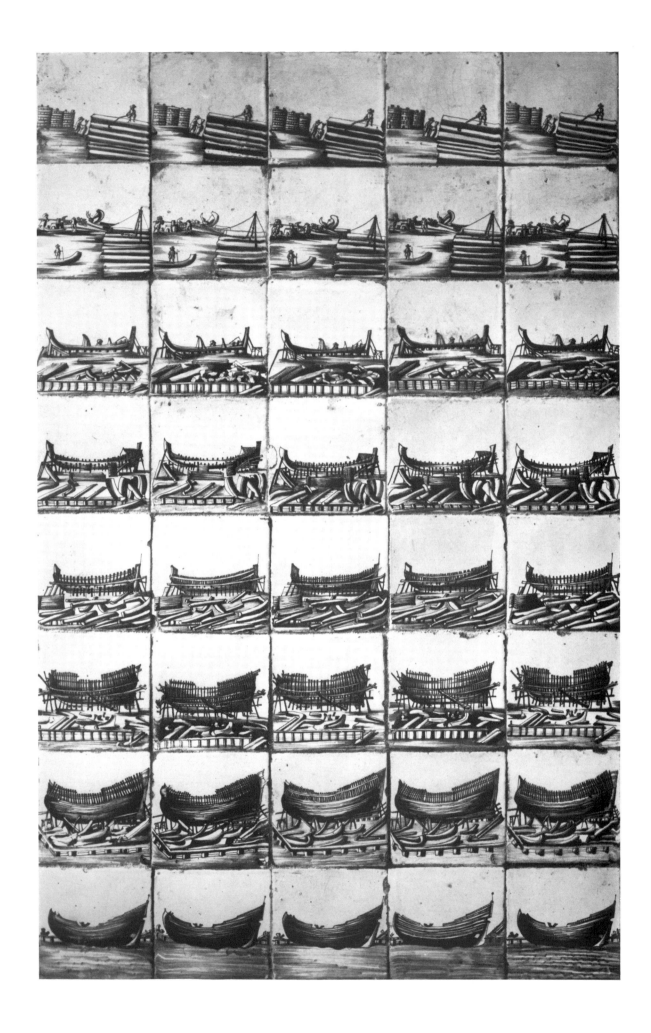

which departed both in scale and rhythm from the traditional rules of Dutch tile-decoration.

This whole movement, its rivalries and conflicts of interest must perforce have produced a violent reaction on the part of the native tile-makers who received little protection from the law and thus had no choice but to enter into competition with the intruders by imitating their style and aesthetic values. At the end of the seventeenth century certain workshops in Lisbon approached artists working in the city and requested them to paint *azulejos* "in the Dutch manner", meaning in blue monochrome and with designs of greater delicacy than had been usual. One of the first to respond to the call, a Spaniard named Gabriel del Barco y Minusca, who had lived since his youth in Lisbon, had until then, been engaged mostly upon wall and ceiling paintings. Tile-compositions by him dating from between 1695 and 1700 are known, the most famous being the large wall-facing in the church of the Canons of St. John the Evangelist in Arraiolos (239). Other artists also turned to tile-designing. The one who, through the beauty of his colours and the excellence of his drawing, came next to the Spaniard, created the panels in the church of Santiago at Sardoal (226); his finest works are in the Franciscan churches at Ponta Delgada and Fayal, respectively on the islands of S. Miguel and Fayal in the Azores. In spite of great efforts, it has not been possible to establish the name of this fine artist, who is reputed to have been a Dutchman.

António Pereira was another extremely gifted painter who at the beginning of the eighteenth century worked for the makers of *azulejos*. Only one signed work by him is known in Portugal and that is in the church of the Misericordia in Vidigueira; but there are several in Brazil, one in the Golden Chapel of Recife at Pernambuco and another in the Palacio Saldanha at Baía. Pereira used Flemish engravings or woodcuts, which accentuated the "Dutch style" of his *azulejos*.

It was, however, António de Oliviera Bernardes, the great Portuguese artist, who, taking the tile-pictures of the Netherlands as his models, did more than anyone else to restore the monumental character of the Portuguese *azulejos*. He also founded a whole school of craftsmen who were responsible for the astonishing Portuguese output of tiles during the eighteenth century. When António de Oliveira Bernardes was called upon to paint ceramic tiles he was already an acknowledged master and president of the painters' guild in Lisbon. One of his first large commissions was the decoration of the whole chapel of Nossa Senhora do Monte in Frielas, near Lisbon – today in a private residence in Cascais. He executed the commission with such accomplishment that a writer of the time expressed his astonishment, having taken the tiles for "the best *azulejos* that can be bought in Holland". António de Oliveira Bernardes systematically developed his tile-painting activities; he bought an old work-shop in Lisbon, where he worked and taught tirelessly. One of his first pupils was his son Policarpo, who painted tiles in such an extreme form of the baroque style that we marvel at them today. It is not possible to name all the artists who received their training from Bernardes and whose works are found in their hundreds in churches and palaces both in Portugal and overseas. In the monastery of St. Vincent in Lisbon alone no fewer than two hundred thousand *azulejos* cover an area of four thousand square metres.

The influence of Dutch tiles in Portugal was not restricted to large pictorial compositions; it can also be discerned in the single tiles which were unknown in Portugal until they began to be imported from Holland. In this case the Portuguese artists did not copy the Dutch models but created designs in a totally different spirit which undoubtedly produced a more decorative effect. It was particularly in the provincial workshops, in Oporto, Coimbra and probably Vianna do Castello, that this cheap form of tile was first produced. Large flowers cover the whole surface of the *azulejo*, small figures or caricatured faces (237), stylised animals, small ships, castles and windmills – quite different from the Dutch ones – religious emblems, objects of daily use and so on – all are painted in blue with a free brush-stroke which gives them great charm. Quadrilobes inspired by the *spinekop* were at first used for corner decoration but they were later reduced to small stars or to a simple flower-petal which, in conjunction with those of the contiguous tiles, formed a fleuron.

In the first half of the eighteenth century the workshops of Lisbon too produced single tiles. These were used for reasons of economy in less important rooms or in houses the owners of which could not afford the so-called *azulejos de brutescos* or figurative pictures. The latter cost thirty *reis* apiece, whereas the single tiles, called *de estrelinhas*, cost a sixth of this sum or five *reis*. They became very popular and reproductions are still being made today, as they are in Holland, for sale abroad.

The Dutch tiles of the second half of the seventeenth century undoubtedly exerted a strong influence on the development of Portuguese *azulejos* of the eighteenth century, even to the extent of altering their character. It should, however, be recognised that after António de Oliveira Bernardes and his son became active, this influence was expressed only in the blue colouring and in the efforts made to improve the artistic quality of the tiles, whereas the essentially decorative nature and the monumental scale characteristic of Lusitanian tile-facings surpass anything which the Dutch artists ever created. Large ceramic pictures, such as those produced for Portugal and Cádiz in workshops in Amsterdam and Rotterdam, were unknown in Holland itself. The scale of the houses there allowed of no such gigantic tile-facings and the church, since its faith was based largely on reason and it objected to religious representations, exercised no patronage.

From 1730 onwards tiles ceased to be imported from the Netherlands. It is true that later on a few interested persons commissioned tile-facings from the small provincial workshops of the Netherlands. But neither the price nor the quality of these was such as to lead to the establishment of a market for them in Portugal.

BRAZIL

When the Dutch tile-manufacturers lost the Portuguese market, they turned towards Brazil, which, early in the nineteenth century had become a Portuguese dominion, and were soon the chief suppliers of tiles to the country. The royal family, who had lived in Brazil since the French invasion of Portugal in 1808, settled in Rio de Janeiro and made a decisive contribution to the development of this great city, even preparing the way for the independence of Brazil which was achieved in 1822.

Like the Portuguese, though in fact with even more reason, the Brazilians appreciated ceramic wall-facings. Tiles began to be used on façades, both as decoration and, especially, as a protection against heat and rain, at a very early date. Until 1808 it was only in the South American metropolis that the Brazilians were able to acquire tiles, but just at the time when tiles were most urgently needed for the many new buildings that were being erected, the traditional sources dried up. In Portugal, first ravaged by war and then subjected to military occupation, all artistic and industrial activity had come to a halt. This situation induced Brazil to open her ports to the ships of all the allied nations. Since the builders of the Brazilian cities could not obtain tiles in Lisbon or Oporto, where there were no longer any tile-manufacturers, they turned to countries which were in a position to deliver the goods they needed. One of the first to send *azulejos* to Brazil was Holland. Even today specimens from Makkum and Harlingen are to be found in the old houses of Rio de Janeiro. There was a brisk demand especially for tiles for the outside walls and this led to the entry of English and later French (Pas de Calais), German, Spanish and even Belgian factories into the field of competition.

New designs were created which had nothing in common with the old Portuguese models but were in large part based upon those of Holland. When commercial relations between Imperial Brazil and Portugal were restored in 1832, the old merchants of Oporto and Lisbon began to supply the Brazilian market once more; in the factories which were set up with Brazilian capital, the first products were *azulejos* for the walls or houses, for which Dutch and other models were again copied. Thus Dutch tiles exerted their influence once again on those of Portugal, but they no longer possessed the charm and quality of the *tegels* of earlier times. Once again Portuguese craftsmen managed to create new designs by enlarging the decorative schemes, since in their opinion these were more suitable for facing the large façades which are so characteristic a feature of Portuguese and Brazilian cities.

Opposite top : The hunting-lodge Falkenlust in the park at Schloss Brühl was built between 1729 and 1739 by François Cuvilliés, who may also have been responsible for the design for the pictures on the tiled walls. Scenes of fights between herons and falcons alternate with ornamental tiles bearing the lozenges of the Bavarian arms in allusion to the Elector of Cologne, Clemens August of the house of Wittelsbach, for whom the lodge was built. Bottom : Representation of a heron feeding her young, also set among the lozenges of the Bavarian arms. These tiles, which are of outstanding quality, were made in the workshop of the Aalmis family, known as De Bloempot.

Page 188 : Figures of devils and spooks, droll fantasies such as that showing Venus in a chariot drawn by a stag and Christ being tempted by the devil, were all popular. c. 1700. Top and middle left, Lambert van Meerten Museum, Delft. Middle right and bottom, Tönder Museum.

Page 189 : Sea-monsters in numerous imaginative variations were also among the motifs popular in about 1700. Tönder Museum.

Page 190 top : Chronos flying over a field and a satyr surprising a nymph. Popular, naïve rendering of mythological scenes. Van Teyen Collection, Monnikendan. Middle : The Flood with the Ark was often painted on tiles after pictures by Marc Antonio Raimondi. De Moriaen Museum, Gouda and Jessel Collection, Westerland. Bottom left : Pastoral scenes were relatively rare. Surprisingly, the figures on this tile are elegantly clothed, an expression of the tendency of the time which, as a counterblast to the "back to nature" trend, liked to dress its rural folk in elegant clothing. This relatively large tile is also glazed on the sides and probably served as the floor of a niche. Keezer Collection, Leiden. Bottom right : Naïve imagination is also demonstrated in this simplified but expressive rendering of Jonah and the Whale. Keller Collection, Munich.

Page 191 : Joseph and his brethren before the pit. One of a series of tile-pictures produced for the Rotterdam orphanage by the De Bloempot workshop under J. Aalmis the Younger. The composition, intended as part of the decoration of a large hall, is rendered in a manner unusually bold for Holland. The border is unfortunately damaged. Examples of this series and from the same pounced pattern are also known from pattern-sheets.

Page 192 : Late 18th century tiles produced for Catholic customers. Archaising corner-motifs consisting of shaded oak-leaf and parts of spinnetjes. Lambert van Meerten Museum, Delft.

Page 193 : Whaling. The picture belongs to the Boumeester tradition, although one of Salm's paintings in grisaille may have served as model. The "pathetic" quality of the icebergs in the distance and the primitive rendering of the clouds are extremely appealing.

Page 194 top : Astronomy. From a series of allegories of the arts, of which the pictures of Music and Sculpture are still in existence. Dated 1764. From the De Bloempot workshop, Rotterdam. Fokke Museum, Bremen. Bottom : so-called pillaertjes, or representations of pillars, which were placed near fire-places and are a reminiscene of the original real sandstone pillars which supported the smoke-hood of the fire-place. Left : Two pillars with garlands of grapes and other fruit from a house at Oldsum on the island of Föhr, now in Tönder Museum. Middle : A similar pillar. Feenstra Collection, Otterlo. Right : Two pillars with tendrils and peacocks, from the farm La Chartreuse near Utrecht ; the farmhouse is shown on the base of the pillars. Centraal Museum, Utrecht. All pillars late 18th century.

186

J. Aalmis à Rotterdam

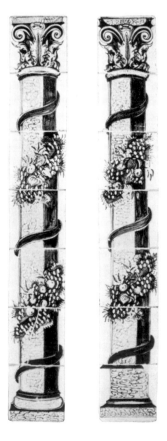

The export of Dutch Tiles to Germany and Denmark

In about the year 1600 – and more particularly after the Peace of Antwerp in 1609 – the Dutch began to produce tiles within the framework of their faience-industry, a development which was to influence the domestic culture of northern Europe continuously for about three hundred years. It was in Germany and Denmark that Dutch tiles were most widely used and most frequently imitated.

Two periods may be distinguished in the history of the Dutch tile-trade: commerce based on quality during the period 1650–1750 and that based on quantity from 1750 to 1900. The first, which was closely bound up with the export of other faience wares, particularly those of Delft, was a whim of fashion within the framework of the baroque culture of the upper classes and of relatively short duration; whereas the commerce of the second period was a matter of popular culture and was of special significance in northern Germany and Denmark, embracing as it did Emsland, East Friesland, Oldenburg, the region of Bremen, the Vierlande round Hamburg and Schleswig-Holstein.

Dutch tiles were imitated in Germany and Denmark in some of the numerous faience factories which had been established throughout central Europe in the eighteenth century to compete with the Dutch industry. They did not, however, achieve any great importance.

Investigation into the distribution of tiles is made difficult by the fact that only in very rare cases were they signed. This often makes it impossible to attribute scattered material to a particular locality and, in cases in which the material available in archives is insufficient, necessitates comparison with tiles in Holland itself. It must be recognized that the production of tiles was for most Dutch faience factories only a branch of secondary importance in relation to their total output and that only in very unusual cases were the most skilful faience painters employed in painting tiles. It must, indeed, even be assumed that in some factories the production of tiles served as training for apprentices. And even when it can be proved that a particular factory exported tiles, there are still very few instances in which we can say which particular tiles were exported. With the exception of the well-preserved factory archives at Makkum, there is no documentary evidence extant in the Dutch tile-producing centres. In spite of this, any investigation of the problem of exportation must start in Holland before examination is made of the exported material abroad.

As early as 1600, according to Hudig, there were fourteen workshops which may also have produced tiles. At least twenty-five factories were established before 1629, principally in Rotterdam, Delft, Utrecht and Haarlem. From 1650 onwards, however, Delft lost in importance as a tile-producing centre and for this reason the expression "Delft tiles", when used for tiles in general, is somewhat misleading. Rotterdam and Harlingen moved up into first position and from 1660 onwards Makkum entered and remained in the field of competition. From the beginning of the eighteenth century onwards the number of tile-factories dropped and those that remained in business must have altered their procedures, for quantitatively production increased rather than diminished, a fact which is related to the demand from farmhouses. After the Napoleonic Wars only eight out of an original eighty factories were still producing: one each in Rotterdam, Delft and Utrecht and five in Friesland; and by the year 1900 the only surviving tile workshops were in Makkum, Harlingen and Utrecht.

Statements relating to the numbers of factories must, however, be taken with certain reservations and it is not known for certain whether all the workshops named by Hudig also exported tiles. Of the manufacture of faience it can in general be said that it was divided among nineteen towns situated in four of the

Dutch provinces: South Holland (9), Utrecht (1), North Holland (5) and Friesland (4); however, only six of these were of importance with regard to the export of tiles; these were Delft, Rotterdam, Utrecht, Amsterdam, Harlingen and Makkum.

It is noteworthy that the Friesian factories took a clear lead as early as the middle of the eighteenth century, a situation which was certainly due to the fruitful commercial relations of this region with north Germany and Scandinavia. As far as the Friesian tiles are concerned, at least 95% of them date from the period 1750–1900, that is, from a relatively late period, for export to Spain and Portugal – principally from Rotterdam and Amsterdam – reached its peak before the Friesian advance into northern Europe.

As has already been indicated, the beginning of the export drive may be dated to the period after 1650 at the earliest and for Germany and Denmark – with the exception of a single region – to 1700. This makes it possible substantially to limit the number of Dutch tile-factories which may be regarded as possible exporters. We may mention the following:

DELFT. Of the thirty workshops in Delft which were active from about 1584 and of which only one, De Porceleyne Fles, still survives, probably at the most a third exported their wares; after 1650 only three did so and after 1750 only one. It may be assumed that the De Paeuw workshop (1651–c. 1772) supplied tiles for the Petit Trianon de Porcelaine at Versailles in about 1670. Some tiles from this source were later used at the Château de Rambouillet, for which in about 1725 Boumeester of Rotterdam supplied his famous marine pictures. This factory probably also supplied tiles for some of the German palaces, to which we shall be returning. This must be assumed also to have been the case with the most important of all the Delft tile-factories, De Roos (1666–1854), which, from 1766 onwards, had the monopoly of tile-production in Delft. It must, however, be emphasised once again that, from the point of view of the exportation of tiles to Germany and Scandinavia, Delft did not play a very important part.

ROTTERDAM. Rotterdam assumes the leading position among the tile workshops of South Holland and it can be taken as almost certain that the earlier tiles of the period before 1700 in Germany and Denmark came from there. So it may well be that an unusual polychrome tile showing the sun, which came from the small village of Emmerlev in northern Schleswig, was a product of the earliest workshop, Goudsche Wagenstraat (1626–1716), which was founded by a certain Cornelis Willemsz Sonnevelt. Sonnevelt was frequently described as a *tegelbacker* or firer of tiles, but nothing more is known about the activities of this concern. Of a number of other factories in Rotterdam numerous details exist to show what types of tile they produced; and when this information is compared with what has come down to us from the northernmost export centres, we find the situation to be strikingly similar. It is recorded, for example, that the Oppert workshop, which in the year 1666 had at its disposal a stock of a good 48,000 tiles, produced tiles with landscapes, shepherds, fruits, men and women, flower-vases, horsemen, biblical scenes and sea-monsters. Companion-pieces to the celebrated tile-pictures showing *poortridders* or riders framed by an archway after designs by Goltzius in the Lambert van Meerten Museum at Delft (156), which show great similarities to the large picture of Julius Caesar ascribed to this workshop, are to be found in the Frederiksborg palace in Denmark (265); these tiles provide the first example in Europe of the exportation of a consignment destined for the interior decoration of a palace. Christian IV (1588–1648) was, in matters of architecture,

Landscape with angler. The picture is painted blue and the border is in powdered manganese. 18th century. Tönder Museum.

the most strongly influenced by the Dutch of all the princes of Europe. The workshops Delftsche Vaart (Boumeester), Het Wapen van Dantzich and Rijstuin (1642–1674) also exported tiles which are found on German and Danish territory.

The most important tile-making concern in Rotterdam was, however, De Bloempot, which from 1692 until 1799, was under the direction of the Aalmis family. The first of the dynasty was Pieter Jansz Aalmis, who died in the year 1707. His son Jan Aalmis (1674–1755) was famous for the hawking scenes which he made in 1731 for Schloss Falkenlust in the park at Brühl (187). In addition to these, a series of pounced patterns has survived which he prepared for his elegant late baroque tiles showing garden scenes (268). His son Jan Aalmis the Younger (1714–1799) and his brother Jan Bartholomaeus Aalmis (1725–1786) produced a series of fine tile-pictures in blue and manganese showing both biblical scenes and secular subjects. They represent a high point in rococo art and their characteristic mark is their rocaille borders. They travelled far, to Cádiz in the south and Altona in the north. This workshop continued until 1852 to export large quantities of tiles even to such distant countries as India, the Argentine and Brazil. Even in 1848 production ran to 470,000 tiles.

UTRECHT. We have no evidence that the earlier tiles of Utrecht, which enjoyed the reputation of being of particularly good quality, were exported to the countries under discussion. After 1760 industrial concerns were established, however, which probably competed against the Friesian factories and possibly exported their wares to the Ems district. These firms were in the hands of Albert Prinse (1760–1855), J. Schillemans, who began in the 1750's, and the Holland tile-factory, perhaps a successor to Schillemans. The last-named copied tiles from old models, a type which is often encountered in the trade today. The factory of Rave-

styen Brothers in Westraven, near Utrecht, however, already established in 1661, is still working today. The production of tiles was started there in 1845 or even earlier. There is a comprehensive pattern book from this workshop of the 1890 period containing types which are well-known in the districts under discussion. Since Ravesteyn Brothers, Tichelaar in Makkum and Van Hulst and Tjallingii in Harlingen, who all had similar pattern-books, collaborated closely, it is hard to decide to which of the four workshops these late tiles should be attributed.

AMSTERDAM. Only two Amsterdam workshops are known: De Oude Prins in the Anjelierstraat and Van der Kloet in the Prinsengracht. De Oude Prins was an exporting firm, as is proved by a collection of thirty-two different patterns for tile-designs which were sent to Philadelphia in 1792. Since this period exactly coincides with the final phase of Dutch whaling, it should be assumed that the wares of this workshop reached northern countries. When in 1802 the workshop had to go into liquidation, a series of tiles of currently popular design was produced but, it should be noted, also imitations of tiles from Utrecht and Friesland. This shows that care is necessary, for it is no longer possible, as it was before, to regard tiles found in north Germany simply as Friesian. They may also come from Amsterdam. With regard to the other factory, the reader is referred to the chapter on Spain and Portugal.

HARLINGEN. The outstanding contribution of Nanne Ottema is his demonstration of the dominant influence of the Friesian factories on tile-manufacture in general; and it is thanks to his intensive examination of the archives that the importance of Harlingen as a tile-producing town has become apparent. It must be supposed that this town was the chief exporter of

197

tiles to Germany and Denmark, particularly in the second period (1750–1900). The oldest workshop, that of Raamstraat, which was in any case producing tiles in the period between 1637 and 1803, was acquired in the year 1684 by Pytter Pyttersee Grauda, a great name in the history of tiles, from whom a large collection of pounced patterns of high artistic merit has come. It has been proved that this workshop exported tiles to Spain; but, in conjunction with the whaling-industry, it also carried on business with customers in the northern countries. The Zoutsloot workshop, whose activities can be traced back to 1684, continued to exist until 1910. Original patterns from this workshop, made by Eybert Pieters, still exist, including the well-known Friesian flowers. Another well-known artist from this workshop was D. P. Danser, who created a number of pictures of whaling. A third tile-painter from Harlingen, several of whose patterns have also survived, is Pieter Ruurds. A tile-picture dated 1779 representing a tannery, which was found at Boldixum on the island of Föhr, is preserved, together with another picture signed by Ruurd showing a mill, in the Schleswig-Holstein Landesmuseum. The third workshop of importance in the exportation of tiles to Germany and Denmark is that of Buiten de Kerkport, which was established in 1672. In about 1850 it passed into the possession of the Van Hulst family. There is in existence a hand-painted pattern-book (268) of about 1800, the earliest known to us, showing all the types of tiles which occur in north Germany and Scandinavia. There is also a printed pattern-book issued by this firm, which, in its last years, was known as J. van Hulst Bouwstofindustrie; the book is entitled *Modelboek van eenige geschilderde Muurtegels* and is similar to that of the Brothers Ravesteyn (c. 1890), which shows how, right up to the present day, tiles have been produced from the old designs, though with a strong *art nouveau* flavour. The Van Hulst factory closed down only in 1933.

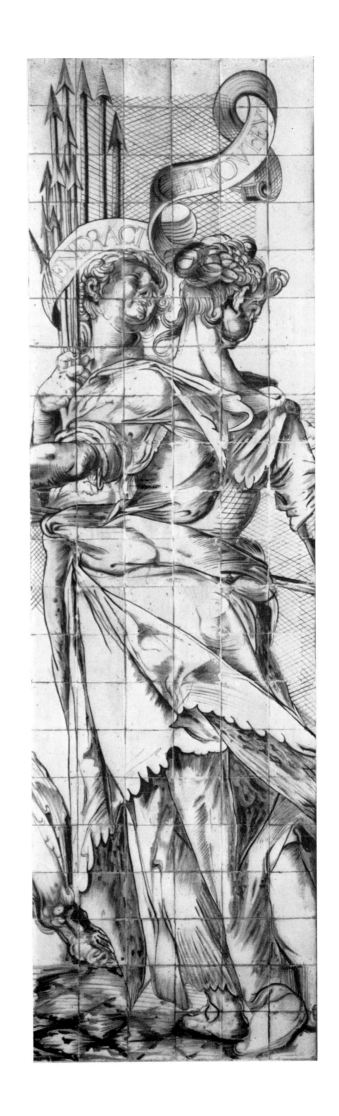

Worckum

MAKKUM. The most interesting of all the Dutch tile-factories is, however, that of Tichelaar. In the first place, it played a decisive part, although on a slightly smaller scale than the Harlingen factories, in the exportation of tiles to north Germany and Denmark; and, secondly, it is the only factory in Holland which has remained since 1660 in the possession of the same family. Thirdly, the archives of the business from about the year 1710 onwards have been preserved. It can thus be ascertained from the production-book for the year 1719 that in that year twenty-seven firings, accounting for 130,000 tiles and 12,500 large plates for food, were undertaken. On the basis of the production-books, the total production of the factory can be assessed at nearly 125 million tiles, eight million large plates for food and fancy-ware and so-called *kleingoed* to the number of half a million. From the earliest lists of creditors it emerges that trade was carried on mainly in Friesland but that, as early as 1712, goods were being exported to Enkhuizen and Hamburg. From 1770 onwards, Amsterdam—whence the wares must have been re-sold to the countries under discussion —Hamburg, Altona, Glückstadt and Friedrichstadt, among others, are mentioned. For a time the factory itself owned two ships *(kuffen)*, *De Rijk en Jouwer* and *De Gebroeders Tichelaar*. Apart from these, exportation was by means of the so-called *Hamburgers*, small wooden vessels of from thirty to fifty tons. Together with their cargo of tiles, these ships carried building materials for which, in Holstein and elsewhere, there was ample demand. They were later superseded, until the railway came, by iron hoys. The careful lists of creditors for the years from 1790 to 1868 provide an entirely new insight into the extent of exportation to the northern countries. They enable us to establish: firstly, the exact extent of the exportation; secondly, the names of the merchants who re-sold the factory's products; thirdly, the wholesale price and, fourthly, the relative numerical proportion of the different types of tile.

Manganese-coloured tiles showing landscapes within borders. 18th century. Tönder Museum.

The following are the export figures for the period 1790–1855:

Hamburg

Johann Georg Büntzendahl 1790–1792....	2,500
Otto Matthias Meyn 1790–1838..........	387,076
Jochem Gerhard Becker 1814–1841	1,089,100
Heinrich Vincent Reimers 1815–1816	17,000
Peter Jacob Meyer 1820–1826	21,000
I.M.C. Boecker's successors 1824–1855....	106,500
I.C. Bajans 1840	10,000
G.J. Krogmann 1840	12,000
J.F. Krogmann 1842–1855..............	751,950
Johann Peter Arnold 1842–1847	148,000
Peter Jacob Meyer's widow 1842–1855 ...	416,200
Total:	2,961,326

Altona

Nicolaus Linnich 1790	7,550
Abraham Ellermann 1790–1791	46,350
Johann Christoph Wedekind 1791–1855...	1,292,854
Georg Ernst Möller 1808–1818	82,100
Adolph Möller 1845–1855	309,804
Total:	1,738,658

Friedrichstadt

Claas Engel 1791–1792	1,394
Peter Karsten 1797	3,016
Total:	4,410
Total export of tiles to north Germany	4,704,394

If we take two guilders as the average price per hundred tiles, the total export for fifty years amounts to 100,000 guilders, or 2,000 guilders per annum. This total is not very impressive when calculated in terms of today's values, but it enables us to understand more clearly how the well-to-do fenland peasants could, without putting themselves out, afford the modest luxury of facing their walls with tiles. When in the eighteenth century people began to face all the walls, not only those where the windows were, with tiles, a large number of tiles came to be required for one room. It is necessary to reckon about 125 tiles a metre, so that it would take 5,000 tiles to face a wall of forty metres. That is the equivalent of about four large rooms. Now in the year 1818, for example, 5,000 landscape tiles cost only 125 guilders, to which, of course, the merchant's profit and transport had to be added – which, however, the whalers, who bought direct in Harlingen, did not have to pay. That brings the cost to between thirty and forty guilders a room at the most. An understanding of these facts demonstrates clearly why tiles, long-lasting and hygienic as they were, were able for so long to compete successfully with wall-papers.

The consignments to the Altona merchant J.C. Wedekind will show what types of tiles were in demand during the first half of the nineteenth century:

Witte (white)		375,025
Landschappen (landscapes)	purple........	196,600
	blue	209,300
Bloempotjes (flower-vases)	purple........	259,900
	blue	154,700
Rozesterren (stars of roses)	purple........	12,000
	blue	2,500
Historien (biblical scenes)	purple........	5,900
	blue	24,100
Weezen ("orphans" or diagonal tiles)		2,500
Kleine bloemen (small flowers)		49,800
Ruitjes (? lozenge-shaped tiles)		400
17 tableaux (tile-pictures):		
Ships, horses and cows		129
Total:		1,292,854

This corresponds exactly to what we know of the tiles in the homes of Schleswig-Holstein, to which Wedekind must have sold. It is noteworthy that the number of tile-pictures exported is not very large. The tiles supplied to the Hamburg merchant J. F. Krogmann follow a rather different distribution; these consignments extend over fourteen years:

Witte		634,800
Landschappen,	purple	10,300
	blue	20,900
Bloempotjes,	purple	26,500
	blue	12,950
Kleine bloemen		11,500
Schildpadjes (tortoise-shell tiles)		2,000
Albasterde (alabaster tiles)		14,000
Blokjes (?) (blocks)		2,000
Marmerde (marbled tiles)		1,000
Slanglijsten (vine-tendril tiles)		8,600
Slanghalfjes (half vine-tendril tiles)		7,400
Total:		751,950

From this it can be clearly seen that this merchant supplied tiles largely for Hamburg kitchens and not so much for the villages. The vine-tendril tiles were used to finish off the decoration at the top.

The really considerable purchases of Abraham Ellermann in the years 1790–1791, when export to Schleswig-Holstein was still prohibited, are noteworthy. They show that this prohibition could not be maintained and indicates that the manufacture of tiles by the faience factories of Schleswig-Holstein was not very profitable, even at Kellinghusen.

Using the Dutch designations, types and prices of the tiles exported by Tichelaar to north Germany and Denmark may be extracted from the voluminous material available. Claas Engel in Friedrichstadt received, in 1791, 600 *landschappen in 't rond* at 42 *stuivers* per 100 (= 2.10 guilders) and 108 *paarse halfjes* or violet border-tiles. Together 17 guilders. One *coffe op* 20 *steentjes* cost 3.50 guilders. In the following year Engel received 400 *paarse roosjes met stelen* (violet roses on stems) for 12 guilders and 12 *stuivers* (the *stuiver* was the equivalent of a *sou* or farthing), but the consignment included 200 landscape tiles. Finally he received a further fifty-four violet border-tiles, one dog and two cats of four tiles each for 4 guilders in all. A tile-picture of the type mentioned would cost about £ 54 today.

Otto Matthias Meyn's widow in Hamburg received in 1790 one thousand blue *kleine bloemen in 't achtkant* at a cost of 3.50 guilders per hundred. *Histories met wolken* cost 3 guilders per hundred. The white tiles which, as we see, greatly outnumber the rest, cost between 36 and 42 *stuivers* per hundred. Landscapes *in 't groot rond* cost 3.25 guilders. Fine landscapes cost 5 guilders per hundred and *herders in 't rond* (second quality) 42 *stuivers* per hundred.

The following prices can be cited from Wedekind's extensive purchases: violet and blue *bloempotjes* at 44 *stuivers* per hundred; blue *rozesterren* at 3.50 guilders per hundred; manganese-coloured *weesjes* at 2.50 guilders per hundred. *Weesjes* are diagonal tiles with blue and white grounds and the name arose from the fact that the orphanage children *(weeskinderen)* wore these colours (212). It is therefore in fact a contradiction in terms to speak of violet *weesjes*. In the year 1838 Wedekind paid for four pictures of ships 1.80 guilders per picture of nine tiles; for pictures of cows and horses 0.90 guilders for every six tiles. The price of a picture of a mill on sixteen tiles supplied in 1797 to Peter Karsten in Friedrichstadt amounted to 2.80 guilders. In a consignment to Jochem G. Becker in Hamburg there is mention of *histories met aawijzingen* (tiles showing biblical scenes with textual references). These were the most expensive tiles, costing 8 Dutch florins per hundred. The blue and violet octagonal landscapes were also expensive, costing 6¼ Dutch florins per hundred. The largest order for tiles of all – over 42,500 pieces weighing between ten and twelve tons – is noted in the *debiteurenboek* on the 4 March 1839 under the name of J. G. Becker, Tichelaar's largest buyer in Hamburg and undoubtedly supplier to the peasants of the Vierlande, the marshy country round Hamburg. *Herders in 't rond* (shepherds within roundels) and *drietulpen* (three tulips) could be bought from Linnich in Altona, who had paid 40 and 42 *stuivers* per hundred respectively. We find fifty-five deals with Adolph Möller of Altona in the period between 1852 and 1855, amounting to 13,600 violet and blue *jacht* (animals within roundels: dogs, hares, stags, foxes) at a cost of 2.50 Dutch florins per hundred. The types of tiles here enumerated are found to this day in the few homes where respect for tradition has caused these impressive witnesses of the past to be preserved. The material mentioned relates to the period up to 1855. For the period between 1856 and 1870, that is, immediately before the general decline of peasant domestic architecture the following maximum export figures from the Tichelaar factory may be cited for the individual types of tiles current at the time:

White tiles	1866:	173,500
Blue flowers	1859:	14,500
Manganese-coloured flowers	1859:	13,500
Small flowers, blue	1861:	6,000
Small flowers, manganese	1861:	6,000
Flower-vases, manganese	1857:	44,500
Flower-vases, brown	1865:	14,000
Landscapes, blue	1860:	18,000
Landscapes, manganese	1856:	26,500
Landscapes, brown	1865:	15,500
Jacht, blue	1864:	3,000
Jacht, manganese	1863:	6,000
Jacht, brown	1863:	7,800
Jacht, without roundel	1861:	2,000
Biblical scenes with clouds	1859:	1,000
Children playing	1865:	200
Horsemen	1869:	6,500
Hamburg octagons	1870:	9,500
Rose-stars, blue	1869:	200
Rose-stars, brown	1869:	200
Dogs, cats, etc.	1865:	88
Mills, ships, ploughs, etc.	1865:	72

This shows that the extant tiles in north Germany and Denmark date in great part from this period and come from the factories of Friesland. The tradition of tile-decoration in this part of the world dates from considerably later than is generally thought; it is contemporaneous with the building of the houses in which the tiles were used, extending, that is to say, from about 1820 to 1900. The printed model-books provide ample information about the production of tiles at the turn of the century. Here are a few more prices for the more popular types of tiles from the catalogue of the Van Hulst factory, in each case per hundred pieces:

The large flowers	4.50 Dutch florins
Animal in a roundel	3.40 Dutch florins
Landscape in a roundel	3.40 Dutch florins
Landscape in an octagon	6.50 Dutch florins
Ships	9.00 Dutch florins
Tiles for walls	5.20 Dutch florins
Biblical scenes	7.50 Dutch florins

"Railway" tiles also occur with great frequency in the area of distribution under discussion. They are bought and sold today as antiques.

DUODECIMA ESTACION

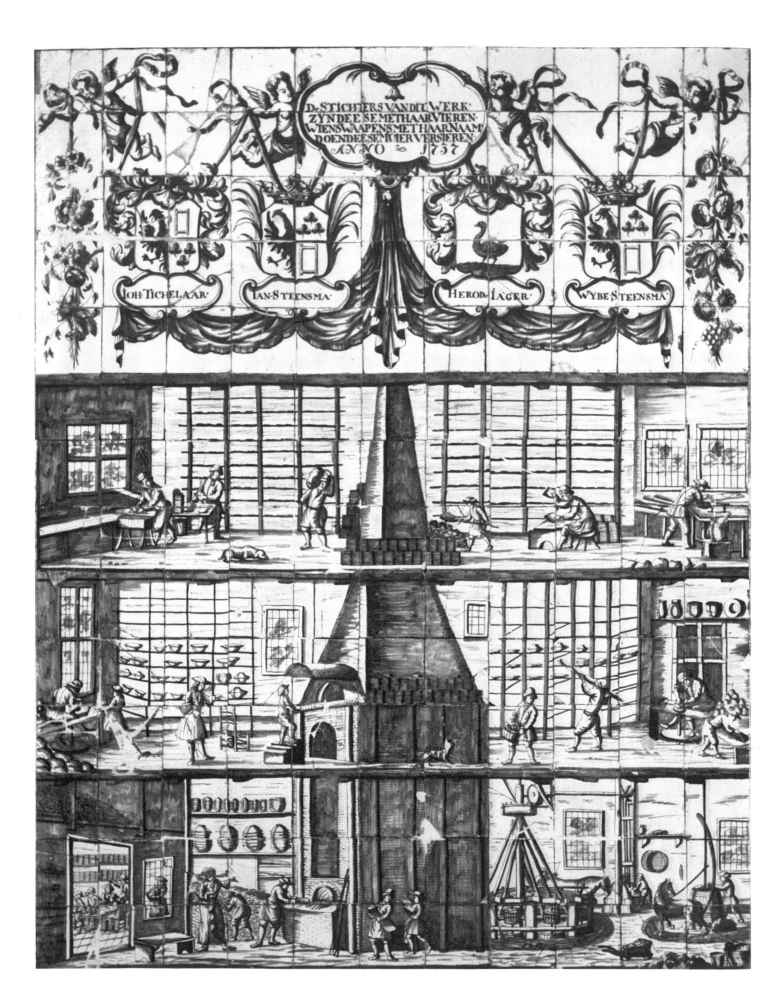

De STICHTERS VAN DIT WERK,
ZYNDEE SE MET HAAR VIEREN.
WIENS WAAPENS MET HAAR NAAM,
DOEN DEESE MUER VERSIEREN.
ANNO 1737

IOH:TICHELAAR   IAN STEENSMA   HEROD IAGER   WYBE STEENSMA

Page 213 top: This crucifixion is, as the inscription shows, the last of twelve Stations of the Cross; it came from the De Bloempot workshop and shows the sad falling off in quality of their later works. The picture was probably made to the order of Spaniards living in Belgium. Victoria and Albert Museum, London. Bottom: Mary in Glory, surrounded by angels, a picture comprising 105 tiles. Antwerp, early 17th century. Musée Royal du Cinquantenaire, Brussels.

Opposite: Large picture representing the manufacturing processes in the Bolsward creamware and tile factory. Above, the arms of the founders of the firm. In the middle, the kiln which rises through several storeys. Dated 1737. Rijksmuseum, Amsterdam.

It remains to add in conclusion that, during the period 1750 to 1835, there was another tile-factory at Makkum. It is easy to assume that this factory also exported to Germany and Denmark. It was founded by a very energetic ship's captain named Hylke Jan Kingma and specialised in tile-pictures. In the year 1823 the business had at its disposal a stock of 348,000 single tiles, 410 flower-pictures, fifteen pictures of mills and forty-four of ships. In the year 1835 Tichelaar bought the remaining stock.

The use of faience—and this included tiles—in the seventeenth century was restricted to the well-to-do strata of society. Throughout the century in the matter of Dutch exports the accent was on luxury. There is no information regarding prices for this period but the occurrence of the earlier tiles in palaces, patrician houses and other places bearing the marks of prosperity, suggest that they were too expensive for the broad masses. Conspicuous differences in quality also suggest that at this time tiles were not the mass-produced articles which they became after 1700.

It has already been stated that in 1686 a Delft workshop supplied the tiles for the Petit Trianon de Porcelaine. Important consignments of the same period to Spain and Portugal are recorded. That the early polychrome tiles were exported is known, however, from a single case in the north-western corner of Schleswig, to which we will return later. The early tiles in the Frederiksborg palace (265) are obviously exceptional. The tiled rooms in the German palaces date, as we have seen, from the period after 1700 and in the Danish castle of Rosenborg Dutch tiles were used as early as 1706. Yet the monopoly of tile-production in Germany and Denmark was not for long left to the Dutch; the numerous local factories soon proceeded to make copies. This was the case at Schloss Favorite near Rastatt as well as at Frederiksborg palace and the Eremitage near Copenhagen.

There is thus no doubt that the protectionist commercial policy practised by the sovereign princes of the eighteenth century, regardless of the profitability of the products, had as one of its effects to force the Dutch faience manufacturers to seek a wider market and to lower their prices by introducing mass-production. They were so successful in this that the indigenous tile-manufacture failed to establish itself either in Germany or in Denmark and even regular prohibitions on imports could not be sustained.

The Dutch manufacturers now turned their attention towards the districts to which tiles could be transported by sea together with other building materials. These trading routes had existed for a long time. In about 1500 there had been in Holland a strong demand for grain and later for oxen, which provided a great opportunity for the fenlands. The first grain-transports were carried by vessels known as *koggen*, a reminder of which is provided by the coat-of-arms of the town of Tönder. Dutch building materials were always mentioned as the return cargo, as, for example, in the year 1531 for the castle at Tönder, in the building of which Dutch craftsmen also took part. For this project bricks, pantiles, lime, floor-tiles, stove-tiles, iron and brass nails and lead were transported from Amsterdam, Makkum and Emden. These stove-tiles cannot, of course, be regarded as wall-tiles. It is an interesting fact that in the period between 1630 and 1650 building materials for the castle of Breitenburg near Itzehoe were supplied from Makkum. It will be seen that similar conditions were described in the rather more northerly Wilstermarsch a hundred years later. The building materials on the north Friesian islands and on Römö also came from Holland.

The trade in oxen reached its peak between 1550 and 1650 and the North Sea coast provided the ports of discharge for the oxen bought in Jutland. The most informative evidence concerning this trade is found in western Schleswig but in broad outline the picture is the same along the whole length of the fenland coast. Tönder and Husum were dependent on trade with Holland, the extent of which is known from customs accounts.

The distribution centres in northern Schleswig were Hojer, Emmerlev and Waygaard in the parish of Risum. The *koggen* were superseded by newer types of ship, including Dundees, galliots, smacks, sloops and boyers – all types which are found a little later on Dutch tiles. The commonest were the smacks, which could carry up to thirty loads or sixty tons, that is, about forty or fifty oxen – not a particularly agreeable form of transport for the beasts. The Dundees could carry only thirty animals at the most, while the so-called Dutch boats could carry up to ninety head of cattle.

These facts are extremely significant for they demonstrate what large consignments of goods could go through by the sea-routes. As has already been shown, the export of tiles did not begin much before 1650. The older polychrome tiles are not found in the castles of Germany and Denmark. An exception to this occurs in the Tönder district where a few particularly prosperous large-scale farmers rivalled the merchants of Tönder as wholesale buyers in Holland and in so doing strictly speaking contravened the law. The occurrence of tiles of the period 1600–1650 in the district of Tönder and Hoyer (129, 135) shows that this small region was the first market-area for Dutch tiles anywhere, the tiles sold there having probably come from Rotterdam by way of Amsterdam and Enkhuizen. They are, however, found only in small quantities and never in the houses in which they were originally hung, so that, from the point of view of trade, it is unlikely that they can have played a significant part. It is noteworthy that the tiles in question were of the standard types and thus were not specially commissioned.

The trade in oxen in this district diminished in significance after 1650, but, thanks to the whale-fishery, relations with Holland remained as close as before. In about 1650 the fisheries were faced with a crisis similar to that of the cattle-trade and the decline of the industry forced the fishermen to look for alternative occupations. Some of them found this in transportation, while others saw new possibilities of making a living in the whale-fishery at Spitzbergen and Jan Mayen and later off Greenland. A contemporary reference, which is always repeated in later writings, says that the great storm of 1634 set this development in train.

The Dutch were the first to make use of those rich sources of livelihood which the English had discovered in the hunting of whales, seals and walruses. In the year 1614 they established their first whaling company and in 1721 they had no fewer than 258 Greenland ships in commission. After Amsterdam, Harlingen was the most popular place with the northerners.

The many fine ship pictures on Hallig Hooge, Amrum and Föhr were doubtless inspired by the works of D. Danser of Harlingen, mentioned above, who, in the year 1747, had made oil-paintings of the fleet of the Harlingen shipowner D. Wildschut. As early as 1701, Föhr and Sylt had an interest to the tune of 2000 men in this fishery, from which a number of more northerly cities soon sought to profit: in 1669 Hamburg invested thirty-seven ships, Glückstadt followed in 1671, Altona in 1685, Flensburg in 1749. Between 1730 and about 1770 even Tönder had a seal-hunting and whaling fleet, though it was on a smaller scale than the others.

The only Greenland voyages of interest at present are those whose points of departure were Dutch ports, Hamburg or Altona. A third of the captains of the Hamburg ships are said to have been natives of Sylt and a third of the Dutch Greenland fleet was commanded by Föhr men.

Landscape within an octagonal frame. Probably Friesian, 18th century. Tönder Museum.

Here again, as in the cattle-trade, smacks were the most important means of transport for both men and goods. Tile-pictures showing these smacks, or the closely related barks, are widely known, An example is found, for instance, in a house at Nebel on Amrum, called the Queden House, once the home of Captain Christian Erichsen (1813–1872). The smack here illustrated has the letters IKSK on the stern. The border is made up of the half-tiles which have been mentioned elsewhere, that is, border-tiles with vine-trails. In the same house at Nebel there is one of the finest tile-pictures of whaling that has come down to us. The whaling-ship, rigged like a frigate, occupies sixteen tiles, adjoining which are four tiles showing two whales and six showing whalers in rowing-boats; below the picture, occupying eight tiles in breadth and two in depth, are the words, in cursive script:

Durch Schip Fahrt und durch Wall Fish Fanst
Unter halt Gott Viel Leut und Land.

The text is clearly inspired by the lines of the ploughing scenes produced at the Makkum factory, which run, in Dutch, "*De Landbouw wacht van s'Heeren Hand veel milden Zeegen opt' Land.*"[1] It is said that Erichsen bought this tile-picture himself in the 1830's – relatively late, therefore – and probability is lent to the story by the flower-vase tiles which surround the whole picture. These two tile-pictures were probably purposely placed in the same house: one ship represents the type used to ply to the trading-cities; whereas the other was used for voyages to the Arctic. In the same way that we know was possible in the English faience-industry, tile-pictures of the ships in which the customer was sailing could be bought to order from the factories. Many ship's captains did this and even had the tile-picture built in above the stove in the parlour. Not many of

these fine pieces, however, have come down to us. The voyage to the harbour in the south at which crews signed on took place round about St. Peter's Day, the 22 February, and, in broad outline, followed the same pattern on all the islands in the North Sea. After various festivities, the men set off, having in advance come to appropriate agreements with the skippers of the smacks in question. In the autumn, when they returned to Amsterdam, Harlingen, Bremen, Altona, Glückstadt, the principal home-ports of the whaling companies, the crews were brought back by the same smacks. This part of the whole enterprise was not without its dangers.

The voyages of the smacks played an important part in the transportation of tiles in the period between 1700 and 1850, when the railways took over most of the freightage. The tiles were presumably brought to the north in the smacks returning from the ports of registration since, when the crews returned in the autumn, there cannot have been much space for goods in the vessels, which were, for preference, closely packed and each of which carried, in fact, up to 200 sailors. It is known that the famous grave-stones which were bought in Bremen, Hamburg and Holland, were transported to the islands in this way and it may be assumed that the sailors also bought tiles in Hamburg and Altona, when they signed off there, while those signing off in Harlingen would, of course, have bought direct from the factories.

It is impossible to say whether the same distinction may rightly be made between the cattle-trade tiles and the whaling tiles as between the castle and farmhouse tiles farther south. It is difficult to show that there was an unbroken tradition of tile-decoration in the northern part of Schleswig from about 1630 to 1900. No early tiles are found on these islands and the obvious supposition is that, when poor islanders suddenly became prosperous, they sought to emulate their more fortu-

217

Opposite top: Popular ceramics provided the models for these pleasantly coloured tiles in slip and sgraffito techniques. Limburg, 19th century. Lambert van Meerten Museum, Delft. Bottom left: Farmer with his horse. The way in which the shadows are painted suggests a mid-19th-century date. Bottom right: Windmill, probably portraying one in the possession of the customer. Both tiles clearly of Friesian origin. First half of the 19th century. Tönder Museum.

nate neighbours on the mainland and to surround themselves with the symbols of affluence, among which, during the period when the cattle-trade was brisk, tiles came to be counted.

A large number of men from the mainland, however, also took part in these voyages, either as crew or whalers. For this reason, tiles also penetrated as far as the districts of Ribe and Ringköbing. And it must be said in conclusion that the Danish islands of Manö and Fanö were also important centres of tile-decoration—but the tiles there were of later date.

There is no doubt that Tönder occupies a special position in the history of the exportation of tiles, as does, in its own fashion, north Friesland. It is surprising that the tradition here extends so far back, a fact that one would sooner have expected of Friedrichstadt on the Eider, in the preponderantly Dutch environment of Schleswig-Holstein. As is well known, this city was founded in 1621 by Dutch Protestants at the instigation of Duke Frederick III. No nothern city shows as many signs of Dutch influence as Friedrichstadt. Although Dutch influence on the structure remains unmistakable to this day, scarcely a single interior of the seventeenth century has survived. Only the impressive Friedrichstadt room in the Flensburg museum gives a hint of former grandeur. The tiles in Friedrichstadt, however, are all of later date. The assertion that "white Delft faience tiles" are to be found in every old house in Friedrichstadt and that they were a novelty at the time when the city was founded, is refuted by the material to hand. The tiles in the room in the Flensburg museum are of the late eighteenth century and there are no examples in Friedrichstadt of polychrome tiles, such as have been found, uniquely, in Koldenbüttel in Eiderstedt. In this case also, excavations or similar finds would have to be made before the possibility of a tradition of tile-decoration in the first half of the eighteenth century could be assumed. The asser-

Page 220: Wall faced with white and green azulejos in the church of the former convent of the Bom Jesus in Setúbal. This form of tile-decoration was very popular at the beginning of the 17th century.

Page 221 top: Decoration of a fountain in the Penha Verde at Sintra. Polychrome grotesques on a mother-of-pearl ground. Lisbon, dated 1631. Bottom: Continuous polychrome azulejo-compositions decorated the whole gallery of the Santo Amaro chapel at Lisbon. Lisbon, c. 1600.

Page 222 top: The walls of the church of S. Maria at Obidos are totally faced with tiles. Lisbon, c. 1685. Bottom: Wall faced with tiles in the church of São Roque at Lisbon. They are signed by Francisco de Matos and dated 1582.

Page 223 top: Singerie from the Leitão Collection. One of the tile-pictures which came from the Quinta da Viscondessa, of which another is today in the Museu do Azulejo, Lisbon. Lisbon, c. 1640. Bottom: Tile-picture of a halberdier on the staircase of the former palace of the Lisbon Patriarch at Tojal, near the capital. Similar figures line the ramp. A type called portier frequently found in the work of the Lisbon school. c. 1630–1650.

Page 224 top: Wall faced with blue and golden-yellow tiles which harmonise with the gilt carving. Church of the former monastery of Santa Maria at Almoster. Lisbon, c. 1630. Bottom: Tile-facing forming the antependium for an altar. Polychrome tiles inspired by oriental embroidery, with the Portuguese royal arms in the centre. Lisbon, c. 1650. Church of the former abbey of St. Theresa at Carnide near Lisbon.

Page 225 top: Garden of the palace of Marquês de Fronteira at Benfica, Lisbon. Pool of the knights with large tile-pictures of historical scenes on the surrounding walls. Lisbon, c. 1640. Bottom: The nave-walls of the church of Montes Guararapes in Recife, Brazil, are totally faced with azulejos patterned in blue and white. Imported from Lisbon, c. 1670.

tion that the use of tiles passed from the trading and seafaring circles to the farmhouses is thus untenable. In northern Schleswig it happened the other way round and along the rest of the coastal strip of Schleswig-Holstein the tradition did not set in until long after 1700. The tiles can not be said to represent "sunken cultural treasure."

From the point of view of trade, conditions on the mainland are not so interesting, but tiles are encountered everywhere where there were seafaring connections and where the Dutch had trading interests. A typical example is the county of Bentheim, where Vechta served as the link with Holland. The complaints, cited by Riesebieter, of the potters of Danzig, who lamented the fact that the ships which came to collect grain brought tiles from Friesland as ballast, is a further proof of the importance of the seaways in this branch of export.

The numerous tiled interiors have not fared happily in the course of time. Perhaps later interest in tiles as antiques has had more to do with robbing the old farmhouses of their noble wall-decorations than the desire for change and rebuilding. Thus, if we wish to experience the effect of the old tiles, we have largely to rely upon the reconstructions of tiled interiors in museums. In general they are to be found in the districts in which tiles were formerly of importance but there are also many which are far removed from their original surroundings. Such is the case, for example, of the Saxon farmhouse from Diepholz (Hanover), in the Germanisches Nationalmuseum in Nuremberg.[2] In the open-air museum at Sorgenfri near Copenhagen there are tiles from houses on Fanö, Römö, Ostenfeld, near Husum, and Eiderstedt, which, however – like a number of interiors from other northern parts in the Dansk Folkemuseum in Copenhagen – have been much restored. The most valuable are undoubtedly the small, local museums. The following may be selected from many: the King's Parlour on Hallig Hooge (265), the old Friesian house in Keitum on Sylt, and the *Kommandörgaard* of the National Museum in Toftum on Römö. The Ems country is represented by the Saxon house in the local museum in Lingen, the Altes Land, on the shores of the Elbe, by an Empire room from Jork in the museum at Altona; a marshlands room from Winsen in the Museum at Lüneburg also shows tile-pictures of shipping on the Elbe. Bentheim is represented by a kitchen in the Niedersächsisches Heimatmuseum at Hanover, and the Vierlande by a parlour from Kirchwärder in the Bomann Museum at Celle.

The richest interiors from the point of view of tiles are, however, in the museums at Altona, Schleswig and Flensburg. Thus, for example there is at Altona a room from Gross-Wisch near Wewelsfleth in the Wilster-marsch – the counterpart to the one from Urendorf in the Dansk Folkemuseum in Copenhagen – and one *(Marnestube)* from Kattrepel. Interiors from the Holstein Geest have been preserved: one from Todenbüttel at Altona, and one from Kellinghusen and Lohbarbeck in the Schleswig-Holstein Landesmuseum at Schleswig. And in conclusion two more interiors from Süderdithmarschen may be mentioned, both originally from Dingen, one now at Schleswig, the other at Meldorf. The most important tile-pictures are to be seen at

227

Flensburg and Schleswig, while single tiles in their manifold varieties – although removed from their rightful contexts – may be seen to best advantage at the Tönder Museum and at the Focke Museum at Bremen. The progress of the tile from its origins as a piece of utilitarian craftsmanship by way of mass-production to the status of museum exhibit has been long. Only in the present century have tiles been properly appreciated. They deserve to be valued perhaps not so much for their artistic qualities as for their sociological importance. Or, as it was so well put in a small article in the *Grafschafter Nachrichten* of 1960, "There was a 'European Economic Community'. Spontaneously and with no clear political guidance, an exchange of goods was developed, which was conditioned by natural demands and worked efficiently. Neighbouring peoples worked and lived side by side, with and for one another."

German and Danish Tile-Factories

The sentiments cited at the end of the preceding chapter were unfortunately vitiated by the fact that the neighbours lost no time in endeavouring to check the competition to which their primitive industries were subjected by the efficient Dutch faience factories. To do this they established, with the assistance of Dutch experts or of men who had been trained in Holland, a large number of factories in both Germany and Denmark; their aim was to produce – and this is characteristic – "Delft porcelain" or imitation porcelain "in the manner of Delft"; and they remained in existence for varying lengths of time.

In many respects, this meant the prelude to an important new development in the sphere of faience production; where tiles were concerned, however, none of these factories, as has already been stated, succeeded in rivalling the Dutch. One gains the impression everywhere that tiles played a very modest part in the programmes of the indigenous factories. Signed tiles are exceptional and in many cases we know only from the factory-archives what tiles were produced. Frequently the similarity between indigenous and Dutch tiles is so complete that it is impossible to distinguish the provenance.

To summarise the information available, the factories from which tiles have survived, or of which it is known or may be assumed that they produced tiles, are named below in chronological order of their founding. The dates are those of the founding of the factories but this does not necessarily mean that the factory in question produced tiles from the first.

FRANKFURT AM MAIN. 1666. Two-thousand tiles are mentioned in an inventory of the year 1693. These are probably the earliest German tiles known. Johann Kaspar Rib, so well-known in the history of German faience, who had learnt faience-painting in Delft, worked at Frankfurt from 1702 to 1708. There are records in the archives of tiles bearing paintings of horsemen, which are moreover said to have been exported to Holland.

BERLIN. 1678. After Frankfurt, it was the factories at Berlin and Potsdam which came most strongly under Dutch influence – to such a degree, indeed, that their wares have often been confused with Delft-ware. There are no records of tiles having been produced in the first factories; but it is probable that the third Berlin factory, and its associate factory in Rheinsberg, under the direction of Carl Friedrich Lüdicke, who had learnt his craft in Holland, were engaged in tile-production during the period between 1756 and 1779. Tiles are mentioned in the stock-list, but without more detailed description.

BRUNSWICK. 1707. Johann Kaspar Rib, mentioned above, and the Dutchman Daniel Kayck, whom we shall meet in Zerbst, were probably responsible for tile-production at Brunswick also. In the Städtisches Museum in Brunswick there are tiles in manganese and blue of the kind which occur at Rosenborg Castle and in the Dansk Folkemuseum (Boyken, fig. 11). They are traditionally Dutch. The date of these tiles is not known; if, however, the Rosenborg tiles are identical with those which were bought in 1737 for the Dutch kitchen, they are earlier than one would think at first glance.

DRESDEN. 1708. There is mention at the time when this factory was founded of a ceramist named Rüllener, who had been trained in Holland and was exclusively conversant with the art of tile-painting but who was dismissed because, in the year 1710, 20,000 tiles miscarried. He was, however, reinstated after acquiring a collaborator from Brunswick.

ANSBACH. 1710. We have here an example of a factory which was established comparatively early but did not until later acquire a tradition of tile-making. In 1763, 2,800 tiles, of which a few are signed and dated, were made for the Residence at Ansbach. These differ markedly from the Dutch tiles both in regard to their size and their decoration and may be considered the peak of original German tile-production (259). For further details, the reader is referred to Boyken who also cites tiles from Ansbach in the hunting-lodge of Gunzenhausen and in middle-class houses; they are not, however, of the same high quality. (Illustrations: Hüseler, fig. 296; Riesebieter, fig. 82; Boyken, figs. 17, 18).[1]

NUREMBERG. 1712. Johann Kaspar Rib, whom we have already mentioned more than once, was active here during 1712 and 1713.[2] The following year a series of tiles was produced for the dining-room at Schloss Favorite near Rastatt (Boyken, fig. 28), which were somewhat smaller than usual and very much like the Dutch tiles. Riesebieter (fig. 106) illustrates a tile signed with an R painted in bright enamel colours with a polychrome bunch of flowers in a baroque cartouche reserved on a purple ground; this tile belongs to the so-called *Hausmalerarbeiten*[3] but whether it comes from Nuremberg is doubtful.[4]

ERFURT. Signed Erfurt tiles of the period between 1728 and 1734 are known from the castles of Dornburg near Jena and Belvedere near Weimar. Help in dating them is provided by tiles bearing the monogram of Duke Ernst August and his first wife Wilhelmine Eleonore. Apart from these there are a few signed tiles. The Dutch prototypes are easily recognised, but there can be no question of confusing the Erfurt tiles with tiles of Dutch provenance, the differences in the corner-decorations and borders being among the most distinctive features. Hüseler says in this connection that attempts at localising tiles must be based on stylistic comparisons alone, but that such attempts can be suc-

cessful only in regions which, because of their position, were not involved in the importation of cheap Dutch tiles by water. In regions to which coastal shipping returned with Dutch tiles instead of ballast all competition was pointless.

ZERBST. 1721. This factory was founded by Johann Kaspar Rib in collaboration with the Dutchman Daniel Kayck of Delft. Thus it is no wonder that there is early mention of tiles being produced here. In the year 1723, 2,000 tiles for the pleasure palace were delivered to the duchess at Friederikenberg, exactly the same number as to the castle of Frederiksborg near Copenhagen. It is not known what these tiles were like; there must however, have been large and small ones, white ones, and ones with blue and brown powdered decoration. "Large quantities of them were lying a few years ago" in the cellar of the castle at Zerbst.

COPENHAGEN. 1722. Delfs Porselins-eller Hollandsch Steentöys Fabrique – this was the name of the first faience factory in Copenhagen with which, under the direction of the Holsteiner, Johan Wolf, newly come from Nuremberg, and with the collaboration of ceramists from Zerbst, faience-production was established in about 1724 in Denmark and at a later date in Sweden. Wolf, who had originally been a painter, had to leave Copenhagen on account of fraudulent practices and was succeeded by the Thuringian Johan Ernst Pfau. Although no tiles are known from the short period of Wolf's directorship, one may perhaps detect a connection between the tile-production at Zerbst and the somewhat later Copenhagen production. At all events, in 1735 "2000 tiles from the porcelain factory of this city" were produced at a cost of 33.2 Riksdalers for the "pancake kitchen" in the Frederiksborg palace near Copenhagen. And a year later 360 small tiles were supplied for the "Dutch kitchen" in the garden of the

Rosenborg Castle. These were possibly the tiles which were later incorporated in a privy by the tower at Rosenborg. The Copenhagen factory also supplied in the year 1737 "blue and white tiles in the Dutch style" for the hunting-lodge of Eremitage near Copenhagen. 133 Rdl. 2 Mk. 11 Sk. were paid for the consignment. Tiles similar to those known from Brunswick and from Rosenborg were also found in the middle-class houses in the vicinity of the factory and are now exhibited in the Dansk Folkemuseum. However, the production of tiles proved not to be a profitable concern in Copenhagen either.

WRISBERGHOLZEN. 1737. Some unusual tiles carrying proverbs (Boyken, fig. 15) date from the year 1749; they are in fact stove-tiles but were used as wall-tiles in the castle at Wrisbergholzen. The factory also, however, produced traditional tiles in the Dutch style, of which a signed one is known from the Heinsen property near Hamelin. (Boyken, fig. 16).

GÖPPINGEN. 1741. Christian Rupprecht, who was trained in Hamburg and Delft and who was connected with both Ansbach and Wrisbergholzen, stated in the year 1749 that he could produce, among other things, "small, square flags, otherwise called tiles", that the German factories were not as yet successfully geared to tile-production and that the Dutch in Rotterdam and Delft far surpassed them, since their costs were half as much; that tiles, however, were half the price of wall-paper. No tiles from Göppingen are, however, known.

HANNOVERSCH-MÜNDEN. 1746. Tiles are mentioned in a price-list of 1786. These are manganese-coloured biblical tiles and ornamental tiles in the Dutch as well as in a more original style, with different corner-decorations, in the museum at Münden[5] and in the Goethe-haus in Frankfurt.

GÖGGINGEN. 1749. Tiles for a cabinet in the castle of Dillingen are said to have been made here; they are, however, no longer in existence.

MAGDEBURG. 1754. In this year, two years before the actual foundation of the Magdeburg factory, the proprietor, Johann Philipp Guichard, is said to have made small tiles in the Dutch style. Riesebieter's collection included tiles from Magdeburg in manganese-purple and green, signed with the M mark.

SCHLESWIG. 1755. It is stated in the Copenhagen directory for 1787 that a man from Schleswig arrived in Copenhagen with blue, white and purple earthenware including small tiles. In the year 1800 one hundred tiles cost 2 Reichsthalers. It has not so far been possible to establish which tiles these were. It is worthy of note that as early as 1770 the selling and offering for sale of foreign wares such as "English, Friesian, Stettin, Delft and others of the same kind, whatever they may be called, as also the Dutch wall-stones or so-called clinkers" was prohibited and the decree was repeated five years later. This establishes beyond doubt that the Friesian wares represented a considerable import and it was probably impossible to sustain this prohibition.

RHEINSBERG. 1762. Under the directorship of the former Berlin faience manufacturer Carl Friedrich Lüdicke, this factory delivered in the year 1776 a consignment of tiles to the Empress Catherine II of Russia for the *salon* at the Admiralty at St. Petersburg. The Empress mentioned in a letter the "*épreuves de jolies* (sic) *carreaux de porcelaine.*"

KELLINGHUSEN. 1763. It has already been stressed elsewhere that the superiority of the Dutch tiles was marked by the fact that the six factories in Kellinghusen near Itzehoe, otherwise so productive, failed to

233

Faience factories in Germany and Denmark in which tiles were produced.

Representation of a sailing-boat on a Kellinghusen faience plaque. c. 1800. Schleswig-Holstein Landesmuseum, Schleswig.

assert their influence upon the interiors of the houses in the surrounding marsh country. It is true that comparatively large numbers of tiles clearly attributable to Kellinghusen are still in existence in the district, but at no time were they as widespread as the other Kellinghusen faience. Dutch models were, in part, directly imitated, as, for example, in the case of the so-called *rosesterren* and perhaps also the composite stars in blue and manganese; the most interesting, however, are the typical Kellinghusen tiles which, in contrast to the Dutch, were made without pounced patterns and with lobed leaves as corner-ornaments. There are also polychrome tiles in the characteristic Kellinghusen colours of yellow and green, in the same style as the dishes. The most famous is "Dr. Grauer's room" of about 1775 which is now in the Schleswig-Holstein Landesmuseum (260). Thanks to excavations of faience in Kellinghusen it has been possible to determine the special characteristics of the various factories. During these excavations in the autumn of 1953 there were found among other things a number of vine-tendril tiles which have not yet been attributed to any factory. An interior with a character of its own is a room from the Altdeutscher Gasthof on the Störbrücke in the Schleswig-Holstein Landesmuseum, where there is yet another room set up with tiles from Kellinghusen.

HUBERTUSBURG. 1770. In the deed of concession granted to the famous faience painter from Kiel, Johann Samuel Friedrich Tännich, "wall-tiles and stove-tiles of all kinds" are mentioned but until now no tiles have been traced either to Kiel or to Hubertusburg.

It must be assumed that other German and Danish faience factories also produced tiles. In Wittmund, for example, there is mention in 1798 of a factory making tobacco-pipes and plaster flooring. Tännich stayed here and in Jever, where Sebastian Heinrich Kirch also

lived for a time before going to Kellinghusen, and both were men with experience in the production of tiles. But the Dutch competition was too close at hand and the Dutch system of production worked too well for there to be possibilities of survival for concerns of this kind, in spite of the import prohibition in East Fries-

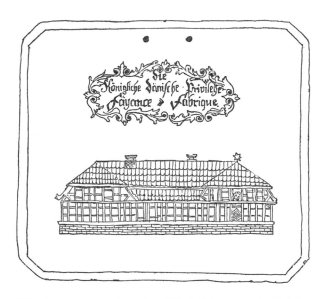

Tile-plaque representing the "Königliche Dänische Privilege Fäyance-Fabrique" in Kellinghusen. c. 1800. Schleswig-Holstein-Landesmuseum, Schleswig.

land in the year 1769. There are also records of faience tiles decorated in blue on the island of Mors in north Jutland.

From the point of view of sales, it can be said in general that tile-manufacture in Germany and Denmark was a fiasco, although in certain cases it was artistically superior to the Dutch.

The imitations of Dutch tiles which were produced in the Black Forest are more provincial than the Kellinghusen faience. They are often so clumsily painted that one might think that oil-colour had been used. Animals

Opposite left: Gastronomic motifs in manganese in a kitchen of the palace of the Correio-Mór (postmaster-general) in Loures. The hanging hams provide a most unusual touch. Lisbon workshop, c. 1730. Right: Blue azulejos *showing busts, characteristic of the Oporto school. c. 1680. This detail comes from the former São Lázaro Museum in Oporto.*

Page 238 top: Vault of the parish church at São Lourenso de Almancil, Algarve. The ceiling painting is by Policarpo de Oliveira Bernades. Dated 1720. Bottom: The Birth of Christ, a tile-picture attributed to Antonio de Oliveira Bernades of Lisbon. Dated

1711. The colouring is a strong blue. The picture comes from the chapel of the Virgin Mary at Peninha in the Serra de Sintra.

Page 239: Detail of the light-blue tile-facing of the nave, chapels and choir of the church of the Canons of St. John the Evangelist at Arraiolos. From the workshop of Gabriel del Barco. Dated 1700.

Page 240: Crucifixion. One of the fourteen tile-pictures of the high altar of the Convento de Nossa Senhora da Esperança at Ponta Delgada on the island of São Miguel in the Azores. Lisbon, signed by Oliveira Bernades and dated 1712.

were among the most popular motifs in the Nagold valley and in Raeren on the lower Rhine. Emigrants took these industries to America; this accounts for the German pottery in Pennsylvania, which locally is wrongly called "Pennsylvania Dutch pottery" and of which there are examples in the Pennsylvanian Museum at Philadelphia. The confusion arose from the fact that the German emigrants called their native wares "deutsch", which was understood by the Americans as "Dutch". The wall-tiles from Schloss Bedheim at Ummenstädt near Meiningen, are extremely attractive with their brown figures in green grass on a light-yellow ground. The goats and the birds on perches are painted in a particularly lively fashion and might be regarded as the very distant relations of the Dutch animals of the sixteenth and seventeenth century.

In the Cologne district during the first half of the eighteenth century many polychrome tiles were given a transparent glaze; they have been known since the middle of the eighteenth century by the name of Marburg tiles. Dutch tiles were their antecedents, as may be seen from the landscapes, biblical scenes and cavaliers. But there are also birds and other beasts, travelling packmen and much else which is reminiscent of the Ansbach manufacture, to which, presumably, Cassel gave the stimulus. The Marburg tiles stemmed from country handcrafts. The lively manner in which the movements of the horses and their riders are presented is extremely attractive. In about 1789 a certain Burkhard Keppler made a name for himself. The Marburg tiles were used specially for wall-facings behind stoves.

Particularly valuable from the artistic point of view are the porcelain tiles from the Meissen factory, with specimens of which the walls of a bathroom at Schloss Brühl at Pforten are faced. The motifs are little bunches of flowers and *fleurs semées.* Other German porcelain factories too produced tiles to order.

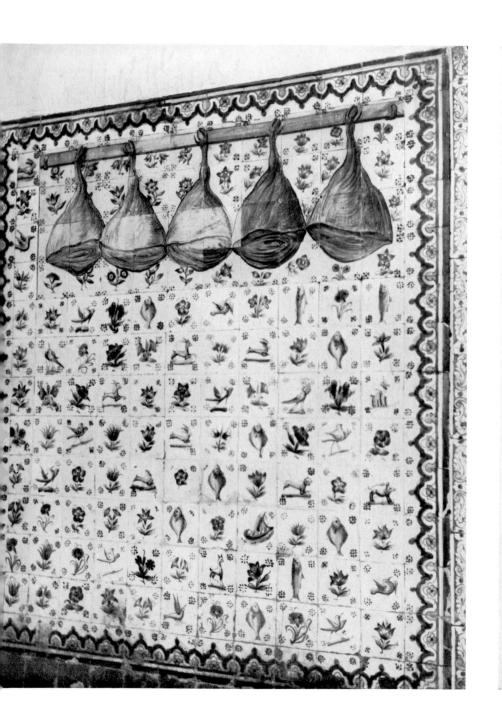

Materials and Methods of Production

It is unfortunately impossible for a study of the production of tiles to be anything but incomplete. There are two main reasons for this. The first is that no early documents relating to the making of tiles have survived —if, indeed, they ever existed. The second reason lies in the fact of the enormous variety of types in which tiles occur, which makes it impracticable within the framework of one chapter to go deeply into the details of every type. In the hope of making a clear survey, we shall therefore explain the technique of tile-production according to the manner of their manufacture, as demonstrated in the table on p. 242.

Since, however, in the course of time, the manufacture of tiles came to be closely connected with the manufacture of pottery in general and of faience in particular and was undertaken in conjunction with these, the obvious course in describing the technique of tile-manufacture is to refer to the manufacture of faience, of which certain evidence has survived.

The earliest account is that of Abulqasim, written in the year 1301, and deals with the manufacture of faience at Kashan in Persia.[1] The next is the much quoted work of Piccolpasso on the manufacture of maiolica in Italy, which appeared in 1556.[2] The third, issued in the year 1794, is by Gerrit Paape and describes the work of the *Delftsch aardewerkmaaker*.[3] Although nearly two hundred and fifty years elapsed between the appearance of each of these works, little had changed during the whole of this period. And what is true of table-ware, will undoubtedly have held good for the generally simpler methods of producing tiles.

Now, these methods of production should not be understood too literally, for the divisions adopted in the earlier chapters based on appearances take virtually no account of the actual procedure which is the shaping of the tile, but nearly always concentrate on the enrichment of the surface, which, in fact, forms only the last phase in the process of production.

The first thing to do, therefore, in describing the technique is to deal with the many questions which are common to the manufacture of almost all tiles and subsequently to go into the particularities of the decorative techniques. This will be found to tie up with the table, the main division of which is based on the number of firing processes which were required to give proper value to the enrichment of the surface, that is, the refining process. A further division has its basis in the nature of the materials, such as clay (slip), glazes, coloured or uncoloured, transparent or opaque and so on, used to enrich the surface. It must be said that not every tile manufactured can be fitted into this diagram, for there are specimens which belong to more than one group. Thus, for example, we have tiles which are partly glazed and partly unglazed; other tiles have both transparent and opaque glazes; others again are partly treated in underglaze and partly in on-glaze techniques; lustre is to be found both on transparent and opaque glazes. But for the sake of a clear survey all these small variations have been omitted from our table.

TYPES OF CLAY
AND THEIR COMPOSITIONS

With very few exceptions, clay is the raw material from which tiles are made; it is produced by the decomposition of rocks. Clay is very seldom found free of other minerals, being most frequently mixed with quartz or sand (SiO_2). After the sand has been removed by washing, the clay remains in its purest form as kaolin, an aluminum silicate ($Al_2O_3 . 2SiO_2 . 2H_2O$). This silicate is called clay-substance. Its special property is its plasticity; this means that, when the clay has been worked into a paste with water, it retains whatever form it has been given even after the added

241

CLASSIFICATION OF TILES ACCORDING TO METHODS OF DECORATION

	Basis	Material applied
One firing		None
	Unfired tile	Colourless transparent glaze
		Coloured transparent glaze

	Slip	Colourless transparent glaze
		    Cracknel (or poured slip) technique
		    Sgraffito technique
		    Sgraffiato technique
		    Inlay technique

		Coloured transparent glaze
Two firings	Fired tile	Colourless transparent glaze
		Pigment coated with colourless transparent glaze
		Coloured transparent glaze
		Opaque (white) glaze
		Opaque (white) glaze with pigments applied
Three firings	Glaze on wares which have been fired twice	Metals Gold Metallic compounds Lustre
		Pigments *Petit feu* (enamels)

water has disappeared by evaporation. Usually, however, the mined clay contains other minerals as well as quartz, such as feldspar, mica, lime, ferric oxides, and organic materials.

The clays are divided into those which are mined at the sites where they were formed, called primary clays, and those which have been carried by water and deposited elsewhere, called secondary clays. These latter have in the course of their movement attracted many other minerals and are the most strongly adulterated; examples are sea- and river-clay.

Although the clay-substance forms the plastic component of the clay, a very high percentage of clay-substance does not always make for the most plastic clay. On the contrary, pure kaolin, for example, almost exclusively clay-substance, is much less plastic than many clays with a lower substance-content. It is, in fact, not only the chemical composition which is decisive in determining the degree of plasticity, but rather physical properties such as shape and size of the particles. A less plastic clay needs less water in the shaping process and when dry produces a less cohesive whole. These clays are called lean; they show only slight shrinkage when dry.

Plastic clays need more water to make them suitable for working and when dry produce a brittle substance; these clays are called fat; they shrink much more considerably when dry and are much more susceptible to being distorted or split if too quickly dried.

It is certainly remarkable that clay played only a subordinate part in the earliest Egyptian tiles. The body of most Egyptian ceramics consists, in fact, mainly of sand quartz with very little clay and some alkalis, as was shown by an analysis[4] carried out by Le Chatelier in 1899.

When the clay used contains a certain percentage of iron, the colour will be red when it has hardened in the fire. When lime is also present, the colour will be reddish, ochre or even yellow, according to the amount of lime in proportion to the iron. In applying the covering tin-glaze so frequently used in tiles, it is necessary to have about 25% calcium carbonate in the body in order to guarantee that the glaze adheres well and without crazing to the clay. We know in the case of a certain Persian clay that this lime content was indeed present;[5] whether this was also so in Italy is not known. Where, however, as in the Netherlands, the available clay contained insufficient lime, marl was added to raise the lime content and a strongly calcareous clay was produced. This discovery was probably not made until later: most of the vessels and tiles of the early seventeenth century have a red body and only the later ones are yellow. Paape in 1794 names Tournai earth, a Belgian marl, as one of the components of Delft clay. This raw material was used at Makkum as early as 1716.[6]

MINING THE CLAY

Although exceptional cases are known when, in earlier times, clay for making ceramic wares was brought from a great distance, it is generally assumed that the potter used the clay available in his immediate neighbourhood. In other words, the ceramic trade developed principally in places where suitable raw materials were obtainable. These were then usually mined by simple methods, being dug out of deposits lying at no great depth.

Abulqasim in his writings describes only the origin and mining of his raw materials. Piccolpasso, however, describes two methods of raising the raw material used in Italy. By the first method, the clay was simply dug out of the river-beds after the rainy season, when the river had brought the clay down from the mountains. The second method consisted in digging trenches one behind

Opposite top: Detail from a tile-picture from the church of the
Convento da Graça, the former Augustinian monastery at Torres
Vedras. It shows the arrival in Goa in September 1595, a scene from
the life of the Archbishop of Goa, Dom Aleixo de Menezes. Lisbon,
workshop of a pupil of Bernades. Bottom: Decorative composition
in blue, with the arms of the Caldura family in the chapel of the
Quinta das Centieiras in Abrantes. Lisbon, c. 1740.

Page 246 top: Naked men fighting a duel, greyish-blue decoration
of a salon in the bishop's palace at Viseu. Coimbra, c. 1745.
Bottom: Bull-fight in bright blue. Detail of the decoration of a
salon in the palace of the Correio-Mór (postmaster-general) at
Loures. Lisbon. c. 1730–1740.

the other in the river-bank and joining them by means of small canals. This was done during the dry season; when the rains set in, the river water flowed fairly sluggishly through the system of trenches, so that the clay it brought with it sank to the bottom. When the rains ceased, the clay could be lifted and the trenches made ready for the next season.

In the Netherlands it was diluvial sea-clay which was most often used and sometimes also river-clay.

PREPARATION OF THE CLAY

The preparation of the clay mass is simple when the clay can be used as it was found, with admixture of water only. When the clay is too dry to be worked, it is necessary only to add water and to work the clay. If the clay has to be mixed with other minerals, it is difficult to achieve a perfect mixture "dry". In the fracture of the old tiles, it is sometimes possible to tell from the variations in the colour of the body that the mixing has not been a complete success. In the Netherlands at a later period, presumably specially for the benefit of the table-ware production, this was obviated by washing the clay, in the way that Paape describes. In the Netherlands the strongly calcareous clay which was used in other countries – Persia, for example – was not available. It was therefore important for the Dutch factories that, in order to increase the lime content, Tournai earth should be well mixed with the clay mined locally. According to Paape, this washing was done by the clay-washer on a piece of land outside the city. He would stir the raw clay in a wooden vessel until it formed a slip. This slip was then sieved to free it of sand and dirt. It was then run into water-troughs in which first the solid particles sank to the bottom and afterwards the clay dried. When it had been sufficiently dried, the layers of clay were cut into rectangular

pieces, which at a later stage were stored in a cellar which was kept damp so that they might begeren or "yearn", that is to say, achieve an even distribution of humidity, and "sour", which increased the plasticity. Since this whole process could only be undertaken in the summer, it was the responsibility of the clay-washer to see that the quantity of washed clay at the end of the summer was at least large enough to last until the next washing season.

During the process of sinking in the troughs the material became separated, the coarser particles sinking more quickly than the finer. For this reason in the factory at a later stage the clay was kneaded and mixed in a flat pan by the clay-treader, who walked up and down barefoot in the clay, adding water as it was required. Such was, according to Paape, the customary method of work at Delft in 1784. It should, however, be noted that the tile-picture of 1737 giving a schematic representation of the Bolsward factory shows this work being done by a vertical clay-cutter driven by a horse. The blades on the vertical axle stir and blend the clay (214). Ottema[7] points out that on the 15 May 1635 the states of Friesland granted a patent for this apparatus, which was at that time used in the brick kilns.

A special method of preparation was doubtless required for the Egyptian quartz fritwares mentioned above. This body absorbs water very easily but a substance containing 90% quartz, however fine-grained it may be, is so "lean" that it is not only extraordinarily difficult to give it the desired form but also to preserve its form when it is dry. An article published by Lucas in 1936[8] shows how it is possible to do this in spite of the difficulties. He came to the conclusion that a certain percentage of common salt must have been dissolved in the mixing water which gave the body sufficient firmness when it was dried, but which partly evaporated during firing, so that analysis reveals, in the form of sodium, only a part of the salt which was originally

244

present. This part combined with quartz and the glass-substance which resulted served to produce a "fired" object.

SHAPING THE CLAY: RELIEF

The most obvious way of shaping the clay consisted of banging out a piece of clay with the hand to make a flat slab, from which, with the help of a knife and a wooden block, the tile was cut to the desired shape and size. A tile is usually square, but examples in the shape of diamonds, oblongs, triangles, hexagons, hexagons with two parallel sides double the length of the other sides, octagons and eight-pointed stars, with pointed crosses to place between them, are all known.

Decoration in the form of relief can also be executed at the time when the tile is shaped. The relief can be fixed to the underside of the wooden block and impressed upon the soft tile. Since in the process the soft clay would always spread outwards, it is essential to enclose the tile in a frame. This led to a method by which the piece of clay, after it had been roughly shaped, was rolled with a wooden roller, in the early days into a wooden frame and later into an iron one, and afterwards removed from the frame. In this way whatever was desired in the way of more complex shapes could be produced without much trouble. This method was also used in the case of tiles without relief.

We will leave the other shapes out of account and in describing the further processes of manufacture restrict ourselves to square tiles and in particular to the methods used in Friesland.

After the tile has been removed from the frame it is laid on a board, which, when it is full, is placed on a stand to dry. As soon as the tiles are partly dry, they are all turned through an angle of 90°, so that the edges which were lying on the board close to one another and

so could not dry sufficiently now lie free, and vice versa. When the tiles are dry enough not to stick to one another, they are stacked fronts to backs and "put in the corner" to allow them to *begeren* or "yearn" so that the humidity is distributed as evenly as possible. When this process has gone far enough, the tiles are removed from the corner and rolled. They are then laid, their sand-free front sides uppermost, upon a heavy wooden plank covered with lead with two parallel laths about 15 cm. apart following the length of the plank and fixed to the lead. The tile-maker now rolls a greased lead roller sheathed with copper over the tiles, usually twice backwards and forwards, to smooth the surface. The tiles are again stacked and put into another corner. They have to dry further ready for the next process, that of cutting.

In order to cut them, the tile-maker lays out a few tiles on his bench, takes a small square board edged with iron in his left hand and puts it on a tile, using it to draw the tile towards himself; in his right hand he holds a long cutting knife which is set in a haft down its whole length. With this knife he makes a vertical cutting movement along the cutting-board and then turns board and tile three times through an angle of 90° until all four edges have been cut. The pieces that have been cut off go back to the clay-cutter and the tiles are then laid in stacks of thirty round the kiln chimney to dry (214).

The rolling process was not originally a part of tile-making, early tiles being much less flat than the later ones; but by about 1700 we already find rollers in a factory inventory, which shows that by that time at any rate they had been introduced.[6]

The cutting-board appears at the beginning to have had a copper nail in opposite corners of its underside; this made a small hole in the surface of the leather-hard tile which remained visible even after the tile was finished. It was doubtless discovered that two diagonally placed nails sufficed to prevent the tile and cutting board slipping when they were turned. In the end it was found to be equally satisfactory with no nail at all, provided that the tile and cutting board were flat enough. The presence or absence of these holes is thus some indication of the age of the tiles. The thickness of the tiles must also be mentioned in this connection. Since it was evolved from the floor-tile, the wall-tile was originally about 2 cm. thick but in the course of time diminished to about 6 mm.

RELIEF

According to Forrer[9] two techniques were used to produce relief. One consisted of carving the relief in negative in the bottom of a moulding box, pressing the clay into the box and flattening it. The moulding box with the tile in it was then tipped up on to a board so that the tile fell out. When it was dry enough, the edges could be smoothed off, after which it was further dried and finally fired. Moulding boxes of this kind were made either of wood or of clay and, if of the latter, were fired before they could be used. By the other method, the tiles were shaped in a wooden frame, were laid on a plank strewn with sand and smoothed. After this, the relief was applied with one or more decorative stamps to the front surface while the tile was still in the frame and the frame was then removed.

Neither of these two techniques, however, is suitable for use when the relief becomes extensive and takes on the nature of a piece of sculpture, as is the case with certain early Persian tiles; or when the relief includes angles of more than 90⁰ to the surface of the tile. In this case, the leather-hard surface of the tile has to be worked with knives, wire loops and similar modelling tools. Each tile or each unit of decoration thus became a piece of handmade sculpture.

DECORATION OF TILES REQUIRING A SINGLE FIRING

Something has already been said about the techniques of decoration in the previous section dealing with the execution of relief as a part of the process of shaping the tile. We know that once-fired flat tiles as well as tiles with reliefs as the only form of surface-enrichment were extremely popular in Europe between 1300 and 1500.[10]

Both these types of tiles could be glazed before they were fired and, in the firing, acquire their glassy coating. This glaze was a simple lead-glaze consisting of a mixture of clay and lead sulphide suspended in water. This technique of lead-glazing was doubtless taken from the manufacture of floor-tiles or paving-stones. The production of these paving-stones preceded that of wall-tiles by many years and the production of wall-tiles made according to the same techniques followed directly upon it. Two stone marbles were used to control the correct composition of the glazes. One served to test the specific gravity and thus the relative quantities of lead ore and clay. The other served to test the viscosity, which depended on the relative quantities of glaze and water. This viscosity was a decisive factor in determining the thickness of the layer which remained on the tile when it was glazed.

The lead-glaze is transparent but usually has a light-yellow tinge in consequence of the presence of impurities, among which are iron compounds. Spanish lead ore was reputed to be the best. It was possible by mixing to produce colours other than yellow. Copper oxide was used to produce green, manganese to produce black. Obviously clay which had been turned red by firing was no suitable ground for the colours yellow and green, so that we find this clay used only as a background for the transparent and black glazes. For the colours yellow and green a layer of clay was used which, after firing, had a white, or at least a light, colour. Before this tile was glazed the creamy clay mixture, called slip, was applied and then glazed. By this means, four colours could be used in this particular technique: red and black (glaze on red clay) and yellow and green (glaze on slip).

The slip did not, however, serve only as a ground: certain decorative techniques are based on the different colours to which slip and tile will fire.

TRAILED SLIP TECHNIQUE. It is possible, instead of covering the whole tile with slip, to use the mixture to apply figures to the background, just as the pastrycook decorates his wares with sugar or cream.

SGRAFFITO TECHNIQUE. According to this process, the whole tile was covered with slip and lines scratched with a pointed tool in the coating of slip, through which the colour of the undercoat could be seen.

SGRAFFIATO TECHNIQUE is a variation of the foregoing. It consists in scratching not only lines but removing larger parts of the slip, producing light decoration on a dark ground or vice versa.

INLAY TECHNIQUE. The starting-point here was a tile with a counter-relief, the sunken areas of which were filled with slip.

In all these cases a single firing was sufficient, since the tile, together with the layer of slip, if present, could simply be coated with lead-glaze and then fired.

Further variations could be achieved by colouring the slip and using it in different combinations.

This exhausts the possibilities which can be achieved by a single firing of the tiles. In order to produce subtler results, the tiles must be fired twice or sometimes even three times.

THE KILN: FIRING.

The kiln is a simple, oblong chamber furnace. Below the area in which the wares to be fired are stacked, the furnace, is the fire-place, roofed with a gently curving vault which supports the floor of the furnace. The furnace is roofed with a similar vault, which is sometimes flattened on top. The fire-place is connected with the furnace by holes in the vault. The fire which burns in the fire-place rises through these holes into the furnace and escapes through similar holes in the upper vault.

In the southern countries, the kiln usually stood outside the factory building, perhaps under a pent-house, as is shown by the drawing in Piccolpasso's manuscript (fol. 35). In the countries of western Europe it was customary to set up the kiln inside the factory building and for this reason it was necessary to equip the kiln with a tapering chimney which rose above the buildings. Such a kiln is illustrated in the tile-picture of the Bolsward factory (214).

The kiln was heated with wood which was thrown into the fire-place through a "mouth" or stoke-hole which was in the short side of the lower part of the oblong. Above the mouth is the "door", which gives access to the upper chamber, and which, during firing, is walled in with stones and smeared with clay. In the chimney immediately above the vault of the furnace, there is an arched observation hole through which, during the final phase of firing, it can be ascertained that all holes are "burning" well or, in other words, that the flames are rising properly. This is necessary in order to achieve the required temperature of about 1000^0 centigrade.

Wood seems always to have been the usual fuel in Egypt, Persia and Italy. Piccolpasso writes: "…light the fire, which with well dried wood should be made up very gently for about four hours, and afterwards let it be increased but with caution, because, if the fire becomes too fierce, ...the wares will warp and become *frogni* (overfired) ...and keep the fire so that the kiln appears white, that is, all flame, and when it has had about twelve hours' fire, it ought in reason to be done. Also you should know that at about the sixth hour the embers of all the wood that has been burnt will be found at the mouth of the kiln; then take that implement called the *caccia bragie*, which is a board a palm wide and two long pierced through the middle, stuck at the end of a pole. With this ...the embers are thrust over to the back wall, scattering them well on all sides; this being done the wood is gathered up in the fire which is made up as at first. Let there not be made, however, so great a pile of wood as to block up the mouth of the kiln, but follow this plan that there always remain open an aperture of about a palm's breadth. When it is finished let down the fire, and within an hour, if it appears cool enough, draw off all the embers from underneath..."[11]. This quotation shows that the firing process has changed little compared with the old practices still known to us in Friesland. The noticeably short firing time of eighteen hours mentioned by Piccolpasso compared with the thirty-six hours customary in Friesland may be explained by the much smaller size of his furnace, which was only six foot long, five foot broad, four foot high at the edges and six foot high at the centre of the vault.

When the stoker thinks that the furnace is nearly "ready", he draws out a few tiles which were put in expressly as test-pieces through a temporary opening in the furnace door. It depends on the evidence of this "draw-tile" whether he decides to stoke the furnace further or not. If he decides not to do so, he allows the fuel to burn almost through, shuts the mouth, walls it up, then uncovers the holes in the roof.

After the furnace has been left for a few days to cool, it is emptied and further work on the tiles proceeds. The filling of a furnace with tiles which need to be fired only once does not, in fact, involve any special arrangements. It is otherwise with the filling of furnaces in which tiles are going to be fired simultaneously some for the first and some for the second time. Following again the method of work practised in Friesland, the unfired tiles are stacked one on top of the other on the floor of the furnace and against the walls with a little space between the stacks so that the flames can lick round them. They are the least vulnerable and are exposed to the highest temperature, which is essential for a good product.

Above these are placed, back to back in pairs, the tiles which are being fired for the second time: it is important that only the backs should touch one another. The upper layer of the unfired tiles which are lying on the floor of the furnace is now covered with tiles which have already been fired once. Between the stacks of unfired tiles placed against the side-walls are laid two thin rolls of clay. The kiln-filler presses one edge of each of the glazed tiles arranged in pairs into the roll of clay so that they stand upright. On the upper edges he lays two more rolls of clay into which he fixes the "roofing stones" which at the same time become the floor of the next storey. Thus he forms a "range".

From the bottom upwards these "ranges", together with the unfired tiles, form a *rode* or rod and four *roden* form a *boog* or arch. A *boog* of this kind occupies a quarter of the floorspace of the furnace, separated by paths for the fire, through which the flames lick. When the tiles are put in, care is taken to stand the white tiles in the lowest ranges and in the outermost *roden* of the *boog*; thus leaving the most favourable position to the decorated tiles.

Since the layer of glaze is somewhat thicker on the side of the tile on which the glaze has run down from the tile into the tub, care is taken to place these edges uppermost in the furnace. These "heavy edges" are then evened off after firing.

Every kiln holds more unfired than glazed tiles because it must be assumed that a certain number of tiles will be unusable, so that, whatever happens, there are enough biscuit tiles for the next filling of the furnace. The number of tiles per furnace varies according to size between 16,000 and 30,000 flat tiles. Thus there are in the furnace altogether between about 35,000 and 65,000 unfired and flat tiles – assuming that it is only tiles which are being fired.

DECORATION OF TILES
REQUIRING TWO FIRINGS

It is a sign of great technical skill that such outstanding results were achieved in antiquity with the primitive means and imperfect chemical knowledge which were then available. Several thousand years before the beginning of our era the Egyptians were already producing magnificent blue colours. They used, however, not cobalt but copper compounds, as emerged from an analysis by J. Clifford made on behalf of A. Lucas who has devoted an exhaustive study and many experiments to ancient Egyptian and Mesopotamian ceramics.[8] This glaze consists of 75% quartz (sand), 20% oxides of potassium, sodium and calcium, 1.8% copper oxide and certain other compounds, none of which exceeds 1%. Because of its high coefficient of expansion this blue, strongly alkaline, glaze was excellently suited to a body so rich in quartz.

If the colour of the body was not light enough, a white slip was first applied in order to sustain light blue; sometimes also a part of the upper surface was covered with slip in order to produce a contrast of darker and lighter blue. If the white covering layer of clay was used in this case as a ground for the glaze, it was possible in principle to use the slip as a ground for polychrome decoration executed with a brush, even if the decoration thus produced could not be of any great delicacy. A more suitable ground was a white covering glaze, which could be worked in the maiolica or faience technique. According to this technique, once-fired objects, which were porous and made of clay which did not fire white, were given an opaque glaze, often with a high tin content; then, if decoration were required, it was applied to the unfired glaze and fused with it in the course of a second firing. Details of this method of production will be described in terms of the methods current in Friesland which, for practical purposes, are entirely similar to those of Piccolpasso and differ from those Abulqasim only in a few inessential points.

PREPARATION OF THE CALCINATION
FURNACE

The production of the tin-glaze for the maiolica technique is a fairly complicated procedure, requiring special plant. By simplifying the question somewhat, we may describe tin-glaze as a transparent lead-glaze to which tin is added to make the glaze white and opaque. Lead and tin are fused in the calcination furnace. This alloy is calcined, that is to say, it oxydises and becomes "tin-ashes". Three parts lead and one part tin are usually employed. Since tin is expensive, the proportions have from time to time been altered, but they cannot be reduced beyond four parts lead to one part tin, since the glaze would then be insufficiently opaque. Having discussed the proportion 3:1, Abulqasim writes, "...and if a more full-bodied and better glaze is desired, then take tin to as much as half" – that is, two parts lead to one part tin.

Over a long period, the calcination-furnace probably had a flat, oblong floor, sloping upwards a little towards the

255

back, with a flat-arched roof parallel with the long sides of the oblong. The furnace is heated with wood behind the pan. At the front of the pan, above the arched roof, stands a chimney so that the flames strike over the pan. The lead is pushed into the pan through an arched opening a little above the floor in the back wall of the chimney. The correct amount of tin is added to the melted lead to force the melting process of the tin, which melts less easily than the lead; to help the process further, the metal is stirred from time to time. Once the metals are melted, the temperature is raised and the upper surface of the molten alloy begins to oxydise. The lighter oxide floats on top of the alloy and is pushed towards the back wall at the highest point of the furnace floor, on which there is no alloy. When enough alloy or ash has accumulated, it is removed with a long-handled scoop. This is repeated until the whole of the alloy has been transformed into ash.

When it has cooled, the ash is passed through a revolving sieve and rid of incompletely oxidised and coarser components. The finely sieved ash is used for first-quality glaze, the rest for poorer quality.

The other component of tin-glaze is the so-called *masticot*. This *masticot* or, as Piccolpasso calls it, *marzacotto*, is produced in the large furnace which has been described above by burning white sand and soda or potash or both together on the floor of the fireplace. *Masticot* was also known in Persia as a special ingredient. There, however, it was prepared in a separate furnace and its composition comprised less sand and more potash, with which a complete fusion was achieved. The fused product was scooped out of the furnace with an iron spoon and cooled off in water. When it was suddenly cooled, the molten material spattered in all directions, which meant that it could be broken up more easily.

Finally, the tin-ashes and the finely crushed *masticot* are mixed with salt and potash and fired on the floor of the fire-place of the large furnace so that they combine to form a white cake of glass about 8 cm. thick. After the furnace has been cooled, the cakes of glass are broken into large pieces and the sand, which was strewn on the glaze-mass to prevent it sticking to the floor of the furnace and which has now been baked on, is scraped off. The large lumps are crushed to grit and poured with water into tubs. These tubs are half-wooden vats set in the floor with a large hollowed-out block as bottom. A stone which has been rounded on one side to fit the hollow is laid upon it. This stone is moved by mechanical tackle, but in former times it was turned by horse-power.

The whole apparatus, comprising a number of tubs set in a circle, can be seen in the illustration of the Bolsward factory (214), at the bottom on the right, next to the furnace. The grit is ground in the tubs to a fine powder. The resultant sludge is scooped out and put into a wooden tub.

GLAZING OR "GIVING"

The "rough" tiles which have been taken from the furnace, having been once fired are called "biscuit". These are now sounded. That is to say, they are tapped one by one in quick time with a small fragment of tile; the sound produced indicates whether the tile is perfect or cracked – which is often impossible to tell by looking.

After this, dust and loose sand are wiped off. Then follows a short immersion in water, the so-called "baptism", the purpose of which is to prevent the extremely dry, porous tile absorbing too much water from the glaze, which would produce too thick a layer of glaze. When it is "given" or glazed, therefore, the tile is already half saturated with water. The "baptiser" lays the tiles down on the left of the "giver", who takes them up one at a time in one hand and, with the front edge pointing obliquely downwards, holds them over the tub containing the liquid glaze, while, with a small basin in the other hand, he twice pours the glaze over the upper surface of the tile, covering it completely. He then lays the tile glazed side uppermost on a drainer. The tile still absorbs from the liquid glaze so much water that the *opkapper* can in a few minutes stack the tiles twenty-five at a time on *kappen* or "roofs".

Finally the *spatser* removes with a knife the glaze which has run down one side of the tile. Those tiles which are not going to be decorated are now ready for the second firing.

COLOURING AND PAINTING

Although the transparent glaze, *kwaart*, is used for other purposes as well, it may be included among the painter's raw materials. *Kwaart* is similar in composition to the white glaze, although it contains no tin oxide. The method of production is also similar except for the process of oxidisation in the ash-furnace. Since there is no addition of tin, lead is added to the mixture in a different way, usually as red lead. *Kwaart* acts as a flux in the painter's colours for otherwise these would require too high a firing temperature.

The different pigments for the painter are for the most part produced in exactly the same way as the glaze, the tin oxide being replaced by the pigment: for blue a cobalt compound, either smalt or zaffre, is used; for violet brownstone, a manganese compound; for yellow an antimony compound; for red, bolus, an iron compound.

These colours are also fired, though not on the floor of the kiln but in a refractory crucible in the fireplace and afterwards ground in the tubs. The pigments in fact require a lower temperature than the

white, and the quantities needed are smaller. Green is obtained by mixing blue and yellow; a copper compound being also used. Orange is a mixture of yellow and red.

As well as the colours, the painter uses perforated or pouncing patterns, the so-called *spons* or *poncif*, and brushes. The *spons* or pouncing pattern is a piece of paper in which holes are pricked with a needle in the lines of the drawing in order to reproduce the outline of the pattern which is to be applied to the tile (268, 269). The painter lays this pricked paper on the glazed tile and pats it with a little linen bag full of finely ground charcoal. The charcoal dust seeps through the linen and the holes of the stencil and is fixed by the still damp, unfired glaze.

The painter makes his own brush. He bundles hairs from the ears of cattle into a thimble and cuts his brush into the shape he desires. The *trekker*, used for drawing the outlines, is given a fine point; the *dieper*, for the shading and half-tones, is given a strong, broad shape. The painter handles a *kap* of twenty-five tiles at a time using whatever brushes and colours are required; he draws first the outline then the details. For the outline he uses violet, or blue which has been made a little darker by the addition of purple or iron red.

This procedure makes the painter's work easier, for the contrast in colour between the light grey unfired glaze and the lighter blue drawing, which before firing has the pale tone of zaffre, would be so slight that, in view of the extreme fineness of many of the outlines, it would be impossible to get a clear picture. Furthermore, the outlines after firing become darker than the rest of the design, which improves the final result.

Although this painting is by a long way the most important means of decoration, there are other more practical ones. According to one, for example, leaves are rendered not with a brush but with a small sponge. A second was the so-called technique of "spattering" with which the whole surface was decorated. A stencil and a brush full of colour were used, a knife was passed over the brush and the colour spattered over the part of the tile which was not covered by the stencil.

SPECIAL METHODS OF DECORATION DERIVED FROM THE MAIOLICA TECHNIQUE

MOSAIC. We are concerned here not really with a production technique but with a form of treatment by which a composition is built up of small pieces of tile of varying shape and colour which are embedded in plaster or cement.

The pieces required can be cut into the desired shapes from finished tiles, but this is laborious work. The shape can, of course, be much more easily obtained by shaping the tile before it is fired, that is to say, by cutting the tile when it is leather-hard. These small pieces are then fired, glazed to the colour desired and fired again. In this way, mosaic does in fact become a production technique, although only to the extent of giving a specific shape to the pieces.

CUENCA AND CUERDA SECA. A similar result can be achieved by producing the dividing-lines between the forms and colour surfaces of the composition in two other ways.

By the first method, the dividing lines required are cut in a stamp which is impressed upon the clay tile while it is still soft. The recessed surfaces produced are then filled with glazes of different colours. In Spain this method is called *cuenca*. The other technique starts with a flat tile to which the dividing-lines are applied in a dark composition which does not melt easily and has a high manganese content. The areas between the lines can then be filled with glazes as in the *cuenca* technique. This method is called *cuerda seca*.

DECORATION OF TILES REQUIRING THREE FIRINGS

A third firing is necessary when materials are being used for the decoration which would not stand the firing temperature required for the glaze or which need a different atmosphere in the furnace.

LUSTRE. The main point about lustre is the reducing atmosphere which is required to achieve the desired results and which thus differs from the more or less oxidising atmosphere of the normal fire. The temperature required is also lower.

Abulqasim gives a highly detailed and complicated description of gold lustre, the essence of which is that the silver or copper compounds – possibly in combination – are ground together with ochre and water or vinegar and applied to the glaze.

Since firing takes place in a reducing fire, which means that smoke develops, the metal oxides which have been applied are transformed in smallest possible particled sizes into the metallic state and, because the temperature is considerably lower than in the previous firing, the glaze and the decoration, if there is any, are not so soft that the smoke could harm them. For this process a special furnace was used which was stoked for three days and nights. When they had cooled, all the pieces had to be rubbed with damp earth so that they took on a fine metallic sheen, "And everything which has had a fire of this kind glistens like red gold and shines like the light of the sun."[1]

GOLD. Abulqasim also describes the technique of gold decoration. Leaf gold is beaten and laid between sheets of paper which have been coated with plaster. The shapes desired are cut out of these sheets and stuck with gum to the object to be decorated. The piece is then fired for half a day in a gentle kiln, which produces a regular design.

Musketeer with his weapon, reproduced from a pricked pattern.

Opposite left: Tile-pictures of soldiers from Frederiksborg Castle near Copenhagen, each made up of twelve tiles. They came in all probability from the same workshop as the horsemen illustrated on p. 156. Middle 17th century. Opposite right: Corner of a room in the "King's Parlour" on Hallig Hooge. A typical and fully preserved tile-decorated room of the year 1767. The tile-picture of the ship over the stove is dated 1766 and shows the frigate Hanna Maria Dianna, *commanded by the owner of the house, Captain Tade Hans Bandix. The tiles were probably imported by sea direct from a factory in West Friesland.*

Page 266: Dish of fruit with parrots and branches springing from the fruit. A most unusual composition of the first half of the 17th century. Although it is not completely finished, it gives a good impression of the manner of composition of the Dutch tile-painters. Lambert van Meerten Museum, Delft.

Page 267: Pages from a pattern-book for tiles from the Harlingen creamware and tile factory belonging to the Van Hulst family. 18th century. Top: A little church and children playing, below them a star and a bloempot. *Bottom: A dog, intended for a typical Friesian tile-picture comprising four tiles, of the kind usually placed near the fire-place or stove. Hannemahuis Museum, Harlingen.*

Page 268: Pounced patterns as used in the painting of tiles. Stencils were made of strong paper on which the original drawings were done. The outlines were then pricked with a needle. These pricked patterns or sponsen *were laid on the tiles after they had been fired once and coated with white tin-glaze; they were then dusted through the pattern from a pouch which contained ground charcoal. The design thus obtained was then gone over in ceramic colour, glazed and afterwards fired. Top left: A design which has not yet been pricked. Middle and bottom left: Pricked patterns. Right: The finished tiles made from these patterns.*

THE UNSURPASSED TILE-ARCHITECTURE OF PERSIA

1 Omar Khayyam, the 11th-century mathematician and poet, is known in the West for his delightful quatrains, which have been finely translated by Fitzgerald. To his contemporaries, however, he was more important as a mathematician, because this discipline was regarded as the prime introduction to the study of mysticism and the occult. The Seljuks obtained his services and he distinguished himself at their court by his astronomical studies.

2 Sultan Mahmud of the Seljuks (997–1036) commissioned the great Persian poet Firdausi to write a Persian rendering of the *Book of Kings* of the Pahlavi. In his version of this epic poem, Firdausi writes about the mysticism of the adherents of Sufism. Many teachings and affirmations were expounded in his tales. He professes belief in the universality of God, who is everywhere present in the visible and invisible world, and believes that the human soul must struggle constantly to be merged in the divine substance and to find eternal peace.

3 A kiosk and a pagoda are buildings the exteriors of which are covered with glazed ceramic.

4 Byzantium was called Rum by the Arabs, an allusion to the Roman conquest of the city, which became the last remnant of the Roman imperial power; the inhabitants considered themselves "*romanos*". In general, Turks and Byzantines respected one another and each valued the civilisation of the other.

5 Koran school.

6 The Turkish name for Adrianople.

TURKISH TILES

1 Lane, *loc. cit.*, p. 22.

2 It was called the Kiosk because it was supposed to be an imitation of a kiosk in Baghdad. There is, however, nothing Persian about it.

EARLY ENGLISH TILES

1 *Illustrated London News*, 27 June 1964.

2 This pavement is so badly worn that the designs, published

in the middle of the 19th century, can now barely be distinguished.

3 Lane, *loc. cit.*, p. 30.

4 Lane, *loc. cit.*, p. 32.

5 Selden *supra* 38.

EARLY TILES IN FRANCE, GERMANY, THE NETHERLANDS AND SWITZERLAND

1 R. Lantier, Plaques funéraires de terre-cuite mérovingienne, in *Jahrbuch des Röm. Germ. Zentralmuseums Mainz*, Vol. I, 1954, p. 243, p.l 22.

2 Cf. Julius Baum, Karolingische Bildnerkunst aus Ton und Stein im Iller- und Nagoldtal, in *Beiträge zur Kunstgeschichte und Archäologie des Frühmittelalters*, 1958, p. 174f., Herbert Pé, the director of the Ulm museum, writes that examination of the material has proved that the tiles found in 1958 at the Weinhof in Ulm in the immediate vicinity of the former palace building—already in ruins in the 14th century—were manufactured locally; it has so far, however, not been established whether the models may have been imported. An authoritative report on the excavations is still awaited.

3 R. Forrer, *Geschichte der europäischen Fliesen-Keramik vom Mittelalter bis zum Jahre 1900*, Strasbourg, 1901, pl. XXX.

4 Gunnar Tilander, Inscription débattue du carreau octogonal du début du 15e siècle, etc., in *Mededelingenbladder Vrienden van de Nederl. Ceramiek*, 30 (March 1963), p. 25f.

5 J. Renaud, Middeleeuwse vloertegels, in *Mededelingenblad Vrienden van de Nederlandse ceramiek*, 12, (July 1958) p. 6f.

6 Heinz Stoob, *Hamburgs hohe Türme*, Hamburg 1957, p.20f.

DECORATIVE BRICKS ON FIRE-PLACE WALLS

1 L. F. Salzman, *Building in England down to 1540*, Oxford, 1952, p. 98.

2 J. Hollestelle, Haardstenen, in *Bulletin van de Koninkl. Ned. Oudheidkundige Bond*, Vol. IV, no. 6.

3 The Pillars of Hercules at Gibraltar, a reference to America, the land which the *conquistadores* had conquered for the

Spanish monarch and which was far larger and richer than his empire in Europe.

4. The "Zaun" of the German text is etymologically identical with the Dutch word "tuin", meaning "garden". This word originally means "enclosed space"; the "Hollands tuin" or "Dutch garden" refers to the safely protected Dutch territory.

RENAISSANCE AND HUMANISM AS REFLECTED IN ITALIAN TILES

1 G. Liverani, *Five Centuries of Italian Maiolica*, 1957, pl. 56a.

2 L. Ozzola, Mattonelle Isabelliane, in *Faenza*, XXXIX (1953), p. 5.

3 G. Liverani, Spigolature, in *Faenza*, XLVIII–V (1962), p. 102.

4 This liking for Persian motifs is apparent also from scattered tiles decorated with Persian scenes by Francesco Avello, a cultivated artist from Urbino. His colours are mainly warm ones: orange, yellow, blue and green.

5 Liverani, *Five Centuries of Italian Maiolica*, p. 23 ff.

6 G. Liverani, Spigolature: Mattonelle da pavimentazione a Saluzzo, in *Faenza*, XLVIII–V (1962), p. 102.

7 G. Bolognesi, Su di un pavimento maiolicato nella chiesa di San Sebastiano a Venezia, in *Faenza* XLIV (1958), p. 104.

8 The Italian clay is extremely red and dark and for this reason a white slip is used much more often than is usually believed, thus making faience into semi-faience.

FRENCH TILES

1 Jean Thuile, *La céramique ancienne à Montpellier du 17e et 18e siècle*, Paris, 1954, p. 373.

ANTWERP

1 Philippen has recommended, for reasons of linguistic purity, that these ceramics should be called "maiolica" up to the moment at which imports were no longer effected by way of Majorca but were brought directly from Italy. From this moment onwards the designation "faience", derived from Faenza, becomes the correct one. *Geleymakers* means workers in *glaise* = clay (potters).

2 Nicaise has established the correct spelling of his name, see *Les origines italiennes des faienceries d'Anvers et des Pays-Bas au XVIe siècle*, p. 117.

3 Nicaise, *loc. cit.*, p. 119.

4 Nicaise, *loc. cit.*, p. 119.

5 L. J. M. Philippen, *De Oud-Antwerpsche Majolika*, Brussels, 1938.

6 Another product of the contact with Spain was the porringer, a splendid example of Antwerp maiolica, the flat handles of which indicate its Spanish origins. A fairly complete collection of these vessels is still to be found in the Maagdenhuis in Antwerp, the establishment for which they were originally made.

7 N. Rodot, *Les potiers de terre à Lyon au XVIe siècle*.

8 M. Laurent, Guido di Savini and the earthenware of Antwerp, in *Burlington Magazine*, XII (1922), p. 288.

9 Philippen, *loc. cit.*, p. 10.

10 Nicaise mentions the procession of the Chambers of Rhetoric of 1480 in Lierre. It was entitled *The Mill of Paris* and showed God the Father, the Madonna, the Apostles, the Pope, the Emperor, the King of France and others. Many plays and contests of these Chambers provided sources for ceramic works.

11 P. Coecke, *De Triumphe van Antwerpen 1549*, Antwerp, Gillis van Diest, 1550. A book with many plates of cartouches and arabesques resembling those under discussion.

12 J. Floris, *Veilderhand cierlyke compertimente*. Hans Liefrinck exc. 1564.

13 Nicaise, in *Jaarboek Antw. Oudh. Kring*, X.

14 B. Sylvius, *Variarum protractionum quas vulgo Marusias vocant libellus*, 1554.

15 The glazed stone from a house in Delft in the Vecht Collection, Amsterdam, is an exception (see *Cahiers de la céramique*, 22, 1961). In this case a flat stone slab was glazed according to a technique which it was thought was applicable only to porous materials. By a piece of good fortune, the glaze stuck and the stone withstood the heat of the oven.

16 J. Helbig, *La céramique bruxelloise du bon vieux temps*, Brussels, 1946.

INDIVIDUAL DUTCH TILES

1 A. Groneman, De 16e cenurse tegelolveren in Breda, in *Mededelingen Vrienden Nederl. Ceramiek*, 16 (1959) and A. Dorgelo in *Mededelingen Vrienden Nederl. Ceramiek*, 21 (1961). Dorgelo discusses floor-tiles from Deventer with Italian dolphins and a black reminiscent of Siena and of Spanish geometric dividing-bands. The Spanish and Italian influences were intermingled in Antwerp.

2 Eelco M. Vis and Commer de Geus, *Alt-Holländische Fliesen*, ed. Ferrand W. Hudig, 2 vols., Amsterdam 1926.

3 Vis-Geus, ed. Hudig, pp. 36 and 39.

4 J. de Kleyn, Het met de ringeloor versierde aardewerk, in *Mededelingen Vrienden Nederl. Ceramiek*, 22 (1961).

5 Erich Meyer-Heisig, *Deutsche Bauerntöpferei*, Munich 1955.

DUTCH TILE-PICTURES

1 In 1594 the house was inhabited by Petergen Jansd, who sold tiles there. It was pulled down in 1895.

2 G. de Goederen in *Tijdschrift van de Vrienden van Nederl. Ceramiek*, No. 27, p. 14.

3 G. C. von Helbers in *Mededelingen van Nederl. Ceramiek*, No. 4.

4 C. H. de Jonge, Hollandse tegelkamers in Duitse en Franse Kastelen, in *Nederl. Kunsthist. Jaarboek*, X (1959), p. 175.

5 J. M. dos Santos Simões, *Carreaux céramiques hollandais au Portugal et en Espagne*, 1959.

6 H. W. Mauser in *Mededelingen Vrienden van de Ceramiek*, 15.

DUTCH TILES AS DECORATIONS FOR WALLS AND FIRE-PLACES

1 The Dutch word *smuiger* is related to *smook* = smoke. *Schouw*, the Dutch word for mantelpiece is, as H. B. J. Vlas states in *Speelwagen* III (1948), connected with the words *scouden* or *scouwen*, which are derived from the French *escauder* (modern French *échauder*, Latin *escaldere*) = to scald.

2 C. H. de Jonge, Dix parmi les plus beaux décors en "carreaux de Delft", in *Connaissance des Arts*, 124, June 1962, p. 67.

ROOMS LINED WITH DUTCH TILES

1 Cf. Chapters VII and XII.

2 *Mededelingen Vrienden van de Ceramiek*, 4.

3 Cf. de Jonge in *Nederl. Kunsthist. Jaarboek* X, 1959.

4 C. H. de Jonge, *Oud-Nederlandsche Majolika en Delftsche Aardewerk*, Amsterdam 1947.

5 R. Danis, *La première maison royale de Trianon*, Paris 1927.

6 C. H. de Jonge, *Nederl. Kunsthist. Jaarboek*, loc. cit.

7 A. Lane, in *Bulletin Rijksmuseum* VII (1959), p. 12.

8 R. van Luttervelt, Nederlandes tegeltableaux te New York, in *Bulletin van de Nederl. Oudheidkundige Bond*, VI, 3 (1950).

9 F. Francastel, Le Marmorbad de Cassel et les Lazienki de Varsovie, in *Gazette des Beaux-Arts*, 6e période, Tome IX, p. 138–156, 1933.

10 De Jonge, loc. cit.

ENGLISH TILES FROM THE 16TH TO THE 18TH CENTURY

1 Arthur Lane, *A Guide to the Collection of Tiles*, Victoria and Albert Museum, London, 1960, p. 53.

2 Lane, loc. cit., p. 53.

3 Lane, loc. cit., p. 63.

4 He names as sources (loc. cit., p. 66) *Bell's British Theatre*, 1776/77, *Bell's Shakespeare* and *The Ladies' Amusement* published by Robert Sayer before 1760.

THE EXPORT OF DUTCH TILES TO GERMANY AND DENMARK

1 On an east Friesian fireplace in the Bomann Museum, Celle, there is a blue tile-picture (4×4) with the following text: "*Durch Schiffahrt Und durch Walfischfangst Onter half Got vil Lewte und Landt.*" It is signed PL.

2 A similar example is a room from the Elbe island of Finkenwerder with a tile-picture (*The Judgement of Solomon*, 5×4) in manganese with brown star-tiles in the Bomann Museum, Celle.

GERMAN AND DANISH TILE-FACTORIES

1 Mention should be made of sixteen miniature blue tiles in the Bayerisches Nationalmuseum in Munich (10/37 and 57) as well as the showpieces in the Museum für Kunst und Gewerbe in Hamburg.

2 Rib also worked for a time at the Bayreuth factory (founded 1714). Not he, however, but the later "court porcelain painter" Johann Christoph Jucht was responsible for two very large tiles of about 1740 showing stags, birds and flowers. Bayerisches Nationalmuseum, Munich (34/1908–1909).

3 *Hausmalerarbeit* was work carried out in independent enamelling shops.

4 Three very large tiles of the second quarter of the 18th century in the Bayerisches Nationalmuseum, Munich (21/181) are described as Nuremberg tiles.

5 Among them are also some of the star-tiles which were used in groups; but these are green, a most uncommon colour for tiles, from the Danish island of Fanö.

MATERIALS AND METHODS OF PRODUCTION

1 H. Ritter, J. Ruska, F. Sarre, R. Winderlich. Orientalische Steinbücher und persische Fayencetechnik. German translation, with notes, of a chapter on the technique of faience-making at Kashan by Abulqasim ibn-Abdallah ibn-Ali ibn-Muhammed ibn-Ali Tahir of the year 1301. In *Istanbuler Mitteilungen des Archäologischen Institutes des Deutschen Reiches*, III, 1935.

2 Cipriano Piccolpasso, *I tre Libri dell'arte del vasaio*, Castel Durante, 1556. English translation by B. Rackham and A. van de Put, London, 1934.

3 G. Paape, *De Plateelbakker of Delftsch Aardewerkmaaker*, Dordrecht, 1794.

4 H. Le Chatelier in *Comptes rendus* 129, XII (1899), 477–480.

5 Ritter (c. s. aantekeningen 46).

6 N. V. Tichelaar, *300 Jaar Makkumer Aardewerk*, Makkum, 1960.

7 N. Ottema, Fries'che Majolica, in *De Vrije Fries*, XXVII, Leeuwarden, 1920.

8 A. Lucas, Glazed ware in Egypt, India and Mesopotamia, in *Journal of Egyptian Archaeology*, 22 (1936), pp. 141–164.

9 R. Forrer, *Geschichte der europäischen Fliesen-Keramik*, Strasbourg, 1901.

10 Arthur Lane, *A Guide to the Collection of Tiles*, Victoria and Albert Museum, London, 1960.

11 A. Winter, Alte und antike Brennanlagen, die Regie ihrer Feuer, in *Ker. Zeitschrift*, 8 (1956), pp. 513–517.

12 C. H. de Jonge, *Oud-Nederlandsche Majolica en Delftsch Aardewerk*, Amsterdam, 1947, pp. 153–154.

Bibliography

GENERAL:

ROLLO CHARLES; *Continental porcelain of the 18th century*. London, 1964.
WARREN E. COX; *The book of pottery and porcelain*. 2 vol., 5th ed. New York, 1946.
R. FORRER; *Geschichte der europäischen Fliesen-Keramik vom Mittelalter bis zum Jahre 1900*. Strasbourg, 1901.
EMIL HANNOVER; *Pottery and porcelain*, edited by Bernard Rackham. 3 vol., London, 1925.
ARTHUR LANE; *A guide to the collection of tiles*. Victoria and Albert Museum, London, 1960.
[Exhibition catalogue] *Exp. Oud Aardewerk Coll. Bastert*, Museum Boymans-van Beuningen, Rotterdam, 1940.

ANTIQUITY:

G.B[ALLARDINI]; 'Ceramiche funerarie dell'antica Cina' in: *Faenza XXXV* (1949), p. 65.
F. M. TH. DE LIAGRE BÖHL; *Opera minora*. Groningen, 1953.
K. ERDMANN; *Die Kunst Irans zur Zeit der Sassaniden*. Berlin, 1943.
H. FRANKFORT; *The art and architecture of the ancient orient* Harmondsworth, 1954.
W. C. HAYES; *The sceptre of Egypt*. Cambridge, Mass., 1953.
OLOV JANSÉ; *Briques et objets céramiques funéraires de l'époque des Han*. Collection Loo. Paris, 1936.
R. KOLDEWEY; *The excavations at Babylon*, translated by A. S. Johns. London, 1914.
R. KOLDEWEY; *Das wiedererstehende Babylon*. 4 vol., Berlin, 1925.
G. R. MEYER; [Catalogue] *Durch vier Jahrtausende altvorderasiatischer Kultur im Vorderasiatischen Museum*. Berlin, 1956.
A. PARROT; *Archéologie mésopotamienne*. Paris, 1946.
A. PARROT; *Sumer*. Paris, 1960.
A. PARROT; *Sumeria*, translated by S. Gilbert and J. Emmons. London, 1960.
W. M. FLINDERS PETRIE; *Royal tombs of earliest dynasties*. 2 vol., London, 1900–1901.
H. SCHMÖKEL; *Ur, Assur und Babylon*. Zürich, 1955.
H. WALLIS; *Egyptian ceramic art*. 2 vol., London, 1898–1900.

WILLIAM C. WHITE, sometime bishop of Honan; *Tomb tile pictures of ancient China*. Royal Ontario Museum of Archeology. Toronto, 1939.
CHR. ZERVOS; *L'art de la Mésopotamie*. Paris, 1935.

PERSIA AND TURKEY:

MEHDÍ BAHRAMI; *Recherches sur les carreaux de revêtement lustrés dans la céramique persane du 13me au 15me siècle (étoiles et croix)*. Paris, 1937.
GÉNÉRAL M. E. A. BROUSSAUD; *Les carreaux de faïence peints dans l'Afrique du Nord*. Paris, 1930.
ROBERT BYRON; *The road to Oxiana*, London, 1937.
ERNST DIEZ; *Die Kunst der islamischen Völker*. München, 1917.
R. ETTINGHAUSEN; 'Evidence for the identification of Kashan pottery' in: *Ars Islamica III* (1936).
ROBIN FEDDEN; *Syria: A historical appreciation*. London, 1955.
R. GONZALES DE CLAVIJO; *Embassy to Tamerlane*, translated by G. Le Strange. London, 1928.
JULIAN HUXLEY; *From an antique land*. London, 1954.
CHARLES KIEFER; 'Lés céramiques musulmanes' in: *Cahiers de la Céramique 4* (1956).
A. LANE; *Later Islamic pottery*. London, 1957.
A. LANE; 'The painted pottery of Iznik' in: *Ars Orientalis II* 1957), p. 247.
ROBERT LIDDELL; *Byzantium and Istanbul*. London, 1956.
GEORGES MARCAIS; *Manuel d'art musulman*. 2 vol., Paris, 1926–27.
G. MIGEON et A. SAKISIAN; 'Les faïences d'Asie Mineure du XV au XVIII siècle' in: *Revue de l'art ancien et moderne* XLIII, XLIV (1923–24).
K. OTTO DORN; 'Das Islamische Iznik' in: *Istanbuler Mitteilungen des Archäologischen Instituts des Deutschen Reiches*, 13 (1941).
A. U. POPE; *Introduction to Persian art*. London, 1930.
A. U. POPE and P. ACKERMAN; *A survey of Persian art*. 6 vol., Oxford, 1938.
C. PROST; 'Les revêtements céramiques dans les monuments musulmans de l'Egypte' in: *Mémoires de l'Institut Français du Caire* XL (1916).
TAMARA TALBOT RICE; *The Seljuks*. London, 1961.

273

R. M. RIEFSTAHL; 'Early Turkish tile-revetments in Edirne' in: *Ars Islamica IV* (1937).

H. RITTER, J. RUSKA, F. SARRE, R. WINDERLICH; 'Orientalische Steinbücher und persische Fayencetechnik' in: *Istanbuler Mitteilungen des Archäologischen Instituts des Deutschen Reiches*, 1935.

F. SARRE; *Denkmäler persischer Baukunst*. Berlin, 1901–1910.

F. SARRE; *Die Ausgrabungen von Samarra II: Die Keramik von Samarra*. Berlin, 1925.

F. SARRE; *Der Kiosk von Konia*, Berlin, 1936.

SACHEVERELL SITWELL; *Mauretania*. London, 1940.

SACHEVERELL SITWELL; *Arabesque and honeycomb*. London, 1957.

TASHIN CHUKRU; 'Les faïences turques' in: *Transactions of the Oriental Ceramic Society* XI (1933–34).

H. WALLIS; *The Goodman collection. Persian ceramic art belonging to F. Ducane Goodman; with examples from other collections. The 13th-century lustred wall tiles*. London, 1894.

LOUISE WEISS; 'La chevauchée de Mahomet' in: *Connaissance des arts 89* (1959), p. 65.

H. WILDE; *Brussa*. Berlin, 1909.

K. WULZINGER & C. WATZINGER; *Damaskus*. Leipzig, 1924. 'L'étrange envoûtement des mosques persanes' in: *Connaissance des arts 88* (1959), p. 119.

EARLY ENGLISH TILES

P. B. CHATWIN; 'The mediaeval patterned tiles of Warwickshire' in: *Transactions of the Birmingham Archaeological Society* LX (1936), p. 1.

P. T. B. CLAYTON; 'The inlaid tiles of Westminster' in: *Journal of the Archaeological Institute of Great Britain and Ireland* LXIX (1912), p. 36.

E. EAMES; 'The Canynges pavement' in: *Journal of the British Archaeological Association* XIV (1951), p. 33.

E. EAMES; 'The products of a medieval tile kiln at Bawsey, King's Lynn' in: *The Antiquaries Journal* XXXV (1955), p. 162.

LOYD HABERLY; *Medieval paving-tiles*. Oxford, 1937.

R. L. HOBSON; *Catalogue of the collection of English pottery in the British Museum*. London, 1903.

J. R. HOLLIDAY; 'Hales Owen Abbey' in: *Transactions of the Birmingham and Midland Institute* (1871), p. 49.

M. R. JAMES; 'Rare mediaeval tiles and their story' in: *Burlington Magazine* XLII (1923), p. 32.

W. R. LETHABY; 'The romance tiles of Chertsey Abbey' in: *Walpole Society Annual* II (1913), p. 69.

R. S. LOOMIS; 'Illustrations of medieval romance on tiles from Chertsey Abbey' in: *University of Illinois Studies in Language and Literature* II (1916).

J. B. WARD PERKINS; 'English mediaeval embossed tiles' in: *Journal of the Archaeological Institute of Great Britain and Ireland*, XCIV (1938), p. 128.

PONSONBY OF SHULBREDE and MATTHEW PONSONBY; 'Monastic paving tiles' in: *Sussex Archaeological Collections* LXXV (1934), p. 19.

J. S. RICHARDSON; 'A thirteenth-century tile kiln at North Berwick, East Lothian, and Scottish mediaeval ornamented floor tiles' in: *Proceedings of the Society of Antiquaries of Scotland* LXIII (1928–29), p. 281.

M. SHURLOCK; *Tiles from Chertsey Abbey*. London, 1885.

N. E. TOKE; 'The opus Alexandrinum and sculptured stone roundels in the retrochoir of Canterbury Cathedral' in: *Archaeologia Cantania* XLII (1930), p. 189.

MEDIEVAL TILES IN FRANCE, THE NETHERLANDS GERMANY AND SWITZERLAND

E. AMÉ; *Les carrelages émaillés du moyen âge et de la renaissance*. Paris, 1859.

JURIGS BALTRUŠAITIS; *Le moyen âge fantastique*. Paris, 1955.

JULIUS BAUM; 'Karolingische Bildnerkunst aus Ton und Stein im Iller- und Nagoldtal' in: *Beitr. zur Kunstgeschichte und Archäologie des Frühmittelalters*. Cologne, 1962.

J. HOUDOYE; 'Les faïences de Philippe le Hardi (1391)' in: *Gazette des Beaux-Arts* V (1872), p. 93.

R. LANTIER; 'Plaque funéraire de terre-cuite mérovingienne' in: *Jahrb. des Röm. German. Zentralmuseums Mainz* I (1954), p. 243.

J. RENAUD; 'Middeleeuwse vloertegels' in: *Mededel. Vrienden der Nederl. Ceramiek* 12 (1958).

REINHARD SCHINDLER; 'Zwei glasierte gotische Bildkacheln aus den Trümmern des ehemaligen Mariendomes in Hamburg' in: *Faenza* XXXVII (1951), p. 39.

H. STOOB; *Hamburgs hohe Türme*. Hamburg, 1957.

274

GUNNAR TILANDER; 'Inscription débattue du carreau octagonal du début du XVme siècle appartenant à M. Vecht' in: *Mededel. Vrienden der Nederl. Ceramiek* 30 (1963).

JAC. ZWARTS; 'Ceramische Kunst uit den Utrechtschen Dom van Bisschop Adelbold' in: *Maandblad v. Beeld. Kunsten* X, 4 (April 1933), p. 117.

DECORATIVE BRICKS ON FIRE-PLACE WALLS

J. HOLLESTELLE; 'Haardstenen' in: *Bull. v. d. Kon. Ned. Oudh. Bond* VI, 12/4 (15 Sept. 1959), p. 57.

SPAIN AND PORTUGAL

MARIO BARATA; *Azulejos no Brasil*. Rio de Janeiro, 1955.

ANDRÉS BATLLORI y MUNNÉ and L. M. LLUBIA y MUNNÉ; *Ceramica Catalana decorada*. Barcelona, 1949.

BURLINGTON FINE ARTS CLUB; *Catalogue of an exhibition of Spanish art*. London, 1928.

EMILIO CAMPS Y CAZORLA; *Cerámica Española*, Madrid, 1936.

CARLOS CID; *Los azulejos*. Barcelona, 1950.

ANTONIO CORBACHO SANCHO; *La cerámica Andalusa*. 2 vol., Sevilla, 1948.

VERGILIO CORREIA; *Azulejos datados*, 2nd ed., Lisbon, 1922.

VERGILIO CORREIA; *Azulejos*. Coimbra, 1956.

ALICE W. FROTHINGHAM; *Talavera pottery*, Hispanic Society of America, New York, 1944.

J. GESTOSO Y PEREZ; *Historia de los barros vidriados sevillanos*. Sevilla, 1903.

MANUEL GONZALEZ MARTÍ; *Cerámica del Levante Español*. 3 vol., Barcelona, 1944–1952.

FELICIANO GUIMARÃES; *Azulejos de figura avulsa*. Gaia, 1932.

JUAN AINAUD DE LASARTE; 'Cerámica y vidrio' in: *Ars Hispaniae*, Vol. X, Madrid, 1952. (With extensive bibliography.)

PLATON PÃRAMO; *La cerámica antigua de Talavera*. Madrid, 1919.

JOSÉ QUEIROZ; *Ceramica portuguesa*. Lisbon, 1907; 2nd ed. 1948.

REYNALDO DOS SANTOS; *O azulejo em Portugal*. Lisbon, 1949.

J. M. DOS SANTOS SIMÕES; *Alguns azulejos de Evora*. Evora, 1945.

J. M. DOS SANTOS SIMÕES; *Os azulejos do paco de Vila Vicosa*. Lisbon, 1946.

J. M. DOS SANTOS SIMÕES; *Carreaux céramiques hollandais au Portugal et en Espagne*. La Haye, 1959.

J. M. DOS SANTOS SIMÕES; *Corpus do azulejo portugues*, I: *Azulejaria portuguesa nos Açores e na Madeira*. Lisbon, 1963.

G. MATOS SEQUEIRA; *Depois do terramoto*. 4 vol., Lisbon, 1934.

JOAQUIM DE VASCONCELLOS; *Ceramica portuguesa*. Oporto, 1883.

ITALY

A. G. ALAJMO; 'Panelli maiolicati a Sciacca' in: *Faenza* XLI 1–11 (1955).

GAETANO BALLARDINI; 'Corpus della maiolica italiana.' Series *Bolletino d'Arte* I and II (1933, 1938).

EROS BIAVATI; 'Bacini di Pisa' in: *Faenza* XXXIV, 3 (1948).

EROS BIAVATI; 'Bacini di Pisa' in: *Faenza* XXXIV, 4–6 1948).

EROS BIAVATI; 'Bacini di Pisa' in: *Faenza* XXXV, 4–6 (1948).

EROS BIAVATI; 'Bacini di Pisa' in: *Faenza* XXXVII, 5–6 (1951).

EROS BIAVATI; 'Bacini di Pisa' in: *Faenza* XXXVIII, 4–5 (1958).

GIOV. BOLOGNESI; 'Su di un pavimento maiolicato nella chiesa di S. Sebastiano a Venezia' in: *Faenza* XLIV (1958).

G. BRENCI and J. LESSING; *Maiolika-Fliesen aus Siena*, 1500–1550. Berlin, 1884.

J. CHOMPRET; *Répertoire de la majolique italienne*. 2 vol., Paris, 1949.

A. FILANGIERI DI CANDIDA; 'Per il pavimento della capella di Ser Gianni Caracciolo nella chiesa di S. Giovanni a Carbonara in Napoli' in: *Faenza* III (1915), p. 33.

G. LIVERANI; *Five centuries of Italian maiolica*. London, 1957.

G. LIVERANI; *La maiolica italiana*. Milano, 1958.

G. LIVERANI; 'Sulla maiolica di Castello d'Abruzzo' in: *Faenza* XXXVI, 1–2 (1950).

G. LIVERANI; 'Uno sconosciuta bottega maiolicara del primo cinquecento a Faenza' in: *Faenza* XLIII, 1 (1957).

G. LIVERANI; 'Ampliamento delle collezioni al museo' in: *Faenza* XLVII, 1–2 (1961).

G. LIVERANI; 'Spigolature: mattonelle da pavimentazione a Saluzzo' in: *Faenza* XLVIII, 5 (1962).

M. MEURER; *Italienische Fliesen aus dem Ende des 15. und Anfang des 16. Jahrhunderts*. Berlin, 1881; French edition, Paris, 1883.

VICO MOSSA; 'Bacini ceramici di Sardegna' in: *Faenza* XVIII (1952), p. 3.

L. OZZÒLA; 'Mattonelle Isabelliane' in: *Faenza* XXXIX, 1 (1953), p. 8.

BERNARD RACKHAM; *Guide to Italian maiolica*. London, 1933.

BERNARD RACKHAM; *Catalogue of Italian maiolica*. 2 vol., Victoria and Albert Museum, London, 1940.

NINO RAGONA; *La ceramica siciliana*, s. l. 1955.

NINO RAGONA; 'La più antica maiolica siciliana datata: il pannello di S. Calogero a Sciacca' in: *Faenza* XL, 2 (1954), p. 34.

NINO RAGONA; 'Maioliche caltagironesi del primo Cinquecento' in: *Faenza* XL, 6 (1954), p. 125.

NINO RAGONA; 'Note sulla maiolica siciliana dei sec. XVI e XVII' in: *Faenza* XLIII, 1 (1957).

ALBERTO SCATURRO; 'Guiseppe Maxarato, Maiolicaro Saccense (1561–1625?)' in: *Faenza* XLII, 4 (1956).

G. TESORONE; 'A proposito dei pavimenti maiolicati del XV e XVI secolo delle chiese napolitane' in: *Napoli Nobilissima* X (1901), p. 115.

PIETRO TOESCA; 'Maioliche decorative nel Duomo di Lucca' in: *Faenza* XXXVII, 5–6 (1951), p. 94.

FRANCE

J. CHOMPRET; *Les faïences françaises primitives*. Paris, 1946.

H.-P. FOUREST; 'La fayence nivernaise au musée de Nevers' in: *La Revue française*, suppl. au 118 (May 1960).

JEANNE GIACOMOTTI; *Faïences françaises*. Fribourg, 1963.

JEANNE GIACOMOTTI; *French faience*, translated by D. Imber. London, 1963.

ARTHUR LANE; *French faience*. London, 1948

PIERRE MAUROIS; 'La céramique lilloise' in: *Trésors des musées de province*, 4. Paris, 1961.

G. MELLOR; 'French pottery' in: *The Connoisseur* LVIII (1920), p. 133.

ROGER PEYRE; *La céramique française*. Paris, 1910.

HENRY J. RENAUD; *Faïence de Moustiers, XVIIe et XVIIIe siècles*. Geneva, 1952.

JEAN THUILE; *La céramique ancienne à Montpellier du XVI et XVIIe siècle*. Paris, 1943.

EMILE TILMANS; *Faïences de France*. Paris, 1954.

[Exhibition catalogue] *Céramique régionale ancienne*. Musée de Lille, 1951.

[Exhibition catalogue] *Trésors de la faïence de Rouen*. Musée de Rouen, 1952.

'L'étonnante restauration de la Bastie d'Urfé' in: *Connaissance des Arts*, June 1955.

ANTWERP

J. CHOMPRET; 'Essai sur le pavage de Brou et la céramique flamande du XVIe siècle' in: *Antwerpens Kon. Oudheidkundige Kring, Jaarboek* XIII (1937).

ALEX DORGELO; 'Onbekende majolica vloertegels' in: *Mededelingen Vrienden v. d. Nederl. Ceramiek* 21 (1961).

A. GRONEMAN; 'De 16e eeuwse tegelvloeren in Breda' in: *Mededelingen Vrienden v. d. Nederl. Ceramiek* 16 (1959).

J. HELBIG; *La céramique bruxelloise du bon vieux temps*. Brussels, 1946.

J. HELBIG; 'Faïences anversoises postérieures aux guerres de religion' in: *Bulletin des Musées Royaux d'Art et d'Histoire*, Brussels, 1947, p. 1.

CH. VAN HERCK; 'Antwerps plateel. De Saulus bekering van 1547 en enkele aanverwante fragmenten' in: *Antwerpens Kon. Oudheidk. Kring. Jaarboek* XII (1936), p. 62.

CH. VAN HERCK; 'Een Antwerps tegeltableau der Drie Goddelyke Deugden': *ibid.* XIII (1937), p. 73.

CHR. VAN HERCK; 'Een vondst van Antwerpsche tegeltableaux uit het einde der XVIe eeuw': *ibid.* XX, XXI (1944–45), p. 121.

CHR. VAN HERCK; 'Antwerpsche ornament-tegels der 16e eeuw': *ibid.* XVII (1941), p. 28.

CH. VAN HERCK and J. M. DOS SANTOS SIMÕES; 'Antwerpsche tegels van omstreeks 1558 in Portugal': *ibid.* XX–XXI (1944–45), p. 128.

MARCEL LAURENT; 'Guido di Savino and the earthenware of Antwerp' in: *Burlington Magazine* XLI (1922), p. 288.

H. NICAISE; 'Les origines italiennes des faïenceries d'Anvers et des Pays-Bas au XVIe siècle' in: *Bulletin de l'Institut Historique belge à Rome* XIV (1934), p. 109.

H. NICAISE; 'Notes sur les faïenciers italiens établis à Anvers' in: *Revue belge de Philosophie et Histoire* XVI (1937), 1–2.

H. NICAISE; 'Les modèles italiens des faïences néerlandaises aux XVIe et au début du XVIIe siècle' in: *Bulletin de l'Institut Historique belge à Rome, Fasc.* XVII (1936), p. 107.

H. NICAISE; 'Sources d'inspiration flamande des faïenciers anversois dans la première moitié du XVIe siècle' in: *Ann. du XXXe Congrès Féd. Arch. et Hist. de Belgique* 1936, p. 99.

H. NICAISE; 'Les carreaux en faïence anversoise de l'ancienne abbaye d'Herckenrode' in: *Bull. des Musées Royaux d'Art et d'Histoire* IIIe série, VII, 4–5 (1935), p. 92 and 117.

L. J. M. PHILIPPEN; '*De Oud-Antwerpsche majolica*'. Brussels, 1938.

L. J. M. PHILIPPEN; 'Oud Antwerpsch plateelwerk' in: *Gedenkboek Frans Claes*. Antwerpen, 1932.

BERNARD RACKHAM; *Early Netherlands maiolica, with special reference to the tiles at 'The Vyne,' Hampshire*. London, 1926.

F. SMEKENS; [Catalogue] *Glas en Ceramiek, Musea Vleeshuis*. Antwerpen, 1954.

[Exhibition catalogue] *Antwerpens Gouden Eeuw*. Antwerpen, 1955 (De Ceramiek, F. Smekens).

THE NETHERLANDS

CATHARINA BÜLOW; *Das Kachelbuch*. Hamburg, 1956.

ROBERT DANIS; *La première Maison Royale de Trianon*. Paris, 1926.

ELISABETH DHANENS; *Wandtegeltjes*. Bruges, 1947.

OTTO VON FALKE; 'Holländische Fayence-Bilder' in: *Pantheon*, 1937 (Fr. v. Frijtom, Corn. Bouwmeester).

P. FRANCASTEL; 'Le Marmorbad de Cassel et les Lazienki de Varsovie' in: *Gazette des Beaux-Arts* VI (1933), p. 138.

H. C. GALLOIS; 'Over Rotterdamsche Tegels' in: *Meded. van den Dienst van Kunsten en Wetenschappen's-Gravenhage*, 1919.

C. DE GEUS; *Bijdrage tot de kennis van de Nederl. Ceramiek n. a. v. de coll. Arthur Isaac in het Rijksmuseum te Amsterdam*.

G. DE GOEDEREN; 'In duysent vreesen?' in: *Mededelingen Vrienden Nederl. Ceramiek*, 27 (1962).

H. GOETZ; 'Holländische Wandfliesen in einem altindischen Königspalast' in: *Oud-Holland* LXVI (1951), p. 239.

G. C. HELBERS; 'De geschiedenis van het oude Goudse plateel' in: *Mededelingen Vrienden Nederl. Ceramiek* 4 (1958).

J. HELBIG; *Faïences hollandaises. Musées Royaux d'Art et d'Histoire*, Bruxelles. 2 vol., Liège.

A. H. HOYINCK VAN PAPENDRECHT; *De Rotterdamsche Plateel- en Tegelbakkers*. Rotterdam, 1920.

FERRAND W. HUDIG; *Delfter Fayence*. Berlin, 1929.

FERRAND W. HUDIG; 'Een Amsterdamsche Tegelbakkerry' in: *Oud Holland* XLIII (1926; van der Kloet).

FERRAND W. HUDIG; 'Amsterdamsche Aardewerkvondsten I en II' in: *Oud Holland* IV (1928).

C. H. DE JONGE; *Oud-Nederlandsche Majolica en Delftsch Aardewerk*, Amsterdam, 1947.

C. H. DE JONGE; 'Dix parmi les plus beaux décors en 'carreaux de delft' in: *Connaissance des Arts*, 124, June 1962, p. 67.

C. H. DE JONGE; 'Hollandse Tegelkamers in Duitse en Franse Kastelen' in: *Nederl. Kunsthistorisch Jaarboek* 10 (1959), p. 125.

C. D. DE JONGE; 'Holländischer Kachelschmuck in den Schlössern Brühl und Falkenlust' in: Walter Bader and others; *Aus Schloß Augustusburg zu Brühl und Falkenlust*. Cologne, 1961.

J. DE KLEYN; 'Het met de ringeloor versierde aardewerk' in: *Mededelingen Vrienden Nederl. Ceramiek* 22 (1961).

J. B. KNIPPING; 'De voorstellingswereld v. d. Nederl. Wandtegels' in: *Mededelingen Vrienden Nederl. Ceramiek*, 24 (1961) and 25 (1962).

W. PITCAIRN KNOWLES; *Dutch pottery & porcelain*. 2nd ed. London and New York, 1913.

IJSBRAND KOK; *De Hollandsche tegel*. Amsterdam, 1949.

DINGEMAN KORF; *Tegels*. Bussum, 1960.

DINGEMAN KORF; *Dutch tiles*. London, 1963.

DINGEMAN KORF; 'Ovaaltjes' in: *Mededelingen Vrienden Nederl. Ceramiek* 8 (1957).

DINGEMAN KORF; 'Haarlemse tegels' in: *Mededelingen Vrienden Nederl. Ceramiek* 10 (1958).

DINGEMAN KORF; 'Spiegeltegels' in: *Mededelingen Vrienden Nederl. Ceramiek* 11 (1958).

DINGEMAN KORF; 'Ovaaltegels' in: *Mededelingen Vrienden Nederl. Ceramiek* 12 (1958).

DINGEMAN KORF; 'De drietulp' in: *Mededelingen Vrienden Nederl. Ceramiek* 13 (1958).

DINGEMAN KORF; 'Kwadraattegels' in: *Mededelingen Vrienden Nederl. Ceramiek* 17 (1959).

DINGEMAN KORF; 'Kwadraattegels' in: *Mededelingen Vrienden Nederl. Ceramiek* 21 (1961).

DINGEMAN KORF; 'Rijkdom of armoede' in: *Mededelingen Vrienden Nederl. Ceramiek* 22 (1961).

ARTHUR LANE; 'Delftse Tegels uit Hampton Court en Daniel Marots werkzaamheid aldaar' in: *Bulletin Rijksmuseum Amsterdam* VII, I (1959), p. 12.

GIUSEPPE LIVERANI; 'Un insigne complesso di Mattonelle olandesi in Faenza' in: *Faenza* XXV (1937).

R. VAN LUTTERVELT; 'Nederlandse tegeltableaux te New York' in: *Bulletin N.O.B.*, 1950, p. 146.

E. NEURDENBURG and B. RACKHAM; *Old Dutch pottery and tiles.* London, 1923.

H. NICAISE; 'Une effigie de Guillaume le Taciturne sur un carreau de Delft' in: *Bulletin des Musées royaux*, Bruxelles IIIe Serie, V, 6 (1933), p. 134.

JEAN NICOLIER; 'Delft' in: *Connaissance des Arts* 23 (1954), 15 Janvier.

NANNE OTTEMA; *De opkomst van het majolikabedrijf in de Noordelijke Nederlanden.* Leeuwarden, 1926.

BERNARD RACKHAM; *Dutch tiles.* Victoria and Albert Museum, London, 1923.

L. REIDEMEISTER; 'Die Porzellankabinette der Brandenburgisch-Preußischen Schlösser' in: *Jahrbuch der preußischen Kunstsammlungen* LIV (1933), p. 262, and LV (1934), p. 42.

H. M. J. RIJKERS; 'Limburgs Aardewerk' in: *Mededelingen Vrienden Nederl. Ceramiek* 3 (1955).

J. M. DOS SANTOS SIMÕES; *Carreaux céramiques hollandais au Portugal et en Espagne.* La Haye, 1959.

J. M. DOS SANTOS SIMÕES; *Azulejos holandeses no convento de Santo Antonio do Recife.* Recife, 1959.

SIGURD SCHOUBYE; *Hollandske Vaegliser*, Copenhagen, 1963.

N. V. TICHELAAR; *300 jaar Makkumer aardewerk.* Makkum, 1960.

EELCO M. VIS & C. DE GEUS; *Altholländische Fliesen*, übersetzt von H. Wichmann. 2 vol. [text of Vol. II by Ferrand W. Hudig], Leipzig, 1926–1933.

H. B. J. VLAS; 'Over oude tegels.' De schouwen in Heer Hugowaard, in: *De Speelwagen* III (1948), p. 8.

PHILIPS WARREN; 'Introduction to Dutch blue and white' in: *Antiques*, Sept. 1962, p. 258.

E. WIERSUM; 'De rotterdamsche Koorddansersfamilie Magito' in: *Rotterdamsch Jaarboekje* 1920, p. 104.

[Exhibition catalogue] *Uit den boden van Rotterdam.* Museum Boymans 1942.

[Exhibition catalogue] *La faïence de Delft.* Musée de Sèvres. Paris, 1954. (H. P. Fourest.)

[Catalogue] *Oud aardewerk.* Rijksmuseum, Amsterdam, 1920.

[Catalogue] Rijksmuseum 'Huis Lambert van Meerten,' Delft, 1922. (Ida Peelen.)

[Catalogue] *Eelco Vis collection*, sale at American Art Galleries, New York, 1927.

GERMANY AND DENMARK

MARGARETE BAUR-HEINHOLD; *Deutsche Bauernstuben* (Die blauen Bücher), 1961.

ADOLF BAYER; *Die Ansbacher Fayence-Fabrik.* Ansbach, 1928; 2nd ed., 1959.

MARTIN BOYKEN; *Fliesen und gekachelte Räume des 17. und 18. Jahrhunderts.* Darmstadt, 1954.

J. W. FROHNE; *Danske Fajancer.* 1911.

EDUARD FUCHS and PAUL HEILAND; *Die deutsche Fayencekultur.* Munich, 1925.

F. HUDIG in EELCO M. VIS & C. DE GEUS; *Altholländische Fliesen* (see below).

KONRAD HÜSELER; *Deutsche Fayencen.* 1956.

H. C. BERING LIISBERG; *Rosenborg og Lysthusene i Kongens Have*, Copenhagen, 1914.

O. RIESEBIETER; *Die deutschen Fayencen des 17. und 18. Jahrhunderts.* Leipzig, 1920.

SIGURD SCHOUBYE; *Hollandske Vaegfliser.* 1963.

N. V. TICHELAAR; *300 Jahre Makkumer Aardewerk*, Makkum, 1960.

KAI ULDALL; *Danske Fajancefliser.* 1925.

KAI ULDALL; *Gammel dans Fajence.* 1961.

EELCO M. VIS & C. DE GEUS; *Altholländische Fliesen.* 1926–1933. (For full description see section 'The Netherlands.')

GERD WIETEK; *Kellinghusen und seine Fayencen.* Kellinghusen, 1933.

[Exhibition catalogue] *Katalog zur Fayencen-Ausstellung im Ansbacher Markgrafen-Schloss*, 1928 (Dr. Paul Heiland).

[Exhibition catalogue] *Twee eeuwen Duitse Faience*, Gemeentemuseum, The Hague, 1955.

ENGLAND

ESTHER STEVENS FRASER; 'Some colonial and early American Decorative Floors' in: *Antiques* XIX–4 (April 1931), p. 296.

J. HODGKIN; 'Transfer printing on pottery' in: *Burlington Magazine* VI (1905), p. 232.

ARTHUR LANE; 'English Delftware' in: *Cahiers de la Céramique* 6 (1957).

LOUIS LIPSKI; 'An introduction to Bristol delftware tiles' in: *Connoisseur* 1953, p. 80–5.

O. VAN OSS; 'English Delftware in the eighteenth century' in: *English Ceramic Circle Transactions* 3 (1951–5), p. 217.

W. J. POUNTNEY; *Old Bristol potteries*. Bristol, 1920.

E. S. PRICE; *John Sadler; a Liverpool pottery printer*. West Kirby, 1948.

J. A. G. WATSON; 'Some of the less-known Liverpool transfer tiles' in: *Connoisseur* LXXVIII (1927), p. 28.

MATERIALS AND METHODS OF PRODUCTION

R. FORRER; *Geschichte der europäischen Fliesen-Keramik*. Strasbourg, 1901.

C. H. DE JONGE; *Oud-Nederlandsche Majolica en Delftsch Aardewerk*. Amsterdam, 1947, p. 153–154.

A. LANE; *A Guide to the collection of tiles*. Victoria and Albert Museum, London, 1960.

H. LE CHATELIER; *Comptes rendues* 129, XII (1899), 477–480.

A. LUCAS; 'Glazed ware in Egypt, India and Mesopotamia' in: *The Journal of Egyptian Archaeology* XXII (1936), 141/164.

N. OTTEMA; 'Friesche Majolica' in: *De Vrije Fries* XXVII (1920).

G. PAAPE; *De Plateelbakker of Delftsch Aardewerkmaaker*. Dordrecht, 1794.

CIPRIANO PICCOLPASSO; *Li tre libri dell'arte del vasaio*. Castel Durante, 1556, in the original Italian, with translation and an introduction by Bernard Rackham and Albert van de Put. London, 1934.

H. RITTER, J. RUSKA, F. SARRE, R. WINDERLICH; 'Orientalische Steinbücher und persische Fayencetechnik' in: *Istanbuler Mitteilungen des Archäologischen Institutes des Deutschen Reiches*. 1935. (Contains a translation into German, with notes, of an account of the techniques of faience manufacture, written in 1301 in Kashan by Abulqasim ibn-Abdallah ibn-Ali ibn-Muhammad ibn-Ali Tahir.)

N. V. TICHELAAR; *300 jaar Makkumer Aardewerk*. Makkum, 1960.

A. WINTER; 'Alte und antike Brennanlagen, die Regie ihrer Feuer' in: *Keramische Zeitschrift* VIII (1956), 513–517.

Index